Law and Justice in
a Multicultural Society

In memoriam of José Guilherme Negrão

LAW AND JUSTICE IN
A MULTICULTURAL SOCIETY
THE CASE OF MOZAMBIQUE

Edited by
Boaventura de Sousa Santos,
João Carlos Trindade
& Maria Paula Meneses

Centro de Formação
Jurídica e Judiciária

ces

CODESRIA

© Council for the Development of Social Science Research in Africa, 2006
Avenue Cheikh Anta Diop Angle Canal IV, BP 3304 Dakar, 18524, Senegal
www.codesria.org

In association with the Centro de formação Jurídica e Judiciária
Rua de Mutateia, 1752 – Bairro do Fomento – Matola, Moçambique

Centro de Estudos Sociais
Universidade de Coimbra
Colégio S Jerónimo, Apartado 3087, 300-401 Coimbra, Portugal
www.ces.uc.pt

and with financial support from DANIDA

ISBN: 2-86978-191-1   ISBN-13: 978-2-86978-191-7

Typeset by Djibril Fall
Cover image from a painting by Malangatana entitled *O voo das pombas sagradas,* 1993
Printed by Lightning Source

Distributed in Africa by CODESRIA

Distributed elsewhere by
African Books Collective, Oxford, UK
Web site: www.africanbookscollective.com

The Council for the Development of Social Science Research in Africa (CODESRIA) is an independent organisation whose principal objectives are facilitating research, promoting research-based publishing and creating multiple forums geared towards the exchange of views and information among African researchers. It challenges the fragmentation of research through the creation of thematic research networks that cut across linguistic and regional boundaries.

CODESRIA publishes a quarterly journal, *Africa Development*, the longest standing Africa-based social science journal; *Afrika Zamani*, a journal of history; the *African Sociological Review, African Journal of International Affairs (AJIA), Africa Review of Books* and *Identity, Culture and Politics: An Afro-Asian Dialogue*. It co publishes the *Journal of Higher Education in Africa*, and *Africa Media Review*. Research results and other activities of the institution are disseminated through 'Working Papers', 'Monograph Series', 'CODESRIA Book Series', and the *CODESRIA Bulletin*.

Contents

About the authors

André Cristiano José is a lecturer and researcher at the Centre for Legal and Judicial Training, Maputo, Mozambique.

António Alberto da Silva Francisco is Professor of Economics at the Eduardo Mondlane University, Maputo, Mozambique.

Boaventura de Sousa Santos is Professor of Sociology and the Director of Center for Social Studies at the School of Economics, Coimbra University, Portugal; he is also a ILS Distinguished scholar at the University of Wisconsin, Madison, USA.

Conceição Gomes is a researcher and the Executive Director of the Permanent Observatory of Justice at the Center for Social Studies, Faculty of Economics, Coimbra University, Portugal.

Guilherme Mbilana is a researcher at the Center for Studies on Democracy and Development, Maputo, Mozambique.

João Carlos Trindade is a Supreme Court Justice in Mozambique. He is also the Director of the Centre for Legal and Judicial Training, Maputo, Mozambique.

João Pedroso is a lecturer at the Faculty of Economics, Coimbra University and a researcher at the Center for Social Studies of the same university.

José Guilherme Negrão was Professor of Development Studies and associate Dean at the Faculty of Agronomics and Forestry Engineer at Eduardo Mondlane University, Maputo, Mozambique.

Maria Manuel Leitão Marques is Professor at the School of Economics, and a senior researcher at the Center for Social Studies, Coimbra University, Portugal.

Maria Paula Meneses, a Mozambican anthropologist, is a senior researcher at the Center for Social Studies, Coimbra University, Portugal.

Joaquim Fumo is a lecturer and researcher at the Centre for Legal and Judicial Training, Maputo, Mozambique.

Teresa Cruz e Silva is a researcher and Professor at the Center for African Studies, Eduardo Mondlane University, Maputo, Mozambique.

Terezinha da Silva is a lecturer and researcher at the Centre for Legal and Judicial Training, Maputo, Mozambique.

Preface

**Boaventura de Sousa Santos, João Carlos Trindade
and Maria Paula Meneses**

In this book we present the main results of a research project on the systems of justice in Mozambique, conducted between 1996 and 2000.[1] The study was undertaken under the auspices of the Supreme Court through an academic partnership between the Center for African Studies (CEA), Eduardo Mondlane University, Mozambique and the Center for Social Studies (CES) at the School of Economics, Coimbra University, Portugal.

The project was carried out by a research team from two countries directed by two coordinators, one from Mozambique – João Carlos Trindade – and one from Portugal – Boaventura de Sousa Santos. The Mozambican research team consisted of 15 researchers, five of whom were part of the core research team. The Portuguese team included five researchers.

This monograph analyzes the complex network which represents the judicial system in Mozambique by interrogating the role of the multiple entities intervening in the system, both in a colonial and a post-colonial context.[2]

Until the onset of Portuguese colonization toward the end of the nineteenth century, the various peoples of Mozambique did not live under a single political authority; they existed as independent entities, with various forms of political and social organization. The transition to the twentieth century became synonymous with the establishment of colonial rule, symbolizing a critical period of radical change that led to the creation of the Mozambican political scenario. The different economic and political strategies implemented by the colonial state in Mozambique resulted in important changes in the organization of power.

After independence, political-legal cultures as diverse as the Eurocentric, socialist revolutionary culture or the Eurocentric, capitalist democratic culture have been added to the existing mix of legal orders. These *new* cultures added new elements to the resources available locally. The previous resources were structures remaining from earlier periods in the life of the state, some of which, although legally suspended for a while, had continued to survive sociologically (as was the case with the so-called *traditional authorities*).

If, during colonial times it was relatively easy to distinguish, in terms of legal pluralism, between the main legal orders concerned – colonial law on the one hand and native or indigenous customary law on the other – this distinction became increasingly blurred in a postcolonial context. In fact, Mozambique constitutes a heterogeneous state, composed of a mosaic of legal hybrids, reflecting a mixture of elements of different legal orders (official/state law, customary law, various religious laws, etc.). For this reason, the working concept of the project – an understanding of the Mozambican state as a heterogeneous state – incorporates a broad view of law which includes local/indigenous customary practices and religious law as well as state civil law and enforcement institutions and procedures, in order to create an innovative view of human rights that draws on local, cultural and legal norms and institutions and the priorities set by local, national and international structures.

As we shall discuss later, the hybrid nature of the legal framework exists not only on the structural level of the relationships between the different legal orders but also on the level of the legal behavior, experiences and representations of citizens and social groups, a phenomenon Santos describes as *interlegality* (1995: 473). At the same time, in the field of conflict resolution innovative legal bodies, such as the community courts, are being created.

As we will discuss throughout this book, the ongoing legal reforms are aimed at recognizing the *alternative* mechanisms of conflict resolution taking place in a complex and conflictive context in which several distinct legal rationalities coexist: the remains of the Portuguese colonial legal codes, socialist orientated policies, customary law, various religious systems and Western constitutionalism.

The research data analyzed here was designed within the framework of a project on the situation of contemporary justice. The main objective of the project was to promote an empirically sound and dynamic understanding of the relationships between the multiple judicial entities present in the country within the context of cultural transformations in Africa. Therefore, the data analyzed here is the result of monitoring the particular entities involved in conflict resolution, such as the judicial courts, the community courts and other alternative bodies in Mozambique. This research included direct observation of court sessions, interviews, analysis of procedures (whenever possible) and analysis of archival data. This time-consuming research enabled us to access the rich information discussed in the text.

This monograph will hopefully represent a contribution to the current debates on the formation of the state in Mozambique since the nineteenth century. It consists of three parts. In Part I we describe the theoretical, analytical and methodological framework used to analyze the socio-political and legal structure of the multicultural Mozambican society. Part 2 is an intermezzo, aimed at describing the socio-economic evolution of Mozambique over the last fifty years. In Part 3 we describe and analyze the information that was gathered on official justice and community justice. The chapters included in Part 3 present the main findings of the research into official justice (the Supreme Court, the provincial and district courts and the General Attorney's Office), access to the law and justice, and the informal, semi-official or non-official forms of justice that exist alongside the official judicial system in Mozambique and which the majority of citizens use to resolve disputes.

Throughout the research period we benefited from the support of many people and institutions, many more than we can remember. Above all, we would like to thank the Supreme Court, in the person of its Chief Justice, Dr. Mário Mangaze, for its continued support throughout the research period, a task which by its complexity and ambition, was bound to involve some delays. A special word of thanks is also due to Prof. Teresa Cruz e Silva, the Director of the CEA at Eduardo Mondlane University during the period in which the initial research was carried out, for the remarkable way in which she overcame bureaucratic difficulties, managed the complex relationships between researchers and provided the best possible working conditions. We owe her a very special debt of gratitude. We also wish to thank Dr. Isabel Casimiro, Director of the CEA at the time when the protocol between the CEA and the CES was established, for her important contribution towards getting the project started, Ms. Ana Koelhar, the ICEP delegate in Maputo, for her valuable help, Dr. Nina Berg from DANIDA, Dr. Francesca Dagnino, UNDP consultant and Dr. Fátima Fonseca of the Supreme Court. From 2002 onwards, our research into the Mozambican system of justice has been based at the CFJJ (Centre for Legal and Judicial Training). We would like to thank the staff there, whose work has been central to the development of our work.

In addition, on an institutional level, our thanks are due to two institutions that supported the research financially: the Danish Agency for International Development Assistance (DANIDA) and the *Instituto da Cooperação Portuguesa* (Portuguese Institute for Cooperation, now the Portuguese Institute for Development Assistance – IPAD). In an exemplary demonstration of international cooperation these two institutions worked together to make viable a project which, due to its size, would have been too burdensome for one institution alone.

While preparing the book, we relied on the support of several research assistants at the CES. We gratefully acknowledge all their assistance. A special thanks to Jorge Almeida who helped prepare the English version. A word of recognition to Sheena Jean Caldwell for the English translation.

Finally, our very special thanks to João Paulo Moreira, on whose generous time and competence we counted during the last phases of the preparation of the manuscript, and whose outstanding job as a copy-editor was invaluable.

We dedicate this book to the memory of José Negrão. Prematurely deceased, José Negrão was one of the best-known African economists, internationally respected for combining solid professional knowledge with the passionate dream of seeing

Mozambique develop according to the needs of its people, rather than the impositions of international donors and their orthodoxies. We were fortunate enough to have benefited from his collaboration in our project, and pay him homage by symbolically giving him the last word in this book. José Negrão authored the last chapter, dealing with the topic to which he dedicated his best energy in the last years of his life, the land question.

Notes

1   A second project, aimed at preparing the legal reform was initiated in 2003 and is still under way. The research team, coordinated by Boaventura de Sousa Santos and João Carlos Trindade, involves eight researchers both from CFJJ and CES. Several data and information gathered already during the second project found its way into this monograph.
2   Mozambique has a population of approximately 19 million, almost all native Africans, belonging to several ethnic or linguistic groups.

Part I

State, Law and the Administration of Justice

1

The Heterogeneous State
and Legal Plurality

Boaventura de Sousa Santos

Introduction

The end of the twentieth century witnessed a global call for the rule of law and the reform of the judicial systems in many countries of the world. Multilateral financial agencies and international aid non-governmental organizations (NGOs) made such changes one of their priorities for their efforts in the developing world.[1] The global nature of this process and the intensity with which it was implemented, both in financial and political terms, reflected the rise of a new development model: the neo-liberal development model. This model looks to a greater reliance on markets and the private sector and requires a new legal and judicial framework: only when the rule of law is widely accepted and effectively enforced are certainty and predictability guaranteed, transaction costs lowered, property rights clarified and protected, contractual obligations enforced and regulations applied. In most countries across the developing world profound legal and judicial reforms were implemented. They focused exclusively on the official legal and judicial system, conceived of as a unified system, and left out of consideration the multiplicity of unofficial legal orderings and dispute resolution mechanisms that had long coexisted with the official system, many dating back to the early colonial period. The neglect of non-state legal structures, combined with the intense, globally induced call for reform and the changes in the role of the state, ended up widening the gap between the law-in-books and the law-in-action.

The focus of this chapter is the recent history and current nature of this gap in Mozambique. In present-day Mozambique – as in other African countries – the disjunction between the officially established unity of the legal system and the sociological plurality and fragmentation of legal practice is probably more visible than in any other region of the developing world. In the analysis that follows, I will show that this disjunction has a multiple impact on state action and legitimacy, on the operation of the official legal system, on the relationships between political and administrative control, on the mechanisms of conflict resolution operating in society, on the legal and institutional frameworks of economic life and on the social and cultural perceptions of politics and legality.

For several centuries a Portuguese colony, Mozambique became independent in 1975. The revolutionary socialist development path adopted in the first decade after independence was abandoned in 1984 in the face of a deep economic crisis and under the pressure of multilateral financial institutions. It was replaced by a democratic capitalist development path, later on enshrined in the Constitution of 1990. At the end of the 1970s a vicious civil war broke out, initially masterminded and fueled by the Rhodesian and South African secret services. It ended twelve years later with the Peace Agreement of 1992, having left the countryside pulled apart and half a million dead. In 1987 the first structural adjustment agreement was signed.[2] Considered one of the poorest peripheral countries, Mozambique was initially subjected to particularly harsh measures of restructuring, given its status as a 'strong adjuster'. It is today viewed as a 'success story', having experienced in the last decade some economic recovery and having carried out the democratic transition with mixed results but without much turbulence.

As mentioned earlier on in the preface, the empirical research analyzed in this chapter results from an on-going project on the judicial system in Mozambique. The empirical data more directly relevant for the analysis undertaken here comprise extensive research focused on community courts and traditional authorities.[3] In-depth studies were conducted in 5 community courts – Mafalala and Xipamanine (Maputo city), Liberdade (Inhambane province), Munhava Central (Sofala province) and Maimio (Cabo Delgado province) – and 6 chiefdoms: the *regulados* Luis and Mafambisse (both in the Sofala province), Cumbapo (Zambézia province), Zintambila (Tete province), Cumbana and Nhampossa (both in the Inhambane province). The data collection included direct observation of court sessions and dispute resolution settlements, archival data whenever available, and semi-structured interviews.

In section 1, I deal very briefly with the recent transformations on the nature and role of the state in Africa and its impact on legal pluralism. In section 2, I analyze the social and political conditions that account for the heterogeneity of state action and legal pluralism in Mozambique. In section 3, I focus on the community courts, conceived as legal hybrids, and in section 4, on traditional authorities, conceived as alternative legal and political modernities.

1. The Heterogeneous State and Legal Plurality

The Emergence of the Heterogeneous State

The globalizing pressure Africa is experiencing today is perhaps more intense and selective than ever before. Since the fifteenth century Africa has been subjected to various forms of globalization originating in the West, including colonialism, slavery, imperialism, neo-colonialism or structural adjustment. The intensity of the most recent form of globalization lies in the fact that it is almost totally impossible to be resisted locally. It appears as an unconditional and ineluctable imperative.[4]

The impact of neo-liberal globalization in Africa is most visible in the changing structures and practices of the state. The states that emerged from the processes of independence became in one way or another developmentalist states. Although huge differences existed between them – above all the difference between those which adopted the capitalist and those which adopted the socialist path towards development –, the new states presented themselves as the driving forces of development. They were seen as the centers of strategic economic decision-making and as holding total primacy over civil society, a concept little used during that period. This model of the state operated through great bureaucratic apparatuses, many of which had been inherited from the colonial state. Moreover, this 'overdimensioning' or 'overdevelopment' of the state in relation to society constituted one of the most resistant forms of continuity with the colonial regime (Bayart, 1993; Young, 1994).

Between the mid-1970s and early 1980s, this model of the state entered into a crisis. It was during this transition period, in 1975, that the African countries freed from Portuguese colonialism – Mozambique, Angola, Guinea-Bissau, Cape Verde Islands and São Tomé and Príncipe Islands – emerged, and all of them, without exception, adopted the socialist path to development.[5] With the final collapse of the Soviet Union already imminent, the Washington Consensus, adopted by the core countries under the aegis of the United States in the mid 1980s, sealed the fate of nationalist and socialist models of development based on the primacy of the state. From then on, the state, which under the previous model of development had been the solution to the problems of society, became the great problem of society. Inherently predatory and inefficient, it had to be reduced to a minimum, since reducing its size was the only way of reducing its negative impact on the development of society-based problem solving mechanisms. In many African countries, the production of the weak state, combined with the socially devastating consequences of structural adjustment, led some states to the brink of total implosion. As always, external factors have combined with internal ones to create civil wars, inter-ethnic wars, the rise of corruption and, consequently, the privatization of the state and the collapse of its fragile administrative structures, above all in the areas of education and health care policies and basic infrastructures. By the mid 1990s, the World Bank itself recognized that the new model of development presupposed a state strong and efficient enough to ensure an effective regulation of the economy and the stability of the expectations of economic agents and social actors in general. As latecomers, the new states that emerged from Portuguese colonialism in the mid-1970s, after decades of liberation struggles, suffered even more drastically the consequences of the new global impositions which affected in profound ways the most basic tasks of state building. In section 2, I will illustrate this with the case of Mozambique.

As a consequence of the global imperatives just mentioned, the African nation-state has lost centrality and dominance by force of the emergence of powerful supra-state political processes. However, in an apparently paradoxical way, these same processes have led to the emergence of infra-state actors (sometimes very powerful actors) equally determined, albeit for very different reasons, to question the centrality of the nation-state. A case in point is the re-emergence of traditional authorities as social and political actors, a phenomenon which, as I will show below, occurred in Mozambique. These combined pressures have led to a double decentering of the state, at an infra- and at a supra-state level. This does not mean that the state has ceased to be a key political factor. However, the ways in which it is being contested and reformed transform it into an increasingly complex social field in which state and non-state, local and transnational relations interact, merge and confront each other in dynamic and even volatile combinations, making the nature of legal plurality ever more complex. The centrality of the state resides now, to a great extent, in the way in which the state organizes its own loss of centrality. In other words, the withdrawal of the regulatory state – what has been called the deregulation of economic and social life – can only be achieved by state action, most of which must be accomplished through legislation .

The ways in which this state transformation is occurring are contributing to an increase in the functional heterogeneity of state action. Under often contradictory pressures, the different sectors of state action are assuming such different logics of development and rhythms, causing disconnections and incongruities, that sometimes it is no longer possible to identify a coherent pattern of state action, that is, a pattern common to all state sectors or fields of state action. This is related to the increasing duality between the intensely transnationalized sectors of social life and the non-transnationalized or only marginally transnationalized ones. The heterogeneity of state action is itself reflected in the total breakdown of the already shaky unity of state law, with the consequent emergence of different politics and styles of state legality, each of which operates with relative autonomy. In extreme cases such autonomy may lead to the formation of multiple micro-states existing inside the same state.[6] This new political formation I call the heterogeneous state (Santos, 1995: 274-281). It is characterized by the uncontrolled coexistence of starkly different political cultures and regulatory logics in different sectors (*e.g.*, in economic policies and family or religion policies) or levels (local, regional and national) of state action. Among the most significant factors accounting for the heterogeneous state are a disjunction between the political and administrative control over the territory and its people, the lack of integration among different political and legal cultures governing state action and the official legal system, and political and institutional upheavals caused by multiple ruptures occurring in rapid succession. All these factors will be illustrated in section 2 with the case of Mozambique.

Old and New Forms of Legal Pluralism

Legal pluralism in contemporary African societies is more complex today than ever before and in large part this is due to the processes of state transformation mentioned above. Until recently the analysis of legal plurality was centered on the identification of local, intra-state legal orders, which co-existed in different forms alongside the official, national law. Today, alongside local and national legal orders, supra-national legal orders are emerging, which interfere in multiple ways with the former. Nowadays sub-national legal plurality acts in conjuction with supra-national legal plurality.[7]

From a sociological perspective, the articulation among different scales of law becomes,[8] therefore, increasingly complex. We can identify three scales – the local, the national and the global. Each one has its own legal norms and rationale, with the result that relations between them are very often tense and conflicting. These tensions and conflicts tend to increase as the articulations between the different legal orders and the different scales of law multiply and deepen. Whereas in colonial society it was easy to identify the legal orders and their spheres of action and thus regulate relationships between them – European colonial law on the one hand, and the customary law of the native peoples on the other[9] –, in present-day African societies the plurality of legal orders is much more extensive and the interactions between them much denser. Paradoxically, if, on the one hand, this denser relationship makes conflict and tension between the different legal orders more likely, it also shows that the different legal orders are more open and susceptible to mutual influences. The boundaries between the different legal orders become more porous and each one loses its 'pure', 'autonomous' identity and can only be defined in relation to the legal constellation of which it is a part. Out of this porosity and interpenetration evolve what I call legal hybrids, that is, legal entities or phenomena that mix different and often contradictory legal orders or cultures, giving rise to new forms of legal meaning and action. In section 3, I will illustrate the concept of legal hybrid with the case of community courts in Mozambique.

Situations involving legal hybridization as a new kind of legal pluralism challenge conventional dichotomies to the extent that legal practices frequently combine the opposite poles of the dichotomies and contain an infinite number of intermediate situations. Even so, on an analytical level, the dichotomies are a good starting point, as long as it is clear from the outset that they will not provide the point of arrival. The conventional dichotomies most relevant to analyze legal plurality in Mozambique are the following: official/unofficial, formal/informal, traditional/modern, monocultural/multicultural.

The official/unofficial variable results from the political-administrative definition of what is recognized as law or the administration of justice, and what is not. In the modern state, the unofficial is everything that is not recognized as state-originated. It may be prohibited or tolerated; most of the time, however, it is ignored. The formal/informal variable relates to the structural aspects of the legal orders in operation. A form of law is considered formal when it is dominated by written exchanges and norms and standardized procedures, and, in turn, is considered informal when it is dominated by orality and common language argumentation. The traditional/modern variable relates to the origins and historical duration of law and justice. A form of law is said to be traditional when it is believed to have existed since time immemorial, when it is impossible to identify with any accuracy the moment or the agents of its creation. Conversely, a law is said to be modern when it is believed to have existed for a shorter period of time than the traditional and whose creation can be identified as to time and/or author.[10] The monocultural/multicultural variable relates to the cultural universes in which the different laws and systems of justice occur.[11] There is monocultural legal plurality whenever different laws and justices belong to the same culture and, conversely, there is multicultural legal plurality whenever the diversity of laws and justice correlates with important cultural differences (Santos, 1995: 506–19; 1997; 2002c). Taking this set of variables or dimensions as starting points, I will analyze in the following sections some of the most important features of legal plurality in Mozambique.

2. A Palimpsest of Political and Legal Cultures[12]

During the thirty years of its existence as an independent state, political-legal cultures as diverse as the colonial culture, the socialist culture, the democratic culture and the traditional or community cultures have superimposed themselves on Mozambique. The uneven embeddedness of these highly diverse political-legal cultures derives in great part from the political instability caused by multiple ruptures succeeding each other at a fast pace. In fact, over the past thirty years, Mozambican society has experienced a series of radical political transformations, many of them traumatic, which have followed one another at dizzying speed. The following are the most significant: the end of colonialism, which was violent up until its last period (starting with the national liberation struggle from the early 1960s until 1975); a revolutionary rupture which aimed to build a nation from the Rovuma to the Maputo,[13] a socialist society and the formation of a 'new Man' (1975–1984); the aggression of colonial Rhodesia and apartheid South Africa, in retaliation for the solidarity offered by Mozambique to the struggle for freedom in the region (from the late 1970s until the 1980s); the civil war (from the end of the 1970s until 1992); the collapse of the revolutionary economic model and its abrupt replacement, under external pressure, by the neo-liberal capitalist model, which included both structural adjustment and the transition to democracy (1985-1994); and finally the construction of democracy (from 1994 to the present).[14] All these transformations occurred as ruptures, as processes which, instead of capitalizing on the positive features of previous transformations, aimed to sweep away all traces of them and make a new beginning, unable or unwilling to accommodate the immediate past. In reality, however, ruptures coexisted with continuities, blending explicit and self-proclaimed ruptures with unspoken continuities and so giving rise to very complex legal and institutional constellations and hybridizations.

Some of these constellations and hybridizations are the result of political decisions; others have proliferated in a more or less unacknowledged fashion, far removed from political proclamations. In these constellations, the most complex combinations occur between the cultures of greater historical duration (the traditional cultures and the colonial culture) and the cultures of a lesser historical duration (the socialist, revolutionary culture and the democratic, capitalist culture). The colonial political-legal culture, despite having been most thoroughly rejected – as exemplified by the notion of the *'escangalhamento do Estado'* (breaking up of the colonial state) during the revolutionary period – has prevailed up to the present day, not only in its most obvious forms, such as the colonial legislation still in force or the organization of the administration, but above all in terms of habits and mentalities, styles of behavior, representations of the other, etc. (Bragança and Depelchin, 1986; Monteiro, 1999). It was within this culture that most of the senior civil servants who still ensure administrative routines today were trained.

Another legal-political culture that was rejected, although not quite so unconditionally, was the set of traditional or community cultures. Viewed as products of ignorance and as producing obscurantism and reactionary ideas, these cultures were seen as remnants and instruments of colonial culture. This attitude of rejection, which totally prevailed during the early post-independence years, came to coexist with another, more moderate attitude that favored a highly political and selective use of traditional cultures. For example, the creation of the popular courts, after the independence, sought selectively to co-opt traditional cultures, in order to make them serve the revolutionary culture (Sachs and Honwana Welch, 1990).[15] In this early period, the constellation of political-legal cultures was dominated by the eurocentric revolutionary socialist culture (henceforth socialist culture). This culture, though based on the European revolutionary experience at the beginning of the twentieth century, encompassed also other non-European experiences: Latin American (Cuba), Asian (China and North Korea) and African (African socialism, with a much less Marxist-Leninist outlook than the former and, in general, with a much less explicit set of doctrines, as exemplified in the case of neighboring Tanzania). Apparently the only legitimate culture, revolutionary culture coexisted, in fact, alongside with colonial culture and traditional cultures.

From the mid-1980s onwards, it was the turn of the revolutionary cultural component to retreat and give way to the primacy of eurocentric democratic capitalist culture (henceforth democratic culture). In contrast to the former, which was adopted as an autonomous option and mobilized predominantly internal energies, democratic culture was adopted under strong external pressure, which, nevertheless, in no way excluded its genuine adoption by certain national political elites. Just as in the period when the revolutionary political-legal culture prevailed, democratic culture brought with it profound political changes, including peace, subjection to global capitalism and the transition to democracy. Like socialist culture, democratic culture sought to be the only legitimate cultural reference. However, it had to exist alongside an altogether more complex cultural constellation, including not only the colonial and the traditional, the cultures of longer duration, but also the revolutionary culture of the previous period. The latter had transformed itself into an important institutional reality which, despite having been formally revoked, continued to operate on a sociological level. Thus, for example, the community courts, created during this second period (1992) to replace the popular courts of the previous period, ended up by ensuring the continuity of the popular courts, although under very precarious circumstances, as I will show in the following section. Using the same facilities and staffed by the same judges who, in the previous period, had been popular judges, the community courts transformed themselves into a highly complex hybrid institution. In these courts, revolutionary, traditional and community political-legal cultures combined. Eventually, the only absent culture was the one which supposedly had become the official legal and political culture: democratic culture. In other sectors of public administration and legislation, different political-legal constellations were created. The revolutionary component, which was officially replaced by the democratic component, underwent, in fact, different metamorphoses and combined with the other cultural strains.

From this fusion of ruptures and continuities a highly heterogeneous state action and a very complex matrix of legal pluralism have emerged which today dominate the legal and judicial system and, more generally, public administration. But a full account of these features of legal and political life in Mozambique requires that another, more recent, factor is brought under consideration: the heavy pressures of the globalization to which Mozambique has been subjected in the process of 'structural adjustment'. I am referring more specifically to the impact of global factors on local and national conditions, under circumstances in which the latter cannot consistently incorporate or adapt, and much less subvert, external pressures. Such pressures are both very intense and very selective, and by imposing their own specific regulatory logic, they result in profound changes in some institutions and legal frameworks. At the same time, other institutions and legal frameworks are left untouched and are therefore subject to their own logics.

This results in enormous fragmentation and segmentation, which affect the entire legal and administrative system. On the one hand, there are the transnationalized sectors, operating according to regulatory logics imposed by the multilateral financial agencies and the core countries. On the other hand, there are the nationalized or local sectors, operating according to hybrid and endogenous logics, which, being irrelevant for the transnational designs, are left to the national and local elites to exert their own political and personal differences on them. For example, today the law of the financial and economic sector is highly transnationalized and grounded on a single way of thinking promoted by global imperatives that leave little or no scope for internal political decision-making; on the other extreme, family law, for instance, is of little importance to the transnational powers and is therefore left in the hands of the national elites, who can lead intense political and cultural debates about it. The question of whether there is any underlying compatibility between the strikingly contrasting regulatory logics in these two legal domains is never addressed. The heterogeneity of regulatory logics lies precisely in these disjunctions, which, because they are unquestioned, go on being reproduced.[16]

The global pressures that have created legal and institutional plurality are of two basic types: pressures from the international financial agencies and so-called 'donor countries,' which fall very specifically into the economic area, and pressures originating from the same agents, but principally from the foreign or transnational NGOs, which fall within what we may term social policy in the broadest sense. Both these pressures are very strong, so much so that it is legitimate to ask whether we are not confronted with a situation of shared sovereignty between the Mozambican state and the foreign agents. In the field of economics, the segmentation created by structural adjustments between the transnationalized sector of the economy and the so-called informal sector, is immense. It is a matter of two legal and institutional worlds whose actions are very often unfathomable. It is up to the state to keep them apart by managing this heterogeneity. On a strictly legal level, the heterogeneity of regulatory logics and the duality of legal and institutional worlds reproduce themselves in still another form. The two main sub-cultures of eurocentric political-legal culture – continental civil law and Anglo-Saxon common law – are currently engaged in what we could call a 'global legal culture war'.[17] Breaking apart from the post-World War II settlement, common law legal culture, especially in its U.S. law version, has come to play, through globalization, an increasingly important role. This promotion of common law – which at times can be very intense – is carried out in countries with distinctive legal cultures, and operational logics and methods very different from those which prevail in Anglo-Saxon legal culture. Therefore, discrepancies are created within national legal systems, which add up to the already high levels of state heterogeneity and legal pluralism. The official modern legal culture of Mozambique, which is inspired by continental European legal culture, has begun to experience the influence of Anglo-Saxon legal culture from two sides: through the policies of structural adjustment and, due to the proximity of and the close economic ties between the two countries, through South Africa, whose legal culture is Roman-Dutch and Anglo-Saxon in origin. The latter influence is detected both in contract law and in the legislative process.

In the 'social area', the segmentations and shared sovereignties are even more complex. The complexity lies in the fact that the different NGOs and, in many cases, the different core states behind them, have different concepts of what social intervention should be in such different domains as the fight against poverty, basic infrastructures, education, health care, protection of the family economy and the environment, etc. In other words, in the social sphere, global pressure is not only strong but also very differentiated. Its strength still lies in the fact that the pressure, far from being conceived of as an imposition, is conceived of as international solidarity with a legitimate right to establish the terms of its implementation. As these terms vary from NGO to NGO and from donor country to donor country, and as NGOs and countries have concentrated their interventions in different regions or provinces of the country, the heterogeneity of social policies assumes a territorial nature. The ensuing fragmentation and segmentation emerges not only as the result of complex negotiations, between foreign and international NGOs and donor countries, on the one hand, and the national state and provincial and district governments on the other, but also as the result of the unequal relationships between the foreign and international NGOs and the national NGOs, which, in the vast majority of cases, are financially dependent on the former and therefore subject to their conditions.

The ensuing institutional and administrative fragmentation of the state thus results, in many cases, from anarchic superimpositions that generate exclusion and complaints from all those involved. Thus, the district government complains if an international NGO decides to operate directly and autonomously in the community, responding to needs as they see them and their satisfaction. The provincial government (the administrative level above the district) complains at the decision of an NGO to support a municipality directly, without channeling this support through it. One or more national NGOs complain if an international NGO coordinates its aid with the provincial government and does not include the national NGOs working in the area. Provincial and district governments complain if international NGOs have decided to support particular areas or communities 'without plausible reasons'. Lastly, international NGOs complain that the terms of their intervention are not defined by the national government, which means that they are seen as 'parallel governments' when in fact they 'just want to be partners'. These reciprocal exclusions fuel the above-mentioned disjunction between political and administrative control and transform the latter into an appendage of the former. This transformation, which may occur in other contexts, is here particularly intense and its specificity lies in the fact that it often involves the three scales (local, national and global) of both law and politics.

In order to put an end to the most extreme forms of segmentation and fragmentation in state action, the Government sought, through Decree no. 55/98 of October 13, 1998, to establish some measure of control over NGO actions. Article 6 no. 4 establishes that "it is the obligation of the central organ responsible for the NGO activity to indicate the province in which it will undertake its activities, bearing in mind the need to apply the principle of equity to the development of the country", and Article 2 no. 3 stipulates that "in the course of their activities, foreign NGOs are forbidden to undertake or promote any actions of a political nature". This Decree has not yet been put to a test and it is not difficult to imagine the problems its implementation will entail.

In a situation involving great segmentation of state, legal, judicial and institutional practices, official deregulation is always less far-reaching than it is declared to be and re-regulation much less homogeneous than it intends to be. Under these circumstances, the legal and institutional unity of the state is precarious and the state often appears to be a set of micro-states, at varying removes from each other, some local and others national or transnational, and all of them bearers of composite and distinct operational logics. This is the condition that characterizes both the heterogeneous state and legal pluralism under conditions of globalization. The characterization of legal pluralism will be presented in detail in the following sections.

I conclude the analysis of the conditions accounting for the Mozambican state heterogeneity and legal plurality by focusing on the disjunction of political and administrative control, that is, on the state's incapacity for guaranteeing either the separation or the equal territorial penetration of political and administrative control, thus tending to politicize administrative control and exercise the latter selectively. This is one of the most persistent legacies of the colonial state in Africa and it has grown in the last two decades due to neoliberal globalization, especially in the countries that gained independence most recently, as is the case of the Portuguese-speaking African countries. Nowadays the overdimensioning of political control in relation to administrative control is evident in Mozambique. In administrative terms, the state is still confronting the problems of modern state building, among which is, the problem of state penetration, that is, of its effective political and bureaucratic presence in the whole territory. This situation encourages the politicization of the administration, as can be illustrated with the difficulties in transforming election results into the sharing of power. It is feared that sharing power will involve a loss of administrative control, which is always imagined to be in the service of political control.

The disjunction of political and administrative results control also in the fact that, in its everyday practices, public administration has no means of guaranteeing its own efficiency. Therefore it resorts to whatever institutions are locally available, whether they are structures from an earlier period, colonial or revolutionary[18] – which, in spite of having been legally eliminated or superceded, continue to survive as both political and administrative entities – or whether they are the traditional authorities (Geffray, 1990; Dinerman, 1999; Chichava, 1999). These heterogeneous resources – which create a situation of bureaucratic *bricolage* – translate themselves in to heterogeneous acts of administration caused by the coexistence of the formal and the informal, the official and the unofficial, the modern and the traditional, the revolutionary and the post-revolutionary. In the following section some of these complex coexistences will be illustrated.

3. Entangled Legal Pluralities: Community Courts as Legal Hybrids[19]

In this and in the following section I will analyze some of the patterns of legal pluralism in Mozambique. As already indicated, Mozambican society is a vast and vastly differentiated social field of legal pluralism. Figure 1.1 gives a synthetic view of legal pluralism in Mozambique. In constructing it I privileged the official/unofficial dichotomy.

Figure 1.1: Legal Plurality in Mozambique

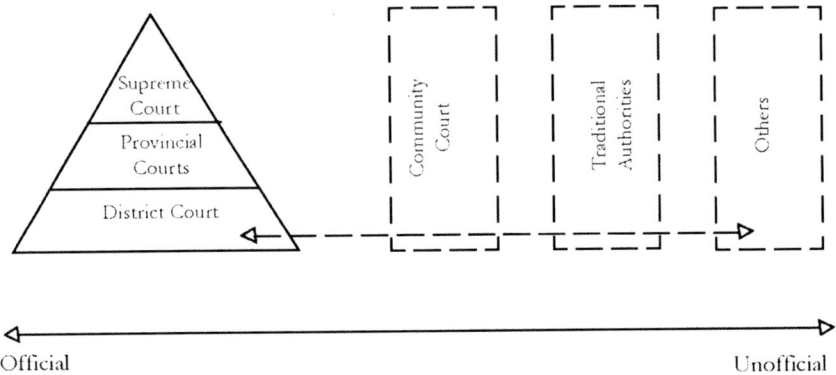

The pyramid on the left hand side represents the official legal system. There are 11 provincial courts and 93 district courts functioning in the country.[20] The district courts are the lower courts and are those with more intense interactions with the non-official legal orders. In the latter I distinguish three instances of conflict resolution which, as the figure shows, are differently located within the official/non-official continuum. The first instance are the community courts, which I conceive of here as a legal hybrid combining official and unofficial components; the second instance are the traditional authorities and the third one is a vast set of associations in which the religious associations, particularly the Muslim ones, stand out. In this section I will concentrate on the community courts.

There are no reliable data on the number of community courts and much less on the number of cases they handle. The number of judges varies from court to court, although a minimum of three judges is required to hear the cases. In the courts analyzed, only about 18% of the judges were women. The judges, whether men or women, tend to be over 40 years of age. Even when they are replaced, recruitment does not, as a rule, alter the age group. However, particularly when the replacements are women, they do tend to be younger. In terms of occupation, the majority may be considered rural workers (most of them women), followed by those who are retired, craftsmen or factory workers. By and large they handle cases relating to family matters, followed by theft, injuries and physical aggression. There are also cases relating to debt, land issues, housing issues and witchcraft accusations.

There are significant differences among the courts in the ways they operate, whether in terms of procedural or of substantive norms. In a few courts there is a selective adoption of the styles, formulas and language of official justice, with all the proceedings being registered in writing. In most cases, however, informality and orality prevail. Even in more formalized proceedings, the use of judicial formulae is combined with the use of common language, directly linked to the oral nature of the surrounding culture. In any event, the formality does not influence the decision. It seems, above all, to have the aim of creating an institutional distance in relation to the parties and of legitimizing the power of the court. All the hearings take place in a context dominated by rhetoric, that is, by common language argumentation. National languages predominate (there are more than 20 national languages in Mozambique) and the court usually speaks in the same language as the parties, with no need for interpreters.[21]

In Mozambique, community courts are the legal hybrid institution *par excellence*, particularly in what concerns the official/unofficial dichotomy. They are recognized by law – they were created by Law no. 4/92, of May 6, 1992 – but their operation is not regulated by law nor are they part of the official legal system (for instance, there is no appeal to the official courts from the decisions of the community courts).[22] The decision to remove them from the judicial system was justified with the new conception of the rule of law introduced along with structural adjustment. The decision was in tune with the political atmosphere of the time, interested in eradicating from the state any remnants of the popular power institutions of the previous, revolutionary period. The community courts were thus left in an institutional limbo. Because they decide cases "with impartiality, good sense and equity" (Article 2, no. 2, of Law no. 4/92) but not according to law, they are not considered part of the judicial system. They should however become organs of justice *"for the purposes of reconciliation or the settling of minor disputes"* (Article 63 of Law no. 10/92) as a type of community justice for which there are words of praise in the law, *"bearing in mind the ethnic and cultural diversity of Mozambican society"* (Preamble to the Law no. 4/92). The Preamble also states that the community courts will "enable citizens to resolve minor differences within the community, contribute towards harmonizing the diverse practices of justice as well as enriching rules, uses and customs and lead towards a creative synthesis of Mozambican law". Being neither entirely official nor entirely unofficial, community courts are a legal hybrid, both inside and outside official law and justice.

Left in this limbo, community courts have taken on the legacy of the popular courts, which have, in the meantime, been formally abolished. The Law that created the community courts determined that the judges of the local and neighborhood courts (that is, the popular courts of the previous, revolutionary period) would continue to exercise their functions until the first elections for judges of the community courts were held. As there were no elections, the judges at the time kept their positions. Death, illness, war and migrations caused the number of judges to be reduced over the years. Moreover, some judges left their posts, due to the loss of the social prestige attached to the position and the feeling of being 'abandoned' by the government. In the absence of any regulatory law to define rules of recruitment, these replacements were made from within the same socio-political environment as that of the previous judges. The new judges were selected by neighborhood structures or by the direct intervention of the ruling party, Frelimo.[23] For this reason, almost all the judges interviewed said they belonged to the Frelimo and many of them also participated in party organizations. This hybridization between political and judicial functions is also at the root of the problems confronting the community courts. Continuity with the popular courts in terms of both personnel and premises has favored the adherence to the Frelimo Party. This fact has led to the political polarization of community justice, in the terms of which community courts are considered instruments of Frelimo and the traditional authorities instruments of Renamo, the main opposition party.[24] This polarization reached some extremes when, for example, a group of judges, who are supporters of Renamo, decided to create a parallel community court in Mocímboa da Praia (in the northern province of Cabo Delgado).

The hybrid character of the community courts does not limit itself to the legal/political or official/unofficial variables. It can be traced in each of the dichotomies that define the terms of legal plurality and also in the constellation of legal cultures (revolutionary, traditional and liberal democratic legal cultures) present in the ways they operate. The extreme variety gives rise to a landscape of chaotic spontaneity. Lacking, in general, institutional support, being in competition with other mechanisms of dispute resolution – ranging from the police and the local political cadres informally performing judicial functions to the traditional authorities and church organizations –, community courts rely on themselves and their skills for improvising, innovating and, in the end, reproducing themselves. Some remain very active, others are moribund; some beat the competition offered by other institutions involved in dispute resolution, while others are rarely resorted to by the members of the community.

The palimpsest nature of the political and legal cultures in contemporary Mozambique mentioned in section 2 is most vividly illustrated in the legal reasoning and procedural style of dispute resolution in the community courts. Some function predominantly within an official, formal atmosphere, whilst others assume an unofficial, informal character. Some operate within a revolutionary logic, placing political loyalty above everything else, while others have fully accepted the new times and the pragmatism demanded by communities mainly interested in peaceful survival. Some seek to affirm their autonomy in relation to the local administrative authorities – which are themselves a political-administrative hybrid –, the religious authorities and the traditional authorities, while others are totally subordinate to the administrative authorities and assume a multicultural character, resorting to the traditional authorities in many cases, such as when dealing with witchcraft or family problems.[25] However, no matter which type of legal reasoning or procedural style predominates, it operates in complex articulations with other types or styles. In this way, and varying according to the courts, the cases, the nature of the dispute or the status of the parties, different 'layers' of formalism and informalism, of revolutionary rhetoric and pragmatic rhetoric, of practices of autonomy and practices of networking are differently combined but always inextricably intertwined.

Finally, though most courts have no working relationship with the district courts, some do. In the revolutionary period, the district courts, then called popular district courts, were the bridges between the law courts and the base popular courts, establishing both complementary and competitive relationships with the latter. This type of articulation continues today, however sporadically and informally. For example, the district courts make use of the community courts and the traditional authorities in order to ensure that court summonses are complied with. In the district of Mueda (Cabo Delgado province), as well as in Angoche (Nampula province), the district court and the community courts in the district capital maintain a stable relationship, which has progressed from the discussion of jurisdiction of the community courts to the joint definition of the sanctions to be applied in various cases and on the rapid handling of cases which are referred to the district court by the community courts. In addition, a form of 'division of legal labor' has developed, in the terms of which family matters, for instance, are referred by the district courts to the institutions of community justice. According to one district court judge interviewed, these types of conflicts "are not for a judge to hear, but should be resolved within the family or in the neighborhood". In this context, the police often takes on the function of distributing the litigation among the different institutions, according to the agreed upon informal rules of jurisdiction.

Through this chaotic web of actions and omissions, of communication and non-communication among different institutions, practices and cultures, the community courts do contribute to 'a creative synthesis of Mozambican law', except that they do so under very precarious circumstances and indeed outside the law. The legal limbo has played against the community courts. A void has been created which has been filled by other mechanisms of social regulation, with the traditional authorities emerging as the most important of all.

4. Multicultural and Multi-ethnic Justices: The Case of the Traditional Authorities[26]

Throughout this chapter I have been emphasizing the multiple and culturally diverse instances of dispute resolution and community justice in Mozambican society, both in rural and urban environments. Besides community courts, traditional authorities and social, cultural, religious and regional associations function as instances of conflict resolution. The most important of the latter associations are the churches and, within them, the Islamic organizations, which have grown in influence in recent years. Because it does not recognize any strong distinction between the religious and the nonreligious, Islamic faith tends to regulate social life as a whole. In the central and

northern regions of the country, where the Islamic presence is historically more powerful, religious law has become an important component of legal plurality, particularly in family matters. This is a field of intense hybridization between the religious law
and traditional law. All this vibrant legal life occurs outside the official legal field, mobilizing legal and political cultures that have very little to do with that underlying the
official legal system. Legal polycentrism merges here with multiculturalism and, thus,
with multicultural legal plurality. But of all the instances of multicultural legal plurality,
the traditional authorities are by far the most important, not only because of their role
in dispute resolution but also because of the political contention around them.[27]

In order to understand the political context in which the traditional authorities
operate in Mozambique it is imperative to locate it in the broader, African context.
Traditional authorities nowadays are the object of debate throughout the African
continent. There are many themes to the discussion and the following may be highlighted: the traditional authorities as local power and administration; the regulation
of access to land; women and traditional power; witchcraft; traditional medicine; the
compatibility between traditional law and official law and, in particular, the Constitution. From the perspective of neo-liberal globalization, the traditional authorities are
the paradigmatic example of what cannot be globalized in Africa. From this perspective, what cannot be globalized is of no interest to neo-liberal globalization, and, as
such, can be easily stigmatized as an African specificity, an obstacle to the opening up
of African societies to the virtues of the market economy and liberal democracy. Yet
what becomes the object of stigmatization may be reappropriated by the subaltern
social groups as something positive and specific, as a source of resistance against an
excluding global (Western) modernity. It is exactly this reappropriation and
resignification that has begun to take place in the area of traditional power. Today, the
recovery of the traditional in Africa, far from being a non-modern alternative to
Western modernity, is the expression of a claim to an alternative modernity. Because
it is occurring throughout Africa and indeed throughout the global South, it is a form
of globalization that presents itself as resistance to globalization.

One of the most visible modernities of the traditional lies in the way in which
modern state elites seek out the 'non-modern', traditional legitimacy to reinforce their
own power. However, this process also occurs in reverse, whenever the bearers of
traditional power seek to promote their children or families to a political career in the
service of the state, to consolidate and reinforce the traditional power they possess
[and see as...] threatened by state competition. This double-edged power struggle
can result in conflicts that are difficult to resolve. The ethical code of modern power
is based on a distinction between public and private and on the primacy of common
interests over sectorial interests. In contrast, the ethical code of ethnic power is based
on community interests and relates to a community made up both of living people
and their ancestors, in which modern distinctions make little sense. Thus, from the
perspective of the modern political ethical code, a particular political or administrative action may be considered as corruption, favoritism, nepotism, patronage or

privatization of the state; but when evaluated from the point of view of the traditional ethical code it may be considered the fulfillment of family obligations and the exercise of community or ethnic loyalties. The popular saying 'the goat eats wherever it is tethered' illustrates this ambiguity or duality.

The question of how to articulate this dual legitimacy feeds one of the most intractable debates in Africa today.[28] According to one argument, the two powers and the two legitimacies must be kept separate, even if they are conferred upon the same person. In other words, state political actions or actions within the public arena of modern civil society must be based exclusively on modern ethical codes, whilst community actions and rituals must be based exclusively on traditional ethical codes. According to another argument, this separation, even if correct – which is debatable – is impossible to sustain, given that individuals cannot keep their multiple identities watertight and uncontaminated. It is better, therefore, to assume that contamination and hybridization between codes is a 'natural' condition.[29]

The rules for this dual-edged power game vary from country to country and according to the historical, cultural and political context. In countries that are officially democratic, these conflicts must be settled by electoral means and according to the rules imposed by the political system in force. Nevertheless, it does happen that, due to the factors already mentioned, electoral legitimacy cannot sustain itself, leading to frequent reliance on community, ethnic or traditional resources. Ethnic power can thus be manipulated, so that in certain situations it functions as a threat and in others as an opportunity. According to circumstances, the political elites wrangle amongst themselves, either for the modern political path, using ethnic power as a resource, or for the traditional political path, using electoral power as a resource. Herein lies a fertile field for the proliferation of political hybrids which are structurally similar to the legal hybrids identified in the previous section.

In the history of Africa this is not the first time that the traditional authorities have been politicized or politically manipulated. This was also the case during the colonial period, particularly from the end of the nineteenth century onwards. It is known that the traditional authorities were used by the colonial powers as a means of ensuring the above-mentioned disjunction between direct political control and indirect administrative control. And indeed the current situation in Mozambique shows a remarkable continuity with the colonial period. To limit myself to the twentieth century, the establishment of a dual, racialized civil society was formally recognized in *Estatuto do Indigenato* (The Statute of Indigenous populations) adopted in 1929.[30] The *Estatuto* established a distinction between the 'colonial citizens', subjected to the Portuguese laws and entitled to all citizenship rights effective in the 'metropolis', and the *indígenas* (natives), subjected to colonial legislation and, in their daily lives, to their customary, native laws. Between the two groups there was a third small group, the *assimilados*, made up of blacks, *mulatos*, Asians, or mixed, who had some formal education, were not subjected to forced labor, were entitled to some citizenship rights (a kind of second-class citizenship) and held a special identification card that differed from the one imposed on the immense mass of African population, the *indígenas*, a card that the colonial authorities conceived of as a means of controlling the movements of forced labor (Centro de Estudos Africanos, 1998). The *indígenas* were subjected to the traditional authorities, who in turn were gradually integrated in the colonial administration charged with solving disputes, managing the access to land, guaranteeing the flows of forced labor and the payment of taxes (mainly the hut tax). As several authors have pointed out (Mamdani, 1996a; Gentili, 1999; O'Laughlin, 2000), the *Indigenato* regime was the political system that subordinated the immense majority of Mozambicans to local authorities entrusted with governing, in collaboration with the lowest echelon of colonial administration, the 'native' communities described as tribes and assumed to have a common ancestry, language and culture. The colonial use of traditional law and structures of power was thus an integral part of the process of colonial domination (Young, 1994; Penvenne, 1995; O'Laughlin, 2000), obsessed with the reproduction of the super-exploitation of African labor.

In the 1940s the integration of traditional authorities in the colonial administration was deepened. The colony was divided into *concelhos* (municipalities) in urban areas, governed by colonial and metropolitan legislation, and into *circunscrições* (localities) in rural areas. The *circunscrições* were led by a colonial administrator and divided into *regedorias*, headed by *régulos* (chieftains),[31] the embodiment of traditional authorities. Provincial Decree No. 5,639, of July 29, 1944, attributed to *régulos* and their assistants – the '*cabos de terra*' – the status of *auxiliares da administração* (administrative assistants). Gradually, these 'traditional' titles lost some of their content and the *régulos* and *cabos de terra* came to be viewed as an effective part of the colonial state,[32] remunerated for their participation in the collection of hut taxes, recruitment of the labor force, and the agricultural production in the area under their control.[33] Within the areas of their jurisdiction, the *régulos* and *cabos de terra* also controlled the distribution of land and settled conflicts according to customary norms (Geffray, 1990; Alexander, 1994; Dinerman, 1999). To exercise their power, the *régulos* and *cabos de terra* had their own police force. This system of indirect rule illustrates the disjunction between political and administrative control referred to above. It continued after the *Indigenato* system was abolished in the early 1960s. From then on, all Africans were considered Portuguese citizens and racial discrimination became a sociological rather than a legal feature of colonial society. The rule of traditional authorities was indeed integrated more than before in the colonial administration.

After the independence, Frelimo took a hostile position vis-à-vis the traditional authorities conceived of in the broad sense of the word, including *régulos*, healers (*curandeiros*), religious leaders, etc. Seen as obscurantist remnants of colonialism and as fomenting regional and ethnic differences, there was no place for them in the construction of a supra-ethnic state, a national culture and a model of development aimed at liberating Mozambique, in a few generations, from the shackles of underdevelopment. The first Constitution of Mozambique, approved in 1975, declared in its Article 4 the "elimination of colonial and traditional structures of oppression and exploitation and the accompanying mentality". *Régulos* were then replaced by the new political structures at the local level, the base-level party cells, called *grupos dinamizadores*.[34] In tandem with the base popular courts, they took over the functions heretofore entrusted to the traditional authorities.

The legal abolition of traditional authorities proved to be a complex political and social problem for the government in the following years. To begin with, there were no resources to deploy the new political-administrative structures throughout the whole country, and where they were deployed they were not automatically accepted by the populations. As a result, the traditional authorities continued to rule under different forms and conditions. Both the popular courts and the *grupos dinamizadores* resorted to them in search of guidance and legitimacy. In the process, some *régulos* became judges of the popular courts, deciding the cases on the basis of traditional law and justifying their decisions in terms of revolutionary legality. Another source of problems for the government came with the rise of Renamo. Renamo, which was initially credibly seen as a product of South African secret services, gradually took roots in some regions of the country feeding on the frustrations of the populations with some misguided state policies and with the immense gaps between promises and delivery. Ostracized by Frelimo, the traditional authorities saw in Renamo an alternative for recuperating their power and prestige. A bloody civil war throughout the 1980s further undermined the administrative and welfare capacities of the state and deepened the political polarization around the traditional authorities. Such polarization, combined with the state's docile compliance with neo-liberal impositions from the mid-1980s onwards, fuelled the process by which the traditional became a way of claiming an alternative modernity.

Since 1992 the government has been trying to address the issue of the politicization of base-level governance: community courts, seen as heirs of the popular courts and close to Frelimo, on the one hand, and traditional authorities, seen as a legitimate source of power and close to Renamo.[35] The government response has been two-fold. On one hand, until recently, as I showed in the previous section, the government has seen no urgency in reforming the community courts. The reform is now under way and it is an open question whether the new law of the community courts will be truly bipartisan and therefore likely to survive any changes in government in the future. On the other hand, the government has been trying to neutralize the hostility of traditional authorities, co-opting them by granting them some kind of subordinate recognition and participation in local administration in the rural areas.

The strategy of co-optation relies on the disjunction between administrative and political control. Decree no. 15/2000, of June 20, 2000, the Law of Community Authorities, illustrates the intention of the state to benefit from the administrative abilities of the traditional authorities and simultaneously to neutralize any centrifugal energy they might harness in terms of the political control of populations. As the preamble to the Decree states, community authorities are recognized within the realms – and therefore the limits – "of the process of administrative decentralization, bettering the social organization of local communities and improving the terms of their participation in public administration". Article 2, in turn, establishes that "in carrying out their administrative functions, local organs of the state will interact with the community authorities, by listening to opinions on the best way to mobilize and organize participation from the local authorities, in the design and implementation of economic, social and cultural plans and programs, designed to benefit local development". No political effect, particularly in terms of participatory democracy, is recognized in these processes of listening and interaction. Finally, Article 3 defines the limits of recognition which refer to the political Constitution and statutory law in general. The general limit is formulated in Article 3 no. 1, and no. 2 underlines the pragmatic and instrumental nature of the recognition of community authorities, since the criteria for participation are based exclusively on the "*needs for administrative service*".

This recognition pattern and the politics underlying it bear a clear continuity with the colonial past, which is also visible in some of the rights and privileges conferred upon the traditional authorities: the use of symbols of the Republic; participation in official ceremonies; the use of their own uniform or distinctive costume; the receiving of a subsidy as a result of helping the state in collecting taxes (Article 5). The main difference in relation to the colonial period lies in the fact that the state seeks to neutralize the traditional authorities not only through the strict separation between political and administrative functions but also through the integration of traditional authorities in a broader set of local government involving base-level administrative structures and even the political-administrative hybrids I mentioned above. The colonial state, on the contrary, emphasized the specificity of traditional authorities in order to justify the racialization of state and society. Specificity meant natural inferiority of traditional authorities vis-à-vis modern colonial rule, African culture vis-à-vis Western culture, indigenous peoples vis-à-vis colonial citizens.

In Mozambique and in Africa, in general, there are today two contrasting views concerning the specificity of traditional authorities: according to one of them, traditional authorities are one among several types of local authority and should be granted no privilege among various other types of authority existing in the same community; according to the other, traditional authorities are not on an equal footing with other local authorities, since they alone control the power of the spirits and the power of the ancestors, so decisive in the government of the community because of their access to rituals and the magical aspects of community life.[36] The already mentioned Decree no. 15/2000 of June 20, 2000, on local community authorities, adopts the first argument. According to Article 1, "under the terms of the present Decree, the community authorities are understood to be the traditional chiefs, the neighborhood or village secretaries and the other legitimate leaders recognized as such by their respective communities".

Underneath or parallel to this official politics of recognition and control there is an intense and chaotic web of interlacings among different legitimacies, local powers, legal cultures and legal practices. While in the revolutionary period the popular courts and *grupos dinamizadores* sought the guidance and support of the traditional authorities and settled many disputes with resort to them, even though they had been officially abolished, today the official patterns of recognition of traditional authorities and the 'return to tradition' say very little about the traditional rule in action. Actually this varies according to the region, the prestige of the *régulo*, *xehé* or healer, the relative penetration of the state institutions, the kinship relationships among traditional authorities, state administrators and base-level party organizations, and, finally, the relative strength and influence of alternative community structures of conflict resolution, such as community courts, Muslim organizations, churches, NGOs, etc. A meshwork of regular or sporadic interactions and negotiations is in place, whose unfolding depends as much on the practice of the different institutions involved as it does on the initiative of citizens and social groups interested in turning to their advantage the existence of such competitive or complementary plurality.

Within this web of meshwork and plurality the 'return to the traditional' seems to have more and more appeal, particularly in rural areas where the vast majority of the population lives. A growing activism on the part of the traditional authorities has been identified and the involvement of political or administrative cadres in traditional ceremonies has been accepted. Respect and mutual tolerance have grown. Although in the early 1990s it appeared that most of the traditional authorities were intervening only in religious or spiritual ceremonies as a way to promote peace (Alexander, 1994; Honwana, 2002), the situation today points to a broader intervention which is particularly sought for whenever other local authorities are unable to resolve problems and conflicts.[37] In these forms of cooperation the abovementioned duality of traditional and modern legitimacies dominating law and politics in Africa surfaces very clearly, especially at the local level.[38]

This is the complex historical, social and political context in which traditional authorities operate today as entities of conflict resolution. Among all the dimensions of legal pluralism in Africa, traditional authorities and their law (traditional law, kinship systems, African customs and customary law are some of the terms currently used) have for a long time been the most significant. What distinguishes the legal pluralism they promote is the saliency of the modern/traditional variable and the monocultural/multicultural variable. What is common to the different conceptions of traditional authorities is the idea that these legal practices are distinct from the eurocentric symbolic and cultural universe that underlies official law and justice. Traditional law and justice, therefore, raise two very complex questions: the question of what is traditional and the question of what counts as multicultural. Both these questions are very widely debated issues today and this debate is not only an academic, but also a political one. What is at stake is, once again, the relationship between the political control and the administrative control of populations and their territories, and particularly the question of the legitimacy of the power needed to secure either form of control.

As dispute resolution mechanisms, traditional authorities are particularly important in issues of access to land, family, debt, bodily harm, damage to property, health/
sickness, witchcraft and petty theft, indeed a very broad range of issues. In all these
matters, traditional authorities are a key node in a network of institutions that may
include the district or even the provincial courts, the police, as well as local political
and administrative agencies. Sometimes they are the first venue sought for by the
parties, sometimes they function as appeal institutions, and in still other occasions
they provide advice, or evidence in cases being dealt with by other institutions.

One of the great strengths of the justice provided by the traditional authorities is
its immediate, public, collective, face-to-face, and relatively transparent character.[39]

This analysis shows that the traditional authorities are carving out their judicial
and political space in the new legal and political framework, both when effectively
implemented and when left to the indeterminate play of competing local legal and
political forces. They are doing so using a vast array of means available to them, some
ancestral and others very recent, but all of them used in modern competitive or
complementary interactions with all the other nodes of a mixed, inherently hybrid
regulatory network. Out of this network new forms of democratic rule may be emerging which call for careful analysis. Under the new laws that regulate the process of
recognition and legitimization of 'local leadership', *régulos* and other community leaders may be required to secure the basis of their legitimacy through a broad process of
popular consultation. By opening some space for negotiation in the choice of *régulos*,
cabos de terra, *madoda*, healers, etc, this process, although incipient, includes elements
of participatory democracy.

Conclusion

In this chapter I have highlighted some hidden dimensions of the current global call
for legal and judicial reform, namely the ways in which it seems to be operating, as if
the developing countries were a legal and judicial *tabula rasa*. The rich social experience of diverse legal and judicial practices thereby ignored was the main focus of this
chapter. More specifically, I focused on the Mozambican state and society and on the
rich landscape of legal pluralism that characterizes them. I proposed the concept of
heterogeneous state to highlight the breakdown of the modern equation between the
unity of the state, on the one hand, and the unity of its legal and administrative
operation, on the other. I explained the most salient features of the heterogeneous
state and of legal pluralism in Mozambique in terms of three major factors: the
impositions of neo-liberal globalization and their impact on the political and social
processes; an African cultural heritage, which is the object of intense debates and has
deep implications on law and politics; the nature and role of the state, bearing in
mind that the latter emerged from colonialism in the last quarter of the twentieth
century. I tried to highlight the complexity of legal and political processes in a country that has been independent for less than three decades; that has undergone, in such
a short period, a turbulent succession of contrasting political regimes and cultures;

has suffered a bloody civil war for more than ten years, and since 1994 has been trying to consolidate a transition to a liberal democratic regime.

I expanded on the concepts of legal hybridization with the purpose of showing the porosity of the boundaries of the different legal orders and cultures at work and the deep cross-fertilizations or cross-contaminations among them. Among the many instances in which these conceptions could fruitfully unfold, I focused on community courts and traditional authorities. I reconstructed the multicultural legal plurality resulting from the interaction between modern law and traditional authorities as a multicultural legal plurality involving alternative modernities

The future of the conditions accounting for the heterogeneity of the state and legal pluralism is tied to the future of the Mozambican state and society as an encompassing process, and will tend to decrease in importance in any scenario in which the following developments will occur: democratic stability and sustained social and economic development that is capable of breaking the cycle of successive political-institutional ruptures; deepening democracy, so that political control and administrative control can develop with reciprocal autonomy; and an increase in the institutional and administrative ability and efficiency of the state, so that respect for the plurality of non-state local and foreign actors involved in social intervention does not result in the fragmentation and segmentation of the polity.

Notes

1   I analyze this phenomenon in great detail in Santos (2002c: 313-52). See also Tate and Valinder (1995).

2   Mozambique is part of the Bretton Wood Institutions since 1984. On this subject, see chapter 4.

3   See also chapter 3, as welle as10 through 13, all of them focusing on different aspects of legal pluralism and community justice.

4   It is true that global pressures are subject to local adaptations, but the latter, especially in peripheral countries, are less open to negotiation, or else are marginal or dictated by the philanthropic whim of international agencies or core countries in particularly extreme situations of social collapse. A good illustration of this is the HIPIC (Highly Indebted Poor Countries) initiative led by the World Bank and creditor countries to alleviate the foreign debt of the most impoverished countries.

5   Africa was the only continent not partitioned by the Treaty of Yalta at the end of the World War II and therefore the one where the Cold War became a permanent 'war of position', to use the Gramscian term. Portuguese colonialism survived for so long, despite its weakness as a colonial power, in part because it served the interests of the capitalist countries by functioning as a barricade against Soviet advances in Southern Africa. Still in the midst of the Cold War, the newly independent countries sided with the Soviet bloc, which was already showing visible signs of decline. The Soviet threat explained the war of destabilization waged by

apartheid South Africa against Angola and Mozambique. The war of destabilization gave way to civil war, which lasted in Mozambique until 1992 and in Angola until 2002.

6 Sometimes such micro-states are clustered around different ministries. For instance, the Ministries of Energy or of Mineral Resources and the Ministry of Environmental Coordination may operate under mutually incompatible political principles and regulatory logics.

7 On this subject, see Santos (2002c: 163-351), where the argument summarized in this section is developed at length. Legal pluralism is one of the core debates in the sociology and anthropology of law. See, amongst others, Nader (1969); Hooker (1975); Moore (1978, 1992); Galanter (1981); Macaulay (1983); Fitzpatrick (1983); Griffiths (1986); Merry (1988); Starr and Collier (1989); Chiba (1989); Benda-Beckmann (1988, 1991); Teubner (1992); Tamanaha (1993); Twining (1999); Melissaris (2004).

8 I use 'scales' in the sense that it is used on maps rather than in the common metaphor 'scales of justice'.

9 This does not mean that the two legal orders existed separately, in two different worlds. On the contrary, the separation was a product of the intense and unequal interactions between them. Chanock was one of the first to show that customary law, far from being a remnant, was created by the changes and conflicts brought about by colonialism (1998). The specificity of South Africa in this regard both in the pre-and post-apartheid period is cogently analyzed by Klug (2000).
   On this subject, on Africa and specifically on Mozambique see, for example, Aguiar,(1891); Lopes (1909); Ennes (1946); Gonçalves Cota (1944, 1946); Mondlane (1969); Mondlane (1997); Sachs and Honwana Welch (1990); Ghai (1991); Hall and Young (1991); Gundersen (1992); Moiane (1994); Moore (1994); Ki-Zerbo (1996); O'Laughlin (2000); Bekker *et al.*, (2002). On post-colonialism and legal plurality, see, for example, Darian-Smith and Fitzpatrick (1999); Randeria (2003); Abrahamsen (2003).

10 The complexity of this dichotomy has been widely debated in African post-colonial social sciences. See Copans (1990a); Ela (1994); Gable (1995); Mamdani (1996a); Werbner (1996); Chabal (1997); Fisiy and Goheen (1998); Mappa (1998); Mbembe (2000, 2001).

11 On the debate on multiculturalism and the law, see Khatibi (1983); Pannikar (1984, 1996); Lippman (1985); Sheth (1989); Le Roy (1992); Ndegwa (1997); Esteva and Prakash (1998); Tie (1999); Sheleff (1999); Khare (1999); Sanchéz (2001).

12 A palimpsest is a parchment or other writing-material written upon twice, the original writing having been erased or rubbed out to make place for the second or, more simply, a manuscript in which a later writing is written over an effaced earlier writing. In archaeology the concept of palimpsest is used to refer to situations in which the same archaeological layers comprise objects and residues from very different periods and times and very often not susceptible to exact dating. I use

the metaphor of the palimpsest to characterize the intricate ways in which very different political and legal cultures and very different historical durations are inextricably intertwined in contemporary Mozambique. Their impact on state functions and actions is rendered by the concept of the heterogeneous state illustrated below.

13 These two rivers mark the north and south borders of Mozambique and are used as a symbol of national unity.

14 For an evaluation of the last 30 years of political and economic history of Mozambique see chapters 2 and 4 in this volume. See also Chingono (1996); Minter (1998); Newitt (1995, 2002).

15 The popular courts were considered to be "like a weapon permanently aimed at the class enemy, the reactionaries and the traitors, saboteurs of the economy and unscrupulous exploiters, criminals and outlaws throughout the country". The popular courts were, therefore, the instrument which enabled the population to "resolve the problems and difficulties which emerge in the life of the community, the local area, the village or the neighborhood". The popular courts were considered a guarantee of the consolidation and unity of the Mozambican people, "the great forge in which the people create the new law which is increasingly routing the old law of colonial-capitalist and feudal society" (Cf. Preamble to Law no. 12/78).

16 This process of legal-institutional segmentation does not exclude the possibility of some legal or administrative sectors trying to bridge the two sets of existing regulatory logics. This is the case of the Land law approved in 1997. It remains an open question whether the building of this bridge, always a difficult task, will be solid enough to be sustained (Negrão, 2003).

17 I use the concept of global legal culture wars to highlight the extreme forms of competition among different legal systems, particularly in peripheral countries, which are often linked to structural adjustment programs. Instances of such extreme forms of competition can be read, among others, in Santos, 2002c: 208-215; Nader, 2002; Dezalay and Garth, 2002.

18 From the revolutionary period, all kinds of local political cadres, such as members of *grupos dinamizadores, chefes de quarteirão, secretários de bairro* can still be drawn upon. Both urban settings and large rural villages are divided into neighborhoods (*bairros*). Each neighborhood had a local *grupo dinamizador*, ruled by a secretary. Although the *grupos dinamizadores* have been formally abolished, the figure of *secretário de bairro* (neighborhood secretary) has been maintained; the large neighborhoods are subdivided into quarters, controlled by *chefes de quarteirão* (more on this below).

19 On the subject of community courts, see also chapter 10.

20 A broader analysis of the official judicial structure in Mozambique is presented in part 3 of this book. The figure for district courts includes also the city courts existing in the country. The data is for 2003.

21 For the official judges this is problematic, since the official legal language – Portuguese – is neither the mother tongue nor the language normally used by the majority of Mozambicans.

22 The law that created the community courts established that before the courts could operate a new law would be promulgated, defining their jurisdiction and their institutionalization. Such law has not been promulgated up until now (2005).

23 Frelimo (Mozambique Liberation Front) was the movement that conducted the struggle for national liberation. After Mozambique's independence, Frelimo underwent a process of political transformation and was established as a party in the late 1970s. After the introduction of a multi-party system, in the early 1990s, Frelimo won the three first presidential and legislative elections, thus being the party in power.

24 Renamo emerged as a movement of resistance against Frelimo, carrying out a civil war for more than a decade. After the 1992 Peace Agreement between Renamo and the Mozambican Government, Renamo transformed itself from a movement of resistance into a political party, becoming the major opposition party in the country.

25 The community courts also resort to the Mozambican Association of Traditional Doctors (Ametramo) in cases of witchcraft (see also Meneses *et al.*, 2003, as well as chapter 3).

26 On this subject, see also chapters 3, 11 and 13.

27 The role of traditional authorities in conflict resolution in Mozambique has been emphasized by several Mozambican researchers. See, for example, Cuahela (1996); Honwana (2002); Bonate (2003).

28 In a different way, the question of dual legitimacy is also present in Latin America today after the emergence of multicultural constitutionalism of the late 1980s and early 1990s (the constitutional recognition of the political and legal identity of the indigenous peoples).

29 This, however, raises serious questions, such as, for example, the issue of determining criminal liability in cases considered by official law to be active or passive corruption or abuse of power.

30 The Statute underwent several transformations throughout the colonial period. This subject is also briefly analyzed in chapter 2.

31 The *régulo* (chieftain) was institutionalized, in colonial times, as the lowest component of the administrative colonial system, working under the control of the local administrator. The *régulo*'s position is passed down from generation to generation, according to a hereditary system. Thus, where such a position still exists, its legitimacy derives from family lineages going back to pre-colonial times. The *régulo* embodies different functions of power: legislative, judicial, executive and administrative.

32 Despite this linkage with the colonial administration, several authors refer to the dual role of some *régulos*, who used their privileged position to promote programs

that improved the life conditions of their populations (Isaacman, 1990; Alexander, 1994). In other situations, they made a decision to confront the colonial system directly, or to flee to neighboring countries (Vail and White, 1980; Centro de Estudos Africanos, 1998).

33 An example of this is Article 2 of the Municipal Decree No, 13.128, of April 1950, which granted traditional authorities certain concessions for their interference in labor contracts.

34 The *grupos dinamizadores* were groups of eight to ten people, chosen by a show of hands during the public meetings of urban neighborhoods, workplaces, or local communities throughout the country. All of those accused of collaboration with the colonial regime were excluded on principle. Popular vigilante groups were also formed to assist the *grupos dinamizadores* and were supported by militias that reported to the Frelimo-appointed local administrators.

35 This formulation represents the general tendency. Of course, there are many traditional authorities publicly siding with Frelimo.

36 On the former view, see, among many others, Ghai, 1991; Nzouankeu, 1997; Mamdani, 1996b. On the latter see, also among many others, Ayittey, 1991; van Rouveroy, van Nieuwaal and van Dijk, 1999; Williams, 2004.

37 Depending on the situation, some traditional leaders directly offered their services to the state without conditions, in order to recuperate the role they had before it was disrupted by politics or by the war; others, concerned with the question of status and social recognition are still waiting for formal state recognition, of their authority (materially translated in goods and services such as housing and uniforms).

38 This climate of cooperation does not prevent traditional authorities from remembering past grievances and from voicing them when deemed appropriate. *Régulos* and their assistants were intimidated and humiliated by their former subjects who came to occupy party secretary positions within the Frelimo, or by higher level state and party authorities (Geffray, 1990; Meneses *et al.*, 2003).

39 A detailed analysis of dispute processing by the traditional authorities can be read in chapter 11.

2

Rupture and Continuity in Political and Legal Processes

João Carlos Trindade

Introduction

The nature and forms that the struggles for independence in former colonial territories assumed are factors which heavily influenced the political configuration of the new states. In formulating their development strategies, these states, as a rule, adopted one of two attitudes: they either favored elements offering structural continuity with the former ruling nations or, conversely, imposed significant and deep ruptures of any links with the past.

In the case of Mozambique, the fact that the struggle for freedom had assumed the nature of a 'prolonged popular war' and that Frelimo[1] had progressively incorporated into its ideas "the destruction of all vestiges of colonialism and imperialism, in order to eliminate the system of man exploiting his fellow man, and to build the political, material, ideological, cultural and social basis of a new society",[2] determined the predominance of elements of rupture, especially those relating to the nature of political power and its ideology, the integration of economic and military areas and the strategic options relating to foreign policy (Moita, 1985: 504). In spite of this, both in the political and in the legal and judicial spheres, there were large areas where very little changed, or, if changes had taken place at all, they were only felt at a formal or *institutional* level. For example, we shall see later that the composition, organization and functioning of the courts and the other bodies devoted to the administration of justice were profoundly altered, but the essential nucleus of the standard system that these bodies were called upon to implement remained practically the same, with continuity clearly favored as a solution.[3]

In order to make it easier to understand our analysis of the evolution of the political and judicial systems over the course of the last twenty-eight years, we have subdivided this historical period into four main phases:

1. 1974-1975 – the phase of the Transitional Government, extending from the time when it took office on September 20, 1974 to the proclamation of independence on June 25, 1975;
2. 1975-1978 – From independence to the approval of the first Law on the Organization of the Judiciary, Law no. 12/78, of December 2nd;
3. 1978-1992 – the phase of the "construction of the political, economic, social and cultural basis of socialism" and of the so-called *Popular Justice*, which, for purely descriptive reasons, we have extended to include the year of the Peace Agreement and judicial reform;
4. 1992-2002 – from the Peace Agreement to the present.

1. The Transitional Government and the Preparations for Independence (1974-1975)

The indigenous regime introduced into the colonial legal-political order at the beginning of the *Estado Novo* (the *New State*)[4] constituted one of the structural elements of Mozambican society prior to independence. In the words of Narana Coissoró, the Statute of the Indigenous Populations of the Provinces of Guinea, Angola and Mozambique, approved by Decree-Law no. 39.666, of 20 May 1954, "established [...] a clear distinction between 'citizens' and 'indigenous populations', although they were all considered Portuguese nationals", subjecting the latter to "the 'protective paternalism' of the state, while denying them civil and political rights in relation to institutions of European origin" (Coissoró, 1966: 3).[5]

Under the terms of this Statute, the indigenous populations[6] would in fact be ruled "by the customs and usage of their own respective societies", which meant "compliance with usage and customs [...] limited by morality, the dictates of humanity and the higher interests of the free exercise of Portuguese sovereignty" (Articles 3 and 1, respectively). For a long time, therefore, they were subject to the jurisdiction of the private courts,[7] and access to the law courts was reserved for the non-indigenous populations (whites, those of mixed race, Indians and *assimilados*).[8] Even after the hasty reforms of the early sixties,[9] this situation did not change significantly.

In fact, the end of the distinction between citizens and indigenous populations would prove to be an important formal measure, with obvious *de jure* implications, but with a reduced practical effect, since it was very limited in its *de facto* application. The field of labor relations provides perhaps one of the most illustrative examples of this: although forced labor and corporal punishment were abolished and the formerly native populations could then choose freely who they wished to work for, reality has come to show that racial discrimination was not eliminated from the urban labor markets and that, until almost the end of the colonial era, black Mozambican workers never benefited from the same unemployment benefits, pension schemes, integration into the trade unions or legal minimum wage that Portuguese workers were entitled to (Penvenne, 1995; O'Laughlin, 2000: 23; Covane, 2001). Industrial statistics from the mid-sixties also show that the wages the Portuguese earned in the manufacturing industry were seven times higher in the district of Lourenço Marques,[10] and eleven times higher in other districts in the colony, than the wages earned by Mozambicans in the same circumstances (Rita-Ferreira, 1967-1968: 346).

As far as the administration of justice is concerned, although the reorganization of the parish and municipal courts had some effect, the fact remained that the basic functions of the judiciary continued to be amalgamated with those of the administration. The law determined that the duties of a second class municipal judge should be carried out "[...] as inherited functions by the registrars of the [...] civil registry in the respective municipality or locality" (Article 11, no. 1, of Act no. 48.033 of 11 November 1967), but when it emerged that the majority of municipalities and local areas had no available registrars, colonial administrators ended up exercising these duties (no. 3 of the same legal precept). An identical solution was adopted in relation to the small claims courts judges (*julgados de paz*) (Article 16).

This concentration of duties within the person of the administrator was, in the end, an important means of political control in rural areas. As Rui Baltazar reported,[11]

> The colonial administrator held [...] in his hands all the tools necessary to secure and maintain colonial exploitation. The administrator supervised the economic sectors (from the distribution of land to the exercise of trade); he ensured the recruitment of forced labor for the plantations, public works or for emigration; he collected taxes; he was in charge of security; he distributed favors and judged and punished of his own free will (1978: 31).

In this way, with the exception of positions in half a dozen of the first-class municipal, courts which were very rarely filled, it was only at a larger territorial level (the actual provincial law courts) and at the level of the Appeals Courts that the system, in principle, possessed career magistrates with formal guarantees of autonomy and independence in relation to the executive power. Even so, these positions were difficult to fill and operate. This is Rui Baltazar again, describing the state of the courts during the final period of Portuguese colonial rule in Mozambique:

> Cases were piling up in the court registry offices and the judicial machinery responded only with great difficulty to those it was expected to deal with, [and then only] in the service of the dominant class and interests. In addition, foreign magistrates – for whom the monopoly on judicial posts was reserved [...] – were also in short supply. It became increasingly difficult to recruit the personnel required to ensure the normal functioning of the judiciary from amongst the citizens of the colonizing country. In fact, in various provinces in our country, long before 1974, there were no judges or public functionaries. Even in the capital there were problems filling all the posts that had been created and

which had to be occupied by career magistrates. The repressive machinery in general, and the judicial machinery in particular, were witnessing signs of rapid decline and decay.

After 25 April 1974 the exodus of foreign magistrates serving in Mozambique accelerated to such an extent that when we reached the Transitional Government, out of the 75 existing positions, the number of magistrates appointed amounted to 25.

When, in accordance with the Lusaka Agreement,[12] the Ministry of Justice was created, you could say we found ourselves in a favorable position, as it was necessary to deal with the problems of justice practically from scratch. (1978: 32)

The organization of the judiciary, designed to serve the interests of the bourgeoisie and the colonial bureaucracy, therefore reproduced the general crisis which heralded the end of the regime.

With its economy weakened by, amongst other factors, the exceedingly high costs of maintaining a war which had to be fought on three African fronts (in Angola from 1961, in Guinea-Bissau from 1963 and in Mozambique from 1964), a set of highly unfavorable international circumstances which had led to diplomatic isolation within the United Nations, an army comprised of soldiers who were becoming increasingly aware of the use being made of them by the political powers (Correia, 1985: 550), and increasing internal challenges led by the movements and political forces of the democratic opposition, Portugal approached the end of its long colonial cycle in the mid-seventies (Fortuna, 1985). The most direct cause, the 'detonating factor' in the process of decolonization, was the *coup d'état* of 25 April 1974 in Portugal, at a time when "recognition of independence for the colonies [...] appeared historically necessary, ethically imperative, obligatory in the light of the law of the international community, militarily advisable, and altogether urgent" (Moita, 1985: 506).

In Mozambique, the formal beginning of this process was represented by the swearing in of the Transitional Government, for which provision had been made in the Lusaka Agreement, and which was composed of eleven members: three appointed by the Portuguese state and eight by Frelimo. The political conditions created by ten years of war and the abrupt retreat of the colonials[13] enabled the liberation movement to maintain control of the mechanisms for the transfer of power and prepare the way for extending its ambitious project for the revolutionary transformation of society – designed and tested in the so-called 'liberated areas'[14] – to the whole of the country.

It was necessary to establish priorities, particularly as the available resources were not abundant. The strategy adopted was therefore directed towards achieving three main objectives: a) the first, to be carried out immediately, consisted of guaranteeing that the period of transition to independence proceeded in an orderly and peaceful manner, in accordance with the established agreements; b) the second, a medium-term goal, was the creation of suitable instruments to gradually endow the country with the structures and human resources essential for its development, in accordance with major planned options to be defined by the Government after independence;[15] c) the third, which would take place over a prolonged period of time (as the conditions required for reforms to be introduced had not yet been created), aimed to ensure that the inherited institutions functioned as normally as possible in order to prevent their collapse, which could have created a dangerous institutional void.

In terms of the first objective, legislative provisions were adopted with the aim of repressing each and every act that threatened the social peace and economic progress of Mozambique. Some of the most significant of these were:

- Decree-Law no. 8/74 of 2 November, which punished the promulgation of false or tendentious news liable to affect public law and order, paralyze economic or professional activity, require the intervention of the authorities or in any other way cause unjustified public alarm;
- Decree-Law no. 11/74, of the same date, which considered crimes against decolonization to be all those covered by the Penal Code and, in subsequent legislation, those that obstructed or endangered the process of decolonization as stipulated by the Lusaka Agreement, and established severe punishments for such crimes;
- Decree-Law no. 12/74, also of 2 November, which established that detainees suspected of committing crimes against decolonization would not benefit from the provision of *habeas corpus;*
- Decree-Law no. 16/75, of 13 February, which permitted state intervention in small or large-scale businesses when they ceased to make a normal contribution to economic development and satisfy collective interests.

Some very important decisions of the Transitional Government formed part of the spirit of the second strategic objective, such as the creation of a commercial and issuing Central Bank (the Bank of Mozambique, whose Organic Law was part of Act no. 2/75, of 17 May), or the appointment of a Research Committee to assess the need for expert skills in Mozambique, not only at state level and in the various services provided by public organizations, but also in private companies.[16] A specific concern had, in fact, already been made explicit in this area by the first Provisional Government in Portugal which emerged after the Revolution of 25 April, that it was "urgent to train specialists qualified in the various areas of the law, in order to replace the growing draining away of overseas magistrates and jurists and to prepare groups of leaders for the foreseeable stages of the future" (preamble to Decree-Law no. 299/74, of 4 July). This diploma, which had introduced baccalaureate and degree courses in Law at the then University of Lourenço Marques,[17] had not, however, been regulated, and the Transitional Government therefore decided to complete the task. Thus, the terms of Decree-Law no. 7/75, of 18 January, established a First Cycle, which lasted two years and corresponded to a baccalaureate. It was obtained by passing in the requisite subjects and also in History of the National Liberation Struggles in the Portuguese Colonies (taught in the Faculty of Arts) and Forensic Medicine (taught in the Faculty of Medicine). The decree also established a Second Cycle, which also lasted two years and corresponded to a degree in either Private Legal Sciences or Public Legal Sciences, according to the options chosen.

However, the training of specialist staff and a state bureaucratic apparatus in Law or other specialized areas was, by nature, too slow a process for the urgency with which the positions left empty by the colonial functionaries needed to be filled. Therefore, it was necessary to call into public service citizens who, although lacking the appropriate qualifications, identified with the social and political project defined by the country, had some academic training and displayed qualities of wisdom and good judgment. Various pieces of legislation were therefore issued defining special regulations for this area, such as:

- Decree-Law no. 7/74 of 17 October, which allowed functionaries from other public services or individuals of recognized merit to be nominated to serve in the administration or secretariat of the Civil Administration Services;
- Decree-Law no. 14/74 of 12 November, which established the necessary internal requirements for suitability to serve on the staff of the secretariat of the General Attorney's Office, the Judiciary Police, the Prison Services, as well as the Government Registry, Notary and Identification Offices, for which individuals could be nominated if recognized as possessing the necessary aptitude for carrying out these functions, regardless of whether they possessed the current legal requirements for the position or not;
- Decree-Law no. 27/75 of 1 March, which authorized for nomination as Inspectors and Deputy Inspectors of the Judiciary Police individuals over 21 years of age who had completed their general secondary education or basic secondary education or its equivalent, respectively, provided that they possessed the genuine qualities to carry out the work.

In this way the third objective referred to in the definition of priorities for the work of the Transitional Government was implemented.

2. From Post-Independence to the Reform of the Organization of the Judiciary (1975-1978)

The period immediately following the proclamation of independence was characterized by a radicalization of discourse and political action directed against the structures inherited from the colonial period. *Revolutionizing the state apparatus* was one of the fundamental tasks attributed to the Government during the first session of the Council of Ministers, which met from 9 to 25 July 1975.[18]

Priority was given to the development of rural areas in all sectors of state activity. This, by necessity, implied the abolition of the *regedorias*, which were considered feudal structures, collaborators with the colonial regime and incompatible with popular power. "Destroying the structures of the past is not a secondary task and it is not an 'ideological luxury'. It is a condition for the triumph of the Revolution", argued the document from the Council of Ministers.

As a political strategy to ensure the intended rural development, it was decided to create community villages (*aldeias comunais*), where it was assumed that the inhabitants – supporting each other with their own resources and using collective means of production – would, in the short term, improve their living conditions. At the same time, this form of organization would facilitate the provision of the material, technical and scientific resources which the Party[19] and the Government were trying hard to supply.

Financial resources, therefore, were directed to the sectors considered a priority in the process of 'national reconstruction': education, health, agriculture and defense.

In education, efforts were concentrated on combating illiteracy and enlarging the network of schools in order to benefit increasingly larger numbers of Mozambicans. In order to allow the Government to exercise direct and immediate control over the education system, private education was nationalized and brought within the state system.

As to health care, and working from the assumption that "the practice of private medicine constitutes a form of exploitation which uses illness as a means of making a profit", it was established that all private clinics were to be nationalized and a National Health Service created. The latter was to be responsible for planning medical and sanitation services and ensuring medical support for all citizens, without discrimination, with priority given to preventative medicine and to the rural areas.

Taking agriculture as a foundation and industry as a dynamic and decisive factor, the Government directed its economic policies towards eradicating underdevelopment and the system of human exploitation, thus giving a concrete meaning to the principle enshrined in Article 6 of the 1975 Constitution. The Ministry of Agriculture was provided with two main objectives: firstly, to guarantee the improvement of the living conditions of the people, in particular the rural masses, by providing a qualitatively and quantitatively adequate diet, and secondly, to support the industrial sector with agricultural raw materials.[20]

In the sphere of national defense, it was established that the tasks to be carried out should be closely linked to the process of economic and social reconstruction of the country, thus ensuring the popular character of the Army through its direct participation in production and close contact with the masses. To achieve this proposal, it was established that a National Service for Defense and Reconstruction should be created.

Consideration of the problems of administration and justice conclued that access to the courts during the colonial period had been a minority privilege, that legal language was difficult for people to understand and could only be interpreted by resorting to specialists and that the penal system adopted by the law did not take into due consideration the need for the re-education of offenders and their reintegration into society.

Seeking to make the best use of experiences acquired during the armed struggle for liberation, the Council of Ministers therefore decided to undertake a progressive drafting of new laws that would serve as an instrument for national unity and the defense of the Mozambican Revolution. This was accomplished by adopting a policy of simplifying the language of the law and launching campaigns to explain its content in order to popularize it, and by giving priority to the re-education of offenders, in collaboration with the Ministry of the Interior and the Ministry of Justice. Private law pratice was also considered incompatible with the existence of a popular system of justice.

In the months that followed, various legislative provisions were adopted with the aim of concretizing these policies. Out of all the legislation approved during this phase, special mention should be made of the following:

- Decree-Law no. 4/75 of 16 August, which banned the practice of advocacy and the functions of legal consultant, solicitor and judicial or extrajudicial attorney as liberal professions. A National Service for Legal Consultation and Assistance[21] was created, subordinated to the General Attorney's Office[22], and new procedural rules were introduced, aimed at making it easier for all parties to put the procedures which affected them into practice;
- Decree-Law no. 5/75 of 19 August, which placed all activities concerning the prevention and treatment of illnesses, as well as the training of health care staff, within the exclusive domain of the state;
- Statute no. 12/75 of 6 September, which banned private education and brought all education under the control of the state;
- Decree- Law no. 21/75 of 11 October, which created the National Service of Popular Security[23] which was given the power to order and carry out any investigations, searches and arrests it considered necessary, proceed with the necessary requisitions, institute legal proceedings, detain individuals and decide a suitable outcome for them, namely by sending them to the appropriate police authorities, courts or re-education camps;
- Statute no. 25/75 of 18 October, which brought the Judiciary Police – soon to become the Criminal Investigation Police – within the structures of the Ministry of the Interior, in order to "avoid the dispersal of authority and to ensure the coordination and efficiency [...] of public services of the same type, and with identical objectives".

In February 1976 the Central Committee of Frelimo held its eighth session in Maputo. It took stock of the first months of government and undertook an exhaustive analysis of the internal situation of the country. Considering that the country was going through a particularly sensitive moment involving "the intensification of the class struggle, as a direct consequence of the state-level consolidation of the power of the worker-peasant alliance and the first revolutionary measures", the order of the day was to unleash a "General Political and Organizational Offensive on the Production Front"

(Frelimo, 1976: 36). From amongst the various resolutions passed, we highlight the following:

- *Resolution on the Structures of State Machinery* – announcing the characteristics that the new structures (the representative Assemblies and their executive organs) would have at each level and the provisional rules for their composition, hierarchy and functioning, in relation to the principle of democratic centralism;
- *Resolution on the Community Villages* – establishing a set of principles to be followed during the process of structuring, establishing and organizing production and labor, as well as the conditions for the founding of the community villages;
- *Resolution on Education* – indicating the organizational forms which should be introduced into educational establishments and literacy programs already under direct state administration, so that they could fulfill their social function and the revolutionary task allocated to them;
- *Resolution on Health* – defining the guidelines for conducting the political and organizational battle in the health sector;
- *Resolution on Justice* – conveying the fundamental political orientation underlying the nature and form of the legal system to be adopted by the country. At one point, this document states that,

It is imperative at this moment to destroy colonial-capitalist law and its judicial structure as part of the destruction of the entire state colonial-capitalist machinery in Mozambique. The new judicial system must express the power of the worker-peasant alliance and reflect the dictatorship of the exploited majority. Its sources of inspiration must be:

a) The experiences of the struggle for national liberation
b) The experiences of the class struggle
c) The revolutionary experiences of other peoples

The organization of the Popular Courts will be as follows:

I. The Supreme Popular Court
II. The Provincial Popular Court
III. The District Popular Court
IV. The Locality, Community Village and Neighborhood Popular Court

In order for all the courts to be truly popular, on a local level they will be entirely composed of non-professional judges, chosen from amongst members of the Party, the FPLM[24] and the Mass Democratic Organizations. In the other Popular Courts, professional judges who are trained for their duties and nominated by the central organizations will, whenever possible, be employed, in addition to non-professional judges. Both will periodically attend training and refresher courses and seminars (Frelimo, 1976: 121).

This line is repeated consistently, both on the occasion of the Third Frelimo Congress (February 1977)[25] and during the First Session of the Popular Assembly (in its provisional form[26]), in August/September of the same year. Within this legislative organ, Resolution no. 3/77 of 1 September, on the Land Law, Nationalizations, and on the Popular Courts was approved, establishing '[...] that the organs of the state will take the necessary measures to accelerate the process of the creation of a revolutionary judicial system, namely through the creation of Popular Courts, from the local to the national level, subordinate at each level to the respective People's Assembly".

In compliance with the accepted political line, the Ministry of Justice concluded its draft bill for the Law on the Organization of the Judiciary and made it available for public debate just as the first students were graduating from the Faculty of Law at Eduardo Mondlane University.

The first elections for the People's Assemblies were held at the end of 1977.[27] *Poder Popular* (Popular Power) consolidated its position in the various territorial hierarchies within the country.

In April 1978, about twenty newly trained graduates from the Faculty of Law, together with some of the most experienced judicial officials, were organized into brigades and dispatched throughout the country. The recent graduates had had experience in local political mobilization campaigns since 1974, as well as in preparatory activities for the General Elections. For about four months, in public meetings held in factories, *machambas* (family farmlands), government offices, army barracks, villages, residential areas and other conglomerations, they moderated debates and collected contributions to add to the draft bill. Simultaneously, in each of the eleven provinces, they prepared to open two pilot popular courts on an experimental basis, one at district level and the other local.

In August of the same year, a national seminar in Maputo brought together the members of the provincial brigades, judges, attorneys and senior staff from the Ministry of Justice to come up with a synthesis of the proposals collected from these public debates. It was the first great reckoning of the revolutionary experiences of justice – from the time of the struggle for national liberation in the liberated zones, to the experience within the local *grupos dinamizadores* (dynamizing groups)[28] after independence – and a unique moment for collective reflection on the need to widen the rupture with the colonial system and make the administration of justice better suited to the new social and political conditions in the country. Out of it came the final version of the bill, which the Permanent Commission of the Popular Assembly was to adopt in its December session later in the year, under the title of the Law on the Organization of the Judiciary.[29] Finally, a legal foundation had been established for the creation of popular justice.

3. The Rise and Fall of the Socialist Experience (1978-1992)

In accordance with our chronology, the phase following the establishment of the People's Assemblies and the adoption of the Law on the Organization of the Judiciary corresponds to the rise and rapid decline of the project for building socialism in Mozambique. It covers the whole of the eighties and extends until the reforms of 1992, which were anticipated in the 1990 constitutional revision.

It is therefore worth defining two sub-periods within this phase: one which corresponds to the concretization of the socialist development strategy, or top-down planning, and another which coincides with the first years of the liberalization of the economy, or outside-inside planning, to use the term coined by António Francisco (see chapter 4).

The first sub-period is characterized, in political terms, by a progressive 'hardening of the regime' as the South Africa-backed[30] war of internal destabilization intensified, and in judicial terms by the widening and consolidation of the network of popular courts.[31]

It was, understandably, an era of profound contradictions and ambiguities. Alongside measures to provide full and effective democratization of the state bodies, including those concerned with the administration of justice, some political decisions were announced and some legal measures approved which were amongst the most repressive of the entire revolutionary process.

The authenticity of Mozambican popular democracy was evident in the voluntary participation of millions of citizens in government activities of a wide-reaching social nature – such as national vaccination campaigns,[32] literacy and adult education programs, elections for People's Assemblies and others, – or in grassroots organizations, such as the local *grupos dinamizadores*, the mass democratic organizations (OMM,[33] OJM,[34] OTM,[35] and the socio-professional organizations), the popular militias, the agricultural and consumer cooperatives and, of course, the popular courts.

Various procedural mechanisms were introduced into the judicial system and new epistemological attitudes were proposed which aimed to secure and widen this participation. These included:

- a collegiate of all the courts;
- the participation of lay judges in the district and provincial popular courts, on the same level as the professional judges and as their equals;
- the composition of grass-roots popular courts, in which non-professional judges, directly elected by the community, could intervene exclusively and judge "according to good sense and justice, taking into account the principles which preside over the building of a socialist society";[36]
- greater interaction between the courts and the community, by hearing trials, in cases of a criminal or social nature, in the areas where the disputed events occurred;

- the chance for all parties to act for themselves in their particular cases, without the need to obtain a legal mandate[37];
- a new attitude towards the law and the way in which it interacted with the social and cultural environment in which it was implemented (Baltazar, 1978: 38).

The most radical, and therefore the most unpopular, political decisions adopted included the so-called *Operation Production* and the various campaigns of the *Political and Organizational Offensive*, as well as the following legislative provisions:[38]

- Law no. 2/79 of 1 May, better known as the Law on Crimes against the Security of the People and the Popular State, of which the main innovations to the legal system were the introduction of the death penalty (Article 6, no. 1, paragraph d) and no. 2), and the equating of complicity in a crime with the actual commission of a crime (Article 4) and attempted or frustrated attempts at committing a crime, with actual crime (Article 13);
- Law no. 3/79 of 29 March, which instituted the Revolutionary Military Court, a special court designated as the only body for judging crimes against the security of the state[39];
- Law no. 5/82 of 9 June – the Law of the Defense of the Economy – which also equated crimes actually committed with those which were frustrated or attempted, and accomplices or recipients with the authors of crimes, in addition to refusing bail, suspended prison sentences or their replacement by fines for certain crimes;
- Law no. 5/83 of 31 March, which introduced the sentence of whipping to punish the authors, accomplices or recipients of certain serious crimes, whether committed, frustrated or attempted, since it was considered that the punitive measures employed until then had not been adequate to deter a crime wave;
- Law no. 10/87 of 19 September, which introduced alterations to various precepts of the Penal Code, making the sentences for violent crimes against persons more severe.

The direction and management of the entire judicial system remained heavily centralized within the Ministry of Justice, in accordance with the powers authorized by Presidential Decree no. 69/83 of 29 December. As a general rule, management was exercised by means of directives, which could be sent directly from the Ministry or through the Higher Court of Appeals and the General Attorney's Office.

Directive no. 3/83, of 6 June can be cited as an example of the first instance. It was intended to "endow the courts with the operational means to guarantee that the offensive taking place [in the state residential area, managed by the APIE[40]] fulfilled its objectives, developed in other cities and took root". Another example is Circular no. 3/84 of 2 June, which concerned procedures for granting parole to prisoners who fulfilled the legal requirements. Typical examples of the second instance are the

Directives of the Court of Appeals no. 3/81, of 25 November, which considered the disposition of Article 18 of the Penal Code[41] 'revoked' whenever it impeded the punishment of anti-social conduct which offended 'socialist values and principles', and no. 1/82 of 27 February, ordering the courts, in cases submitted for their consideration and in derogation of what had been established both in the Civil Code and the Civil Procedure Code, to immediately apply the general principles enshrined in the Act on Family Law in relation to contested and uncontested divorce cases, *de facto* union (legal recognition, dissolution and impediments to marriage) and polygamy. In addition, there was the Joint Directive of the Court of Appeals and the Attorney General's Office no. 1/86 of 14 April, on the handling of criminal cases arising out of the context of the so-called *Operação Chapa Cem*.[42]

From the second half of the eighties onwards, due to a combination of highly unfavorable internal and external factors,[43] the political leadership began to confront the need to take a new line on its global development strategy.[44] The redefinition of alliances and international alignments had already been set, since at least 1982.[45] It is within the framework of this new foreign policy that the 'Agreement on Non-Aggression and Good Neighbor Relations', otherwise known as the N'Komati Agreement, signed with apartheid South Africa in March 1984, must be understood.

An integral part of the country's repositioning was also the decision to adhere to the Agreements established at the United Nations Monetary and Financial Conference held in Bretton Woods, New Hampshire, on 22 July 1944 and, consequently, to comply with the programs of structural readjustment defined by the World Bank and the International Monetary Fund.[46] The launching, in January 1987, of the Economic Rehabilitation Program (PRE), served as a counterpart for obtaining the necessary credit for the recovery of an economy devastated by war and the other previously cited factors. The PRE meant adherence to a new ideology which would soon dominate in the entire world: neo-liberalism. With subsequent measures including the liberalization of prices, the reduction of the budget deficit, the privatization of state companies, monetary contraction, the raising of interest rates and drastic cuts to social spending, the country was definitely set on the course of a capitalist market economy (Anderson, 1996: 12). This initiated the second sub-period of the phase under analysis.

As a rule, this new economic model corresponds to a political superstructure based on multiparty representational democracy and tripartite state power and so the way had to be paved for the constitutional reforms dictated by the circumstances. Alongside the intensification of diplomatic efforts aimed at ending the long armed conflict in which the country was floundering, a series of legal and institutional measures were passed which had the clear aim of, on the one hand, facilitating this end and, on the other hand, winning the confidence of the core countries and international humanitarian organizations. Mention should be made of the main pieces of legislation that emerged at the time:

- Law no. 14/87 of 19 December, which declared "an amnesty for crimes against the Security of the People and the Popular State which had provision in Law no. 2/79 of 1 March, committed by Mozambican citizens who have, in any way, fought against, or promoted the use of violence against the Mozambican People or State, inside or outside national territory, provided that they surrender themselves voluntarily" (Article 1, no. 1);

- Law no. 15/87 of 19 December, which offered a pardon to the authors of crimes against the security of the state who had, by their behavior, "revealed a willingness to peacefully reintegrate themselves into society and redeem themselves through socially useful work" (preamble to the law);

- Resolutions no. 9, 10, 11 and 12/88 of 25 August, in the Popular Assembly, which ratified the African Charter on Human and Peoples' Rights, the Convention on the Transfer of Sentenced Persons, the OAU[47] Convention governing Specific Aspects of Refugee Problems in Africa and the Additional Protocol to the Geneva Convention on the Status of Refugees, respectively;

- Law no. 4/89 of 18 September, which revoked Law no. 5/83 of 31 March (the Law on whipping) and granted pardons to those sentenced to prohibitions or limitations on residence, as well as sentences of whipping which had not yet been carried out.

In the same context, the decision was finally made to found and put into operation the organs at the head of the judicial system – the Supreme Popular Court and the General Attorney's Office[48] –, as foreseen in the Constitution and in Law no. 12/78 of 2 December. Through Presidential Decrees no. 22, 23, 24 and 25/88, of 17 October, the Chief Justice and the Deputy Chief Justice of the Supreme Popular Court and the Attorney General and the Deputy Attorney General were nominated.[49] Law no. 6/89 of 19 September defined the organic statute of the General Attorney's Office.

The pace imposed by the internal process of capitalist economic reconstruction and the precipitation of events in Eastern Europe leading to the downfall of the socialist regimes had, as was expected, a decisive influence on the changes taking place in the political and ideological superstructure. Constitutional reform, which had begun as a series of limited proposals with the simple aim of adapting Fundamental Law to the realities of the market economy – or, in the words of the deputies of the Popular Assembly, "to make it more suited to the new challenges of establishing a national consensus on the normalization of the life of the country"[50] – finally gave way to the approval of an entirely new Constitution.

From the political regime to the system of government, to the catalogue of basic rights and to the organization of the judiciary, the 1990 Constitution had very little in common with that of 1975.

With the new constitutional framework approved and with the PRE acting within the regulations laid down by the BWs institutions, it was now necessary, on the one hand, to proceed with a reform of ordinary legislation in order to make it compatible with the new principles and norms of the Constitution and, on the other hand, to 'encourage' the negotiators who, through the mediation of the Community of St. Egidio in Rome, were seeking to launch the longed-for Peace Agreement.

To a certain extent, this is a possible explanation for the promptness with which certain legislation considered 'politically expedient' was drawn up and approved. Here is an incomplete list of the main standard acts approved in 1991/92:

- Law no. 6/91 of 9 January – which established the regulations that should be obeyed when exercising the right to strike;
- Law no. 7/91 of 23 January – which established the legal framework for the formation and activities of political parties;
- Law no. 8/91 of 18 July – which regulated the right to free association;
- Law no. 9/91 of 18 July – which regulated the exercise of the freedom to meet and demonstrate;
- Law no. 18/91 of 10 August – which established freedom of the press;
- Law no. 19/91 of 16 August – which defined and sentenced crimes against the security of the state;[51]
- Resolution no. 5/91 of 12 December – which ratified the International Covenant on Civil and Political Rights adopted by the United Nations General Assembly on 16 December 1966;
- Resolution no. 6/91 of 12 December – which ratified the Second (optional) Additional Protocol on Civil and Political Rights with the aim of abolishing the death penalty;
- Law no. 23/91 of 31 December – which regulated the exercise of trade union activity;
- Law no. 26/91 of 31 December – which authorized the provision of both for-profit and not for-profit private health care services by individuals or collectives.

In the same manner, important new legislation was produced during this period, in the area of economics and finance, of which the following deserve attention:

- Law no. 15/91 of 3 August – establishing rules for the restructuring, transformation and repositioning of the business sector of the state, including the privatization and transferal – with financial compensation – of companies and other production units;
- Law no. 24/91 of 31 December – liberalizing insurance and reinsurance activities;
- Act no. 28/91 of 21 November (complemented by Act no. 20/93 of 14 September) – defining the means of transfer or privatization of companies, establishments, installations and financial institutions owned by the state;

- Law no. 28/91 of 31 December – establishing the legal framework for credit institutions.

Specially relevant to the system of the administration of justice are Law no. 10/91 of 30 July, which approved the status of judicial magistrates and Laws no. 4, 5 and 10/92, all of 6 May, which concerned the functioning of the community courts, the organic statute of the Administrative Court and the organic statute of the judicial courts, respectively.

Among the various changes that these laws brought to the organization of judicial power, there are two which, due to their significance and implications for the future, should be highlighted: the creation of autonomy for the courts and attorney's offices in terms of their executive powers, and the removal of the community courts from the formal judicial system.

In effect, the Organic Law of the Judicial Courts – issued in accordance with the new constitutional framework – established, in Article 65, that "direction of the judicial apparatus is exercised by the Chief Justice of the Supreme Court and by the Judicial Council".[52] It was the responsibility of these organs, therefore, to, on the one hand, issue instructions and directives of an organizational and methodological nature – intended to ensure the good functioning and efficiency of the work of the courts – and, on the other hand, make fundamental decisions concerning the development of judicial activity, the improvement of judicial institutions, budgetary matters, administrative management and other concerns (see Article 69 of Law no. 10/92). In the same way, Law no. 6/89 of 19 September had already established that "the General Attorney's Office has autonomy vis-à-vis the various state organs [...]" and must "without threatening judicial confidentiality [...], present annual information on its activities to the Popular Assembly" (Article 2, no. 1 and 3).

With the creation of these two organs, the Ministry of Justice – which, as we have seen, under the previous law had exercised full management of the system[53] – was virtually reduced to a coordinating and information-providing role.[54]

As for the removal of the community courts from the formal judicial system, this resulted from a strict interpretation, by the legislature, of Article 161 of the 1990 Constitution. Under the terms of this precept,

1. The aim of the courts is to guarantee and reinforce legality as an instrument for the stability of the law, to guarantee respect for the laws and to ensure the rights and liberties of citizens, in addition to the legal interests of the different organs and entities in official existence.
2. The courts educate citizens in voluntary and conscious compliance with the laws, thus establishing just and harmonious social relationships.
3. The courts penalize violations of the law and decide litigation *in accordance with the law* (our emphasis).

Considering that the community courts decide cases "with impartiality, good sense and justice" (see Article 2, no. 2, of Law no. 4/92) and not according to what is established by law, it was concluded that they neither could nor should be part of the judicial system, but should become organs of justice "for the purposes of reconciliation or the settling of minor disputes" (see Article 63 of Law no. 10/92).[55]

If, as previously stated, the intense legislative activity of the single party Assembly of the Republic, which concentrated on some of the most basic democratic rights and liberties, can be seen as part of the 'pressurizing' (in a positive sense) strategy brought to bear on the peace negotiators, we are then forced to conclude that it was very successful. On 4 October 1992, the Agreement between the Frelimo Government and Renamo was finally signed in Rome, putting an end to the armed conflict that had lasted for nearly two decades.

4. From the Peace Agreement to the Present (1992-2000)

The final phase in the historical period under analysis is that of the replacement of a logic of armed confrontation with a logic of political confrontation without the use of violence – the materialization of the structural and institutional changes planned at the end of the previous phase and of the relative economic growth, within the conditions imposed by hegemonic globalization.

It is therefore natural that, after the Rome Peace Agreement, new legal frameworks emerged to regulate the so-called 'transition to democracy' in areas such as the legitimization of political power, incentives for investment in the economy or the consolidation of the rule of law. The following legislation serves as an illustration:

- Law no. 2/93 of 24 June – establishing the criminal investigation judges;
- Law no. 3/93 of 24 June (the Law on Investments) – defining a basic and uniform legal framework in the Republic of Mozambique for the process of making national and foreign investments eligible to benefit from the guarantees and incentives provided under the law;
- Act no. 12/93 of 21 July – approving the Tax Benefits Code;[56]
- Act no. 14/93 of 21 July – approving the Regulation of Law no. 3/93 of 24 June (the Law on Investments);
- Act no. 18/93 of 14 September – approving the Regulation of Industrial Free Zones;
- Law no. 4/93 of 28 December – establishing the legal framework for holding the first multiparty general elections;
- Law no. 6/94 of 13 September – creating the Institute for Legal Assistance and Representation (IPAJ);[57]
- Law no. 7/94 of 14 September – creating the Mozambique Bar Association and approving its statutes;
- Act no. 39/95 of 2 August – approving the statutes of the Investment Promotion Center;[58]

- Law no. 2/97 of 18 February – defining the legal framework for the establishment of local autarchies;[59]
- Law no. 7/97 of 31 May – establishing the legal regime for the state administrative protection to which the local autarchies are subject;
- Law no. 8/97 of 31 May – defining the special regulations which govern the organization and functioning of the Municipality of Maputo.

After the political openings created by the adoption of the 1990 Constitution of the Republic and the end of armed conflict, the non-governmental organizations (NGOs) also emerged. The most significant of these were the ones that had as their aim the defense and promotion of human rights – whether the so-called first generation rights or those of the second and third generations – and that were part of the embryonic Mozambican civil society.[60]

In the political sphere, the general elections of 1994 and 1999 and the local elections of 1998 were the most significant and relevant events during the historical period under analysis. Although dozens of parties and coalitions have emerged since the beginning of the nineties, the most recent trend is towards a progressive political polarization of Mozambican society.[61]

The process of political and administrative decentralization, begun in 1991 with the launching of a government program to reform the local organs (PROL), has also gained fundamental importance. Decentralization, a controversial issue on which it has not been easy to obtain the necessary political consensus,[62] is seen by many as an empowering element in economic and social development, an answer to regional and inter-regional imbalances, a factor in the re-legitimization of the state and an important instrument for bringing peace and democracy to Mozambican society (Faria and Chichava, 1999: 3; Soiri, 1999: 5).

Designed to press forward with the reform of the local administration system through the creation of new organs – each with its own legal character and endowed with administrative, financial and patrimonial autonomy –, the PROL included the elaboration of a diagnosis and in-depth studies into legal, administrative and financial areas, infrastructures and the environment. These studies later served as the basis for the elaboration of Law no. 3/94 of 13 September, on the institutionalization of municipal districts (approved by the Assembly of the Republic while still under single-party status), which constitued the first regulatory instrument of decentralization. There are those who believe that the objectives and principles enshrined in this legal document contain the ideal format for broader democratic decentralization (Soiri, 1999: 6), defined by James Manor (1997: 7) as a mixture of fiscal and administrative decentralization (deconcentration) and democratic decentralization (devolution of power).[63]

This law, however, did not get to be implemented, because the regulatory legislative bills which were to follow it and which had already been drawn up after the general elections of 27-29 October 1994 (and therefore in a new multiparty political context), were vehemently contested by Renamo and the UD[64] – the opposition forces in parliament – and created serious rifts within the Government party (Faria and Chichava, 1999: 4). The conflict which this created and the debate on the constitutionality of these bills for legislative approval finally led to the delaying of the municipal elections which should have established the new local organs of power.

It was therefore decided to proceed with a timely review of the Constitution (Law no. 9/96 of 22 November). In addition to altering some precepts relating to the chapter on 'Local Organs of the State', a completely new title was introduced into the Fundamental Law, Title IV, with the epigraph 'Local Power', which made provision for the existence of local government, the aim of which was to "organize the participation of citizens in resolving their own problems within their communities, promote local development, and deepen and consolidate democracy, within the framework of the unity of the Mozambican state".[65]

This constitutional amendment determined significant changes in the philosophy underlying the aforementioned Law no. 3/94. Once again, in the midst of great controversy and partisan political dispute, another law outlining the local organs (the aforementioned Law no. 2/97 of 18 February) was soon to be adopted, backed by the votes of Frelimo and the UD. Renamo boycotted not only the vote on this law – which expressly revoked the previous law – but also the elections themselves, which took place in June 1998.

Table 2.1 (taken from Faria and Chichava, 1999: 6) indicates the main differences between the two documents to which we have referred.

Many observers and specialists who have analyzed the path followed from the adoption of this law in 1994 up to the first local government elections in 1998 consider that there has been a clear regression, from the point of view of making the process of decentralization more democratic (Soiri, 1999: 7). The strongest critics point to the fact that Law no. 2/97 applies to a restricted number of cities and towns previously defined as local government authorities – and consequently leaves out the great majority of the rural population and a significant part of the resources that enable local governments to secure their own autonomy – and, in addition, does not take communities into account or promote any form of involvement for the traditional authorities.

Even so, it is generally admitted that, in spite of its limitations, the current policy of decentralization "is a positive step forward towards greater democratization and political openness" (Faria and Chichava, 1999: 8).

The declaration of the government's intention to advance with a vast program of reforms to ensure "the rationalization and modernization of public administration, with the aim of making ongoing improvements to the quality of the services offered to citizens" met with the same expectations. With this objective in mind, an Inter-Ministerial Commission for the Reform of the Public Sector[67] was created by Presidential Decree no. 5/2000 of 28 March and was presided over by the Prime Minister. Its objectives were:

a) to draft and propose a global reform policy for the public sector;
b) to ensure the coordination, management and implementation of reform, namely by facilitating the interaction and harmonization of programs from several sectors;
c) to promote and guarantee the integrated participation of all the services and civil society in reducing bureaucracy, as well as in the simplification, modernization and professionalization of public administration.

Table 2.1: Differences in the Legislative Frameworks Relating to Local Power

Law no. 3/94	Law no. 2/97
Administrative division into 128 rural municipal districts and 23 urban municipal districts.	Creation of local government authorities, subdivided into (urban) municipalities and (rural) settlements. Cities, towns, villages and settlements (544) now eligible for local government status. The 128 districts governed by local administrative organs remain outside the scope of local power and consequently come under central administration.
Direct election by secret ballot of the three municipal organs: the municipal President-Mayor (Administrator, in the rural zones), Assembly and Council.	Direct election by secret ballot of the President (Mayor) and the Municipal Assembly. Half the members of the municipal Council are appointed by the President and half are members of the Municipal Assembly.
Clear enumeration of the functions and services of local governments (including public safety, the use of land and the water supply, among others).	Functions of local governments reduced to essential matters (such as the use of land) and dependent on the existence of local financial resources.
Clear definition of the prerogatives and powers of the central and municipal administrations.	Organs of central administration represented in the territorial jurisdiction of the local government. Possibility of their control of, and participation in, local government (dual administration).

Table 2.1: Differences in the Legislative Frameworks [contd.]

Law no. 3/94	Law no. 2/97
Budgetary, fiscal, patrimonial, planning and organizational autonomy.	Administrative, fiscal, patrimonial and organizational autonomy. Local government administration subordinated to the principle of 'unity of political power'.
Provision for budgetary support in the GSB.[66]	Provision for budgetary support in the GSB.
Traditional authorities included in local consultation and decision-making processes (namely in the arbitration of conflicts and in matters relating to the use of land).	Participation of the traditional authorities substantially limited and subject to ministerial regulation.
The right to form an Association of Municipalities. The principle of gradualism: gradual establishment of municipalities based on socio-economic and administrative conditions and on minimum infrastructures.	No reference to the right of municipalities to form an association. The principle of gradualism. The law on the creation of local governments (drawn up, discussed and approved later) limits the number in the first phase to 33.
Legal and financial guardianship of municipalities by the Ministry of State Administration and the Ministry of Finance, respectively.	Legal and financial guardianship of municipalities by the Ministry of State Administration and the Ministry of Finance, respectively. The law on state administrative guardianship over local governments (drawn up, discussed and approved later) determines that this may be delegated to provincial governments.

This commission is supported by a technical unit, the UTRESP,[68] which is responsible for ensuring the integrated planning, coordination, articulation and supervision of the reform programs and projects.

In terms of structural reforms of the economy, policies aiming to reduce inflation and macro-economic imbalances are generally agreed to have had positive results. However there is also concern that, in terms of human development, the country is still far from achieving satisfactory results. According to PNUD[69] indicators, more than half the population in Mozambique live below the poverty line, less than 40% have access to state health care services and only about 46.5% are literate (UNDP, 1999, 2004).[70]

As for the Judiciary, the reforms initiated by Laws no. 4 and 10/92 of 6 May consequently led to the almost total abandonment of the community courts, due to a lack of clarity with regard to their institutional position and a general growing crisis in formal official justice (the courts, attorneys, legal assistance).[71]

An Inter-Ministerial Commission for Legal Reform was also instituted which, amongst other sub-commissions, included one in charge of the preparation of the Family Law (approved in 2004[72]) and one for the Penal Procedure Code and the Civil Code. The revision of the Commercial Code was entrusted, under contract, to a consortium of specialists, and is awaiting approval. The Commission is also preparing bills on the inheritance law and on fiscal and customs litigation.

More recently, recognition that professional training is a priority for all sectors of the administration of justice has led to the creation of the Centre for Legal and Judicial Training.[73] This Center has developed its activities not only in the training and empowerment of judges, prosecutors, justice officials and assistants, legal staff, public defenders and other sector employees (*e.g.* court registry offices, members of the Criminal Investigation Police, etc.) but also in carrying out research into common law systems for resolving litigation and promoting and leading the national debate on Mozambican law.[74]

5. Concluding Notes

The three decades which have passed since Mozambique became independent have been intersected by two contradictory processes of political, economic and social transformation.

One, typically revolutionary, took place during the Cold War period and therefore in an international context of confrontation between two antagonistic systems. It determined a break with "the traditional structures of colonial oppression and exploitation and the mentality underlying them",[75] and adopted central planning and administration of the economy as a development strategy.

The other, typically reformist, unfolded at a time in which the Cold War had given way to a period of *détente* and neo-liberalism had become the hegemonic model of development. It is now proceeding with the implementation of programs of structural adjustment, deregulation and the liberalization of the economy, as determined by a conference of the multilateral agencies usually known as the Washington Consensus.

As quite profound processes of change, their evolution was neither linear nor peaceful, since they were subject to the dialectics of social transformation itself and the conjunctures in which this unfolded. In our description of the political-economic options and the legal contours which emerged in each of the stated historical periods, different types of situations may be detected: a) the ruptures of the revolutionary period with regard to the colonial period, which are still valid today; b) the ruptures of the revolutionary period, undone by neo-liberalism and replaced with the previous *status quo;* c) the ruptures of the neo-liberal period with both the preceding periods.

Perhaps the clearest example of a political decision of the first category concerns the ownership of land. The regime established under Article 8 of the 1975 Constitution,[76] which established a break with the situation prevailing under colonial law, maintained its continuity in Article 46 of the 1990 Constitution[77] and strongly influenced the debates surrounding the process of drawing up a new Land Law (Law no. 19/97 of 1 October).

In terms of the judicial system, and in spite of the reforms brought about by the new Organic Law, the full panel of courts was maintained, as well as the participation of (elected) lay judges, which had been an innovation of Law no. 12/78.[78]

The second category of ruptures can be illustrated by two examples among many: in the economic sphere, the mutation between market economy/centrally planned economy/market economy and, in the judicial sphere, the permitting/banning/permitting of private legal practice.

Examples from the third category of rupture include the single party/multiparty or subordination/autonomy (of the administration of justice system in relation to the executive) dichotomies, wherein the single party system and subordination are common to both the colonial and the revolutionary periods.

At the beginning of this chapter it was said that the ruptures in the legal and judicial system which have occurred from independence to the present were essentially institutional. The observations woven into our analysis of the various stages of the periods outlined show, in fact, that the fundamental politics and philosophies of official (or state) law remained unchanged during the historical period under analysis. Underlying them are a dogma and a rationality which essentially correspond to the liberal matrix of the modern state, the main ideas of which are the theory of tripartite power, the sacredness of the principle of legality or the rule of law, the reactive and retroactive nature of the function of the judiciary and the logical-formal subsuming of facts to norms as the method of applying the law (Trindade, 1997). There is, however, a structural continuity which is reflected in other spheres of the legal order, namely in codified law – some of which has been in force for over a century[79] – and in the division of the judiciary, which itself has always followed the territorial division of the administration.

Notes

1   Frelimo stands for *Frente de Libertação de Moçambique* (Mozambican Liberation Front) and became a political party after independence.

2   See '*Decisões do Conselho de Ministros*' (Decisions of the Council of Ministers), *Boletim da República*, 1st. Series, no. 15, 29 July 1975.

3   For which, the principle enshrined in Article 71 of the 1975 Constitution (which corresponds to Article 305 of the present, 2004 Constitution) was of fundamental importance, establishing that "All previous legislation which contradicts the Constitution is automatically revoked. Previous legislation which does not contradict the Constitution remains in force until such time as it may be modified or revoked". For a commentary on the issues raised by the implementation of this principle, see Dagnino (1980: 15).

4   See Legislative Diploma no. 162, published in the *Boletim Oficial* no. 22, 1st. series, 1 June 1929.

5   According to Marcelo Caetano, quoted by Braga da Cruz (1988: 66), the indigenous populations were "Portuguese subjects subject to the protection of the Portuguese state without being part of the nation, whether this is considered as a cultural community (since they lack the requisite assimilation of culture) or a political association of citizens (as they have not yet won citizenship)". For an update of the debate on the indigenous system as an instrument of oppression and exploitation and its influence on post-colonial politics, see the critique by Bridget O'Laughlin (2000) of Mamdani's book *Citizen and Subject* (1996a) as welle as the latter author's response (2000).

6   Considered to be "individuals of the Negro race or their descendants who, having been born or having permanent residence [in Guinea, Angola or Mozambique], do not yet [possess] the education and individual and social habits deemed necessary for the full application of the public and private law pertaining to Portuguese citizens" (Article 2 of the Statute).

7   See the *Regulamento dos Tribunais Privativos dos Indígenas* (Regulations of the Private Tribunals of the Native Populations), approved by Legislative Diploma no. 37 of 12 November 1927. Article 3 establishes that

> the private tribunals of the indigenous populations will consist of an administrative authority from the main town in the district, municipality, fiscal or administrative area, who will act as chief judge, assisted by two indigenous assessors of the highest level and authority within the district, one nominated by the governor of the district and the other chosen by the Committee for the Defense of Native Populations. Both will serve for two years and will have the right to meals and a monthly payment, to be decided by the Governor General.

Provision was also made for a Private High Court for Native Populations, with its headquarters in the colonial capital, to hear appeals against the decisions of the private indigenous courts. It consisted of the Governor General, who presided over it, a Chief Judge of Appeals, a representative elected annually by the Government Council from amongst individuals who had worked in local administration, and the Director of Native Affairs (*Director dos Serviços e Negócios Indígenas*).

8   Still within the terms of this statute, the *assimilados* were formerly indigenous people who had acquired Portuguese citizenship after proving that they satisfied the following conditions: a) they were over 18; b) they spoke Portuguese correctly; c) they exercised a profession, skill or office which provided them with enough income to support themselves and any members of their family who were in their care, or possessed enough private means to the same effect; d) they were of good character and had acquired the education and habits deemed necessary for the full implementation of the public and private law pertaining to Portuguese citizens; e) they had completed their military obligations and were not registered as deserters (Article 56).

9   The so-called 'Adriano Moreira Reforms', (Coissoró, 1966: 6), a legislative package approved on 6 September 1961 – after the first armed action against colonial occupation, which took place in northern Angola. It which included the abolition of the indigenous regime (Act no. 43.893), a review of the occupying regime and the concession of land (Act no. 43.894), the creation of *Juntas de Povoamento* (Settlement Boards – Act no. 43.895), the restructuring of the *Regedorias* (chiefdom councils – Act no. 43.896), the recognition of local customs and usage (Act no. 43.897), the reorganization of the *Julgados Municipais e de Paz* (Small Claims Courts and Municipal Courts – Act no. 43.898) and the Registry services (Act no. 43.899).

10 Currently including both Maputo Province and Maputo city.

11 Minister of Justice in the Transitional Government and in the first post-Independence Government (1975-78).

12 The Lusaka Agreement, signed by the Portuguese Government and Frelimo on September 7, 1974, constituted the legal instrument and institutional platform which established the cease-fire and led Mozambique to independence the following year.

13 Already by 1973, 22,000 Portuguese had fled the colony (Verschuur, 1986, cited by Magode, 1998: 112). This number increased to around 100,000 between September 1974 and June 1975 (Gentili, 1999: 363) and continued to rise in the first years after independence. The majority of these people had occupied key posts in public administration and had controlled strategic sectors of the economy, such as the construction industry, the banking system, the small and medium-sized manufacturing industries, the fishing industry, the rural trade network and the large and medium-sized agricultural companies.

14 These were interior areas, mainly in the regions of Cabo Delgado, Niassa and Tete, which, as a result of the rising struggle, had been removed from the control of the Portuguese colonial administration. Here alternative forms of political, economic and social organization had been rehearsed which, after independence, were an inspiration for the Government's development strategies and programs.

15 In a message broadcast via Dar-es-Salaam (Tanzania) on the occasion of the swearing in of the Transitional Government, Samora Machel, the president of Frelimo, indicated the following guidelines for the system of the administration of justice:

> The judicial machinery should be reorganized so that justice is accessible and understandable to the ordinary citizens of our land. The bourgeois system involved the administration of justice in unnecessary complexity, a legal system that was impenetrable to the masses, a deliberately confusing and obscure language and at such a slow pace and such costs that it created a barrier between the people and justice. In short, the legal system that exists in our country serves the rich and is accessible only to them. The path we intend to follow is one of simplifying and accelerating the process of applying justice within the framework of new laws and regulations which the Transitional Government must now study, bearing in mind the existing situation and the gradual transformation which must be undertaken (Machel, 1983: 18).

16 See the Dispatch of the Prime Minister of the Transitional Government of 25 January 1975, published in the *Boletim Oficial* no. 13, 1st. series of 30 January of the same year.

17 The University of Lourenço Marques was later renamed Eduardo Mondlane, after the first president of Frelimo.

18 See the reference in note 1.

19 By then Mozambique had a single-party political system, led by Frelimo.

20 See Article 25 of Act no. 1/75, of 27 June.

21 *Serviço Nacional de Consulta e Assistência Jurídica* (SNCAJ).

22 The SNCAJ would never really come to exist, due to a lack of regulation and of means. Later the National Institute for Legal Assistance (*Instituto Nacional de Assistência Jurídica* - INAJ) was created to replace it. Its evolution into the current Institute of Legal Assistance and Representation (*Instituto de Patrocínio e Assistência Jurídica* - IPAJ) is analyzed in more detail in chapter 9.

23 *Serviço Nacional de Segurança Popular* – SNASP.

24 The Popular Forces for the Liberation of Mozambique, or national army (*Forças Populares de Libertação de Moçambique*).

25 See, in particular, the section entitled *A edificação da Justiça Popular* ("The Building of Popular Justice"), in Point 5 of the Report of the Central Committee to the Third Congress (Frelimo, 1977).

26 See Article 37 of the 1975 Constitution.

27 In accordance with the regulations established in Article 21 onwards, in Law no. 1/77 of 1 September, deputies in the Locality and City Assemblies were directly elected by open ballot at meetings of eligible voters in residential areas and workplaces. In their first sessions, these Assemblies elected delegates to the District Electoral Conference from among their members and from among members of

the Party structure, the FPLM, other defense and security organizations, the mass democratic organizations, the state institutions and the units of production. Following the same procedure, the District Assemblies elected their representatives to the Provincial Electoral Conference and, finally, the Provincial Assemblies elected – this time in a secret ballot – a total of 230 deputies to the Popular Assembly.

28 See note 34 in chapter 1.

29 Law no. 12/78 of 2 December.

30 On the role of the *apartheid* regime in destabilizing countries in the region, particularly Mozambique, see the Final Report of the *Commission for Truth and Reconciliation*, South Africa, Volume 2, Chapter 2, which can be consulted at (accessed in September 2002). On the subject, see also Hanlon, 1991; Minter, 1998. http://www.polity.org.za/govdocs/comissions/1998/trc/2chap2.htm.

31 By 1985, 11 provincial popular courts had been created and had begun functioning, including that of the City of Maputo, in addition to 60 district popular courts and around 700 local popular courts, incorporating approximately 4,000 judges altogether (*Justiça Popular, Boletim* 10: 10).

32 For example, the National Vaccination Campaign, which ran from June 1976 to February 1979, enabled over ten and a half million Mozambicans to be vaccinated against smallpox, measles, tetanus and tuberculosis, thus covering a percentage of people never before achieved anywhere else in the world (see the preamble to Ministerial Diploma no. 88/79 of 4 August, published in the *Boletim da República*, 1st Series, no. 90, 1979).

33 *Organização da Mulher Moçambicana* (Mozambican Women's Organization).

34 *Organização da Juventude Moçambicana* (Mozambican Youth Organization).

35 *Organização dos Trabalhadores Moçambicanos* (Mozambican Workers Organization, the main trade union).

36 See Article 38, no. 2, of Law no. 12/78.

37 See Article 3 of Decree-Law no. 4/75, of 16 August.

38 '*Operação Produção*' (Operation Production) was carried out following the decisions of the IV Frelimo Congress (Maputo, 26 to 30 April 1983), which adopted the slogan *Defend the Country, Defeat Underdevelopment, Build Socialism*. It involved political actions of a repressive nature, which aimed to forcibly remove to the most under-populated rural zones (in particular the northern province of Niassa) all those in the large cities who "lived as delinquents, idlers, parasites, outcasts, vagrants and prostitutes", in order to transform them, through productive work and involvement in the local community, into "useful elements of society, honest workers, citizens who fulfill their civic duties and responsible people, worthy of being accepted into society" (see the preamble to Law no. 7/83, of 25 December). The 'Political and Organizational Offensive', for its part, aimed to provide a "historic contribution to the Mozambican Revolution through the enrichment of Marxism-Leninism", and was a method of work based on "the spirit of rigorous demands, maximum effort, efficiency, productivity, honesty and dedication", through which the central

organs of the Party and the state would make an ongoing assessment of the 'process of building the new society and the new Mozambican man" (see Resolution no. 9/80 of the Popular Assembly, published in the *Boletim da República* no. 33, 1st Series, of 20 August 1980). In spite of their upright intentions, both processes in fact ended up by creating countless numbers of innocent victims, as was later acknowledged.

39 The Revolutionary Military Court consisted of five judges appointed by the Ministry of National Defense. The choice always fell on career soldiers, who had no legal training. Although the law established the principle of public hearings (Article 14), in this Court the hearings took place behind closed doors and there could be no appeal against their decisions (Article 3).

40 APIE – *Administração do Parque Imobiliário do Estado*, that is, the State Real Estate Management in charge of the nationalized real estate.

41 Which gave dispensation for the following:

> Analogy or the deduction of parity or majority reason is not admissible in qualifying any fact as a crime, without it also being necessary to verify the elements which essentially constitute the criminal fact as expressly defined in penal law.

42 A political campaign against illegal overcharging in the transportation of people and goods.

43 Which included the following: intensified armed conflict between the government forces and Renamo; a long and persistent drought which exhausted the region, had irremediable effects on the whole of agricultural production, especially the family sector, and created a chronic dependence on the exterior for food; the failure of the rural development policies adopted; the intensification of the international economic crisis, whose repercussions were felt throughout the continent in a particularly dramatic way, to the extent that some consider the eighties a lost decade for Africa (M'baya, 1995: 62; Abrahamsson and Nilsson, 1996: i).

44 There is a vast amount of literature on the causes of the collapse of the socialist option in Mozambique. From amongst those authors who emphasize external factors (South African destabilization and a difficult set of international circumstances), mention should be made of Joseph Hanlon (1991), John Saul (1990), Bridget O'Laughlin (1992), Abrahamsson and Nilsson (1995). Authors such as Clarence-Smith (1989), Peter Fry (1990), Jean Copans (1990b), Michel Cahen (1996), and others prefer to emphasize internal factors (the denial of ethnic differences, the technocratic model of development, etc.).

45 Abrahamsson and Nilsson (1995: 104) note that in August of 1982, at a session of the Frelimo Central Committee, the decision was made to adopt a new foreign policy based on the principle of 'making more friends and fewer enemies'. This change occurred after the refusal of the former Soviet Union to provide greater

economic and military aid to Mozambique and evident signs of a serious swing in Moscow's own foreign policy.

46 See Act no. 6/84, of 19 September.

47 The Organization of African Unity was an international organization founded to promote unity, solidarity and international cooperation amongst the newly independent African states. In 2002 it became the African Union (AU), aimed at promoting cooperation amongst the independent African countries.

48 Until then both the Higher Court of Appeals, created by Law no. 11/79 of 12 December – which replaced the former Appeals Tribunal – and the General Attorney's Office, whose structure had remained unaltered since the colonial period, had been functioning provisionally. Both organs had been charged with the exercise of some of the powers attributed by the Law on the Organization of the Judiciary to the Supreme Popular Court and the General Attorney's Office and, simultaneously, with creating the conditions to ensure that they could begin to function.

49 The other judges in the Supreme Court were shortly afterwards nominated in a dispatch from the Ministry of Justice, in accordance with the provisions in Article 14, no. 1, of Law no. 12/78.

50 See the "Motion for a Salutation to the Central Committee of the Frelimo Party, the Central Commission and the people of Mozambique", of 2 November 1990, published in the *Boletim da República*, 1st Series, no. 44, of 5 November 1990.

51 Much less severe than the previous law, it acknowledged the contents of Article 70 of the 1990 Constitution ("1. All citizens have the right to life. They have the right to physical integrity and cannot be subjected to torture or cruel and inhumane treatment. 2. The death penalty does not exist in the Republic of Mozambique") and subjects this special type of infraction to ordinary jurisdiction.

52 The Judicial Council is defined as "an organ directed by the Chief Justice of the Supreme Court, the function of which is to analyze and rule on fundamental issues relating to the judicial apparatus" (Article 66). It consists of the Chief Justice and Deputy Chief Justice of the Supreme Court, Justices, the Chief Judges of the Provincial Courts and the Secretary General of the Supreme Court (Article 67).

53 Nominating and discharging judicial magistrates and those of the General Attorney's Office at all levels and exercising disciplinary action over them; determining the specialization of the courts and their respective sections, as well as the commencement of their operations; defining the selection criteria for candidates, rules for procedures and time limits for the election of non-professional judges; establishing the budgets for the different institutions, etc.

54 After the judicial courts and public prosecution became autonomous, the Ministry of Justice was left with part of the prison services, the Registry and Notary Public services, the IPAJ and the community courts. Later on, two more institutions were created which came under the supervision of the Ministry of Justice: a Law Reform Commission, recently transformed into a Technical Unit for Law Reform

(UTREL), and the Center for Legal and Judicial Training (CFJJ). This topic will be analysed in several other chapters in section 3 of this book.

55 We shall return to these issues in part 3 of the book.

56 Some of the provisions in the Tax Benefits Code were subsequently altered under Act no. 45/96 of 22 October.

57 The Organic Statute was approved by Act no. 54/95 of 13 December.

58 CPI – in Portuguese, *Centro de Promoção de Investimento*.

59 The municipalization process is part of broader political and administrative reforms that are being carried out in Mozambique (more on this subject below).

60 This topic is analyzed in more detail in chapter 9.

61 In the legislative elections of 1999, Frelimo obtained 48.5% of the votes, Renamo 38.8% and the remaining 10 parties and coalitions together managed no more than 12.7%. In 2004, Frelimo obtained 62% of the votes, while Renamo dropped to 29.7%.

62 Renamo and almost all of the other opposition parties refused to take part in the 1998 local government elections because they disagreed with the legislative package approved by the Frelimo parliamentary majority and the way in which the process of decentralization was being carried out by the government. The number of abstentions reached the unexpected figure of 85.42%. In most of the 33 municipalities involved in the dispute, only the party in power stood for election. Even so, in the two largest cities in the country, Maputo and Beira, the citizens associations *Juntos pela Cidade* (United for the City) and the *Grupo de Reflexão e Mudança* (Group for Reflection and Change) achieved significant results, obtaining 25.6% and 39.9% of the votes respectively and electing 15 and 17 members to the corresponding Municipal Assemblies (AIM, 1998). In 2003 the second local elections took place; for the first time Renamo (sometimes in coalition with other parties) won 5 municipalities.

63 The difference between 'deconcentration' and 'devolution of power' lies in the fact that, in contrast to the latter the former, does not imply a definitive transfer of the authority of the central administration (the power of decision-making and execution) to the elected local organs.

64 The *União Democrática* (Democratic Union) – a coalition which existed during the first legislature.

65 See Article 188, no. 1, of the 1990 Constitution.

66 General State Budget.

67 CIRESP – *Comissão Interministerial de Reforma do Sector Público*, in Portuguese.

68 See Act no. 6/2000 of 4 April.

69 United Nations Development Program.

70 See also the *1999 UN Resident Coordinator Annual Report*, at as well as the data from the last census. http://www.unsystemmoz.org.

71 On this subject, see chapter 10.

72 Law no. 10/2004 of 25 August.

73 See Act no. 34/97 of 21 October.

74 See *Notas sobre a Formação Jurídica e Judiciária em Moçambique* (CFJJ, 2000). See also chapter 6 in this book, which contains more detailed information on the activities carried out by the CFJJ.

75 See Article 4 of the 1975 Constitution.

76 Which stated the following: "The land and the natural resources situated on and beneath the earth, in territorial waters and on the continental platform of Mozambique are the property of the state. The state decides the terms of its use and benefits".

77 Which states: "1. All ownership of land shall be vested in the State 2. Land cannot be sold or otherwise disposed of, nor may it be mortgaged or subject to attachment. 3. As a universal means for the creation of wealth and of social well-being, the use and enjoyment of land shall be the right of all the Mozambican people". Article 109 of the 2004 Constitution reads similarly, although it differs in point no. 2, which declares that "land may not be sold [...]" thus opening the possibility for private ownership of land.

78 With the new, 2004 Constitutional reform, which introduced – among other changes – the notion of legal pluralism in the country, the need for a reform of the judicial system became more than obvious. The reform of the court system was initiated in 2003.

79 The Commercial Code dates from 1888, the Penal Code from 1886, the Penal Procedure Code from 1929 (although it only came into force in Mozambique in 1931), the Civil Code from 1966 and the Civil Procedure Code from 1961.

3

Toward Interlegality?
Traditional Healers and the Law

Maria Paula G. Meneses

Introduction

Mozambique is a large country, with a population of approximately 19 million, almost all native Africans, belonging to several ethnic or linguistic groups. Until the onset of Portuguese colonization, toward the end of the nineteenth century, the various peoples that made up Mozambique did not live under a single political authority. They existed as independent entities, with various forms of political and social organization: some were kingdoms with centralized governments; others existed mainly as headless units, the largest political units being the tribes or chieftaincies.[1]

The transition to the twentieth century became synonymous with the implantation of colonial rule, introducing a critical period of radical changes that brought about the Mozambican political reality. The different economic and political strategies applied by the colonial state in Mozambique resulted in important changes to the organization of power (where and for whom this power operated). The forms of colonial domination and resistance in different spaces and locations are a reaction to the systems of exploitation that depended on slave and free labor – a situation that explains the colonial regime that existed in Mozambique, as well as the different stages that succeeded it (O'Laughlin, 2000: 11). The *Indigenato* regime[2] was the political system that subordinated Mozambicans to leaders of communities described as tribes. The construction of traditional or common law therefore arose as an integral part of this process of subordination and domination out of which the colonial state emerged (Young, 1994; Gentili, 1999). Political control was highly concentrated under the colonial state, while administrative control was much more selective and decentralized. Thus, in rural settings, the colonial state agreed that the administration would be carried out by local, traditional authorities, applying a private, customary law for the resolution of problems in local societies, whereas in urban areas civilians (mostly Portuguese colonials) operated under the rule of law.

In ideological terms, the colonial system was a dualistic system which attempted to oppose the different forms of governance, legal systems, land possession, and labor regulation (Mamdani, 1996a; Newitt, 1995). The colonial state guaranteed the existence of an official, modern legal system for citizens (i.e., for the colonials and *assimilados*). The state would issue birth certificates and identity cards to citizens. Citizens could use these documents to register goods (*e.g.*, land) under their names, and could appeal to state courts to resolve legal conflicts. Civil identity was, therefore, the identity of the civilized citizen; the only one who retained political and civil rights. On the other hand, indigenous rights were defended by traditional authorities through traditional law. Because indigenous identity was drawn along regional ancestral lines, it was mainly defined according to ethnic criteria.

By attributing a political identity to Africans through local (indigenous) authorities, Portuguese colonialism sowed the seeds of the ethnic, racial and identity-based, widespread opposition that characterized Mozambique in the post-independence period.

As Santos claims in chapter 1, after independence, from 1975 on, diverse eurocentric political-legal cultures were added to the extant mix of legal orders. These 'new' cultures added new elements to the resources available locally. These previous resources were remnant structures from earlier periods in the life of the state, some of which, although legally suspended for a while, had continued to survive sociologically (such being the case of the so-called traditional authorities). As a result, the contemporary landscape of Mozambique can be described as a mosaic of legal hybridization, in which there is a mixture of elements of different legal orders (official/state law, common law, various religious laws, etc.). At the same time, in the field of conflict resolution, innovative legal entities are created out of such mixtures.[3] This legal phenomenon has been described as *interlegality* (Santos, 1995).[4]

In this chapter I seek to explore some of the conflicts in the realm of justice administration in Mozambique. My reason for adopting the global-national-local perspectives derives from the need to interrogate the reasons for the mismatch between traditional and modern law, between the official and unofficial settings of conflict resolution.

The 'traditional' sphere – the institutions which take on the protection of the welfare of the local communities – are simultaneously political, curative, juridical and religious; they cover an extensive field of competencies and functions which place the efficacy of problem-solving within a more enveloping context, bringing into play institutions of authority, normative and symbolic structures, and relations of force, knowledge and power. Nonetheless, until 2004 – when the new Constitution recognized the plurality of legal orders in Mozambique (Article 4), only the judicial instances recognized as official have been the object of support by the state; the other legal structures not recognized as official are tolerated but, most frequently, ignored.

Problems related to witchcraft continue to be one of the most visible areas of activity of the traditional institutions, where culture and power are continuously contested and recreated.[5] In the modern view, the qualifier 'traditional' – when applied to conflict resolution or social integration – refers to practices and knowledge that are perceived as opposing and/or complementing the official conflict resolution system. Using witchcraft practices as a window onto the broad subject of 'other authorities', I try to show some possible ways of approaching the question of law and justice in Mozambique as a problem-solving tool.

Having set the analytical framework, it should be said that the analysis studied in this text is mostly based on the practices and discourses found in Maputo city and its environs, as well as in distinct areas of the Maputo province, in southern Mozambique, where the research has been carried out. Also, I gathered information from libraries and from several research organizations. The major sources of information, however, are interviews and participant observation, since little research has been produced in the country on this subject.

1. The Colonial and the Postcolonial State

In 1975, with Independence,[6] the country adopted a Westernized constitution, with a parliamentary system of government. It also provided for an independent judiciary with the power to review acts of both the legislature and the executive. However, since the Frelimo[7] government's goal was to achieve the level of development to be found in the West, recognition of the ethno-cultural differences was seen as a wrong political move, as a path that would advance internal regional fractions; at the same time, many of the local African traditions were regarded as backward and at odds with the road towards development. During the first decade after independence, it became practically impossible to speak of social differences other than the obvious differences between colonialists and the oppressed, between rich and poor. Reference to other forms of difference – be they cultural or even ethnic — would be condemned as pandering to regional divisions in the country. Literate people became an almost inevitable part of Frelimo's effort to extend the modern state[8] into rural surroundings. Their power came from a form of knowledge that denigrated the 'traditionalism' of the tribal chiefs and the 'obscurantism' of their rural culture (Machel, 1981: 38; Roesch, 1992: 472; Geffray, 1990: 34-44, 78-80). Frelimo had won the struggle against colonialism and, on its ruins, was to transform the mentality of native society. Literacy would bring about a transformation from metaphysical reasoning, typical of a traditional society, to scientific and materialist reasoning. Characteristic of the dominant ideology of that time was the fact that scholars ignored some of the main questions that people were posing in legal terms, such as the theme of witchcraft. Instead, witchcraft was described as an impediment to national unity and to the project of liberation: pernicious evidence of the 'traditional', obscure past (Castanheira, 1979: 12).

The Creation of the Customary

The 'invention of tradition', the 'making of customary law' has become a symbol of 'the traditional' in Africa, a product of the colonial past. In other contexts, tradition has become a symbol of a pre-colonial past.

Despite the fact that the *Indigenato* Code was only adopted in the late 1920s, it was preceded by a complete series of codes and sanction regimes, which demarcated the distinction between 'the civilized' and 'the natives'. The essence of the colonial system, thus, was based on the existence of a 'traditional' ruling system, upon which the colonial administrative and judicial system exerted its action. In colonial Mozambique, local, traditional chiefs were closely linked to the colonial system. Although some of the local chiefs (*régulos*) were of 'noble' lineages,[9] several other people appointed by the colonial authorities often lacked traditional legitimacy.[10] At the same time, the positions to which they were appointed were either created by the colonial administration or had been so corrupted by its demands to collect the hut tax, raise the labor force and regulate the forced production of agricultural products that they no longer legitimately represented autochthonous patterns of authority, but rather the co-optation of complex ruling mechanisms.

In its essence, the *Indigenato* regime symbolized the 'making of customary law' from above, with the support of the colonial administration. Modern law – brought about by the colonial state – regulated relations among the non-indigenous as well as relations between non-indigenous and indigenous. It should therefore be evident that political inequality emerged side-by-side with civil inequality, as both were based on the instituted legal pluralism: the colonial/state law and customary rights. The analysis of this process has shown how a web of actors (including colonial authorities, missionaries and African notables/elders) cobbled together local customs, giving it the form of colonial law. While indigenous law was more like a legal claim than a legal code, contrary to the dominant pattern seen elsewhere in colonial Africa, in Mozambique the attempts to codify the customary (Gonçalves Cota, 1944, 1946) were never given the force of law.

A careful study of the customary clearly shows a call for the preservation of the social fabric, through the social construction of tradition, law and ethnicity, throughout the impositions of the colonial system. For Mamdani, this system of 'indirect rule' – a characteristic of the British colonial administration in Africa – established a "decentralized despotism" as the British learned to marshal authoritarian possibilities in the native culture (1996a: 23). However, at the same time, in a game of mirrors, one has to pay attention to the role played by local actors, as people continually reinterpreted and reconstructed tradition in the context of broader socio-economic changes. As Spear notes, "far from being created by alien rulers, tradition was reinterpreted, reformed and reconstructed by subjects and rulers alike" (2003: 4). Thus, 'tradition' emerged as a multi-dimensional landscape, an interactive historical process that was the antithesis of the 'static' colonial state.

Despite being 'punished' by the colonial state, the chieftaincy and related institutions – specifically in the Mozambican colonial context – were an important factor in terms of cohesion and cultural identity, which legitimized authority and regulated relations among the population by administering any occurrences of local conflict. Far from conveying an unchanging past, tradition undergoes continual renewal as new concepts are brought in or old concepts readjusted according to changing realities. Tradition is then composed of fixed principles and fluid processes of adaptation that regulate societies. In colonial times, the *régulos* represented the consolidation of judicial, legislative and administrative authority at the center of the state. In order to keep their position, these traditional chiefs depended on the support of colonial power. But simultaneously, colonial authorities depended on traditional authorities to make their rule effective and legitimate.

Under the Portuguese, the *régulos*[11] were the repositories, administrators and judges of 'customary law', the rules that governed colonial social, political and economic relations. In short, from a political tool for re-negotiating the social status and access to resources, the customary was transformed into a set of enforceable rules that froze its status and restricted access to it.

In a situation where 'traditional' problems were, by law, to be resolved under the 'customary' rules (but where no codification of these rules was ever officially accepted), both the Portuguese administrators and the *régulos* retained the possibility of adjusting the 'traditional' to respond to different situations. As a result, "Africans [chiefs] determined the content of the law in the course of individual decisions in which they provided a more nuanced interpretation of the law than colonial constructions allowed" (Spear, 2003: 16).

In sum, the administrative and judicial power of the colonial state was quite limited, and it became subject to local discourses of power that state neither fully understood nor controlled, as was the case of witchcraft.

The history of colonization and modernization (both in its European and African guises) has been a history of suppression of the demands for justice in the face of witchcraft. In Africa, colonial authorities dismissed customs found to be 'repugnant' to civilized standards. However, as will be further discussed, from the perspective of Mozambicans, the modern, 'enlightened' and rational legislation came sometimes as a perversion of justice. In pre-colonial and even in colonial times witches were frequently expelled from the community, or killed, or forced to pay compensation for the damage caused. Under the colonial state, in neighboring British colonies, witchcraft practices became outlawed, accused of reflecting 'a retrograde past' (Melland, 1935; Roberts, 1935).[12] The nineteenth and early twentieth centuries witnessed the enactment of 'suppression of witchcraft' legislation, designed less to suppress the practice of evil, as understood by locals (which the colonial authorities took for superstition), than to suppress anti-witch activities (which the colonials deemed barbarism); as a result, sanctions against witches were declared offensive and threatened with long prison sentences (Krige, 1936: 252; Chanock, 1998). In a colonial context, witchcraft victims got the impression that they were rendered powerless in the face of the pursuits of witches. From their point of view it was completely incomprehensible why the colonial administration was particularly eager to protect the most dangerous villains. In a colonial context, as we will discuss further on, the state, while not protecting people from witchcraft spells, emerged as the protector of witches, thus making itself illegitimate in the eyes of the native populations. In what was a slightly distinct approach, probably due to its weakness, the colonial administrators in Mozambique, in order to avoid being portrayed as sponsors of witchcraft, never formally accepted the inexistence of witchcraft practices, and allowed 'traditional' courts to conduct trials against avowed witches (Meneses, 2000). Traditional authorities were even allowed to deal with charges of witchcraft, as long as they did not involve accusations of murder (Meneses, 2000; Honwana, 2002).

What gives tradition, custom and ethnicity their coherence and power is the fact that they lay deep in people's popular consciousness, informing them of who they are and how they should act. Yet, as discourses, traditions, customs and ethnicities are continually reinterpreted and reconstructed as 'regulated improvisations' subject to their continued intelligibility and legitimacy. Thus the postcolonial state, in order to be recognized as a legitimate authority, knew the new 'judicial structure' had to be anchored, at least to some extent, in the everyday life of both rulers and subjects alike. In order to be accepted as legitimate, a new 'legal framework' must bear a semblance to the legal corpus upon which it has been built. This is the challenge that, since 1975, has been posed to the state. Inevitably, when addressing the question of analyzing the socio-legal cultures present in the country, the question of witchcraft emerges as probably one of the major *loci* of conflict between the traditional and the modern.

The Traditional Side of Modernity

Over the last two centuries, the dominant discourse in Mozambique has made constant appeals to 'native' peoples based on the colonial drive to modernize by acquiring the 'right' values and knowledges (Meneses, 2003). Progress towards modernity has been defined as good and desirable, understood in a linear, historical progressive fashion: the indigenous must evolve into modern, civilized citizens. As for the former colonies, they were required to evolve from the time of 'tradition', in which they were still living, to an era of civilization, progress and modernity, where the 'most advanced' countries in the world stood (Santos, 2002a: 243-245).

In the political-legal sphere, the dominant discourse, seen as a means of contributing to development, mirrors the kind of peripheral postcolonial states aspiring to modernization. Both the 'native' and the 'civilized' are given fixed ideological meanings, resulting in the impossibility, in terms of socio-legal theory, of connecting different legal systems from the perspective of *interlegality*. This became particularly notorious during the last stage of the colonial presence in Mozambique. The result of the attempt to apply indirect rule to a colonial process where the colonizing power was –

in terms of social, economic and political intervention – quite fragile, produced a hybrid system of traditional authorities. On the one hand, these chiefdoms – whether 'original' or adapted – represented a guarantee of continuity for the functioning of the communities; on the other hand, they constituted the bases of colonial administration within the local setting. In this sense, the customary represented a safety cushion between the communities and the agents of the colonial administration, who were entrusted with resolving various administrative, economic and legal problems, and allowed for a more or less harmonious relationship between the two. Despite being modified under pressure from the colonial entity, in a certain sense the actions of the traditional authorities continued to be seen as local in origin and as the result of a profound familiarity with the feelings, existing norms and language of the communities. These were the factors that permitted and legitimated their actions.

But the ideological campaign of Frelimo during the period of nationalist struggle for independence, as well as throughout the postcolonial setting, was aimed at reinforcing the dualist nature of the system: the citizens as oppressors and the natives as the true Mozambicans. Yet, the socio-political and legal fabric appears much more complex at the height of independence in Mozambique. Despite the continued importance of coercion and colonial administrative control, there was no binary structure in the country as advocated by Frelimo. In the post-independence period, this policy has prevented the recognition of the existence of a plurality of interactions among distinct socio-legal fields, since the dominant discourse (and praxis) only allowed this interaction to occur either as a confrontation of legal orders, or as competing, rival legal systems. In both cases, one legal order would emerge as the dominant, the remaining ones being classified as subaltern or peripheral. However, as Santos suggests (2002c, 2003), complementarity, cooptation, convergence, assimilation, suppression and junctions, are just some of the many possibilities under which interlegal interactions may take place. Hence, how much of the discussion regarding the modernization of the legal structure indeed allowed for a successful empowerment of Mozambicans? Aren't they, instead, through the recourse to the fixity of the traditional vis-à-vis the modern, promoting the impossibility of contacts between distinct systems of social regulation?

The Mozambican postcolonial state emerged in a context where both chronological and territorial differentiation were achieved by a unitary compulsion that tended to underplay differences, insisting upon the homogeneity of the future, and failing to acknowledge the existing socio-legal heterogeneity. Thus, to be part of the 'present' required freezing everything that represented an obstacle in the historical path to modernity, thus seen as part of the 'old' past, as traditional. The other cultures, viewed as inferior under the colonial order, (re)emerged again now in a post-colonial setting, as backward in the dominant legal discourse. The extremely complex cultural mosaic of socio-legal cultures in Mozambique, with their own characteristics and structures, kept being routinely described as a homogeneous entity, which resulted in the general reference to a single traditional judicial structure (Carrilho, 1995; Nilsson, 1995; Lundin,

1998). In terms of legal systems, this approach justified the dominant presence of an official legal system, built upon the principles of Western rationality.[13]

The initial process of incorporating the newly independent postcolonial states into 'the family of nations' resulted in a process of reinforcement of the differentiation between the universal legal framework and the local, traditional legal frameworks. Indeed, the continuity of the principles of Western rationality in the social ordering of Mozambique resulted in a sequence of attempts (Santos, 2003) to integrate the other, the traditional indigenous, under a dominant legal rationale, without acknowledging the fact that the existing differentiation in terms of rights is the result of specific historical and contemporary experiences. This sort of amnesia regarding the other enables the Western-based legal narrative to remain ever-present, without ever being questioned for the bias provoked against the plural arena of socio-legal orders. As before, during the post-independence period the native peoples were viewed as uncivilized, lacking sufficient legal sophistication for their normative systems to be part and parcel of the new national legal order. The stimulating results of a research project on the heterogeneous nature of the Mozambican state pointed out that one of its main characteristics was the fact that only a very narrow segment of the population would appeal to the official, state-oriented judicial system to try to solve their problems. The presence of a Westernized approach to the judicial culture is an example of the bequeathed suppression of other knowledge and practices in the construction of the legal landscape of the country. The international legal framework became the normative episteme other cultures and countries had to accept in order to be recognized as a state. Instead of building a new legal order based on the realities present in the country, the contemporary Mozambican legal framework may be described as one that establishes overall supremacy over other competing modes of rationality, which are either silenced or appropriated according to the interests of the dominant model. In contrast, we maintain that an autocratic approach to consolidating national unity only results in the amplification of the cultural differences and identities, as we have been observing. These observations require a deeper evaluation of the very character of modernization, since the intransigence of the dominant legal model towards the other socio-legal structures (resulting in their subordination or invisibility) indicates the presence of an inflexible modern state, frozen in its past. As the study led by Santos and Trindade (2003) clearly indicates, it has been possible to detect the development of dynamic legal hybridizations in Mozambique – hybridizations that accept the modern model of law, even creating the space for its action. Seen from this angle, the vitality of traditional normative systems reflects the difficulties of a state legal body, which appears unable to achieve its objectives. The hybridization of legal orders reflects the diversity of knowledges present, which are by no means fixed in space and time, as so often is imputed to traditional values.

Because other political, judicial and administrative entitites have been developing and adjusting to contemporary situations, the result is an innumerable array of metamorphoses in the socio-legal field. The fundamental question to be posed is how the dynamics of hybridization of these legal orders have developed, and which forms they have acquired. Contemporary Mozambique is a mosaic of traditional (i.e., non-official) authorities whose role, functions and performances are quite difficult to fit under a common canon.

Conflicts of Power, Conflicts of Knowledge

Imbued with colonial standards, most of the studies conducted on the subject tend to insist on the role of the *régulos*, thus forgetting the enormous array of entities present, who are legitimized from below by the communities that recognize their authority. Such personages as traditional healers (*tinyanga*[14]) are also part of the concept of traditional, local authorities, despite the fact that their political importance seems to be less visible. Another aspect to bear in mind is the fact that the traditional authorities and their means of dealing with social problems are not confined to the strict ambit of law; on the contrary, they cover several other sectors of social life.

In this sense, they require a reshaping of the concept of 'conflict', which includes the notion of misfortune, and which translates the cognitive, symbolic and institutional order of society itself. The universe under study is a good example of the coexistence of several institutions, which aim at welfare and social integration.

In a community for which the cosmological apparatus is perceived as representing a closed environment, and where the concept of disease is perceived as a shared 'problem',[15] the source of the problem has to be detected and expelled on time, for the problem poses the risk of spreading to everyone. However, the search for the source of the disease becomes broader, including the treatment of the social and the physical ailments.[16] Indeed, society is seen as being threatened by a 'disease' whose etiology has to be discovered and combated: traditional healers treat people at the same time as they treat society itself, whether such treatment is to ensure the reproduction and maintenance of the existing order (norms, representations) or its perturbation (tensions, conflicts, collective misfortunes). The disease results in an ailing body, but the source of trouble can be found in a spell or wrongdoing produced by a witch. To cure someone means to eradicate the source of troubles, including the identification and neutralization of a witch. This task can only be accomplished using 'local' medicines, local knowledge. In this process lies the heart of the internal resilience of the traditional in Mozambique.

2. The Ambiguous Nature of Witches and Healers

In Mozambique, as is the case in many African countries, the threat of witchcraft is very difficult to tackle, as one feels exposed to intangible forces, not knowing exactly how they work and where they originate. This feeling of insecurity helps to explain the desperate attempts to expose the culprits, forcing them to confess what nobody could have observed directly. Witches are considered to be inhuman and not fit to live; thus, they have to be removed from the community or destroyed. But official law seems unfit to deal with this problem.

A sociological analysis of this phenomena provides an understanding of the nature of witchcraft as a regulatory element of dissonant social pressures (Meneses, 2000; Santos, 2003: 85-86). In the context under analysis, witchcraft suggests the manipulation by malicious individuals of powers inherent in persons, spiritual entities, and substances to cause harm to others (Asforth, 1998b). Those who have a lot of money or power are perceived to have obtained or gained it because they have taken 'power' from, and thus have been helped, by someone else. Those who die, who suffer misfortunes, do so because they are sick, have problems with success, or there is someone who dislikes the fact that they are different or that they are trying to be different; it may also be somebody trying to tear apart the micro-network of social belonging in which he/ she has emerged.

This short introduction to the subject of witchcraft unambiguously indicates the presence of two sides to the matter: beliefs and action. Accusations are made and action is taken; thus, beliefs and action reinforce one another. In a sense, witchcraft is a sort of occult wisdom (Geschiere, 1997), used to rule over a group or a community. However, witchcraft can also be used by its practitioners to harm others or to obtain various types of benefits, as when they sell their services. It may be used with malicious motives for acts of vengeance, forming a wide web that holds villagers and urban dwellers together through discourses and images that continually explore the moral dimensions of poverty and prosperity. Because witchcraft is just as likely to be a matter of the wealthy attacking the poor as the poor harassing the well off, it is the prerogative of neither.

Among the Changana and Rhonga people of southern Mozambique, for example, perceived victims of witchcraft took, as they continue to do, the law into their own hands to rid the community of the peddlers of this evil craft. It is this latter component that is crucial for a broader understanding of the nature of conflicts and the processes of dispute resolution in Mozambique.

The Nature of the Accusations of Witchcraft

The Changana apply the term *nòyi*[17] to all 'supernatural' attacks. The term is used to refer to attacks or to the power to kill or injure people by means of spells, including also the use of 'medicines', often generally referred to as *murhi*.

Both men and women, old and young, have been accused or have been the object of gossip relating to witchcraft practices, although more generally one would find older (and often widowed) women to be targets of anti-witchcraft action.

Accusations of witchcraft and witch attacks are not rare events. Almost every person in southern Mozambique knows that witches have the power to make lightening strike to injure or kill people; to damage property; to destroy crops, and to cause calamities or accidents. As a victim of a witch affirmed in an interview, "it is not a question of believing or disbelieving. It's difficult for outsiders to understand, but our daily life relies heavily on the world of spirits, for good or evil."[18]

The people afflicted with acts of witchcraft are usually in more or less intimate relationships with the perpetrators – relatives, neighbors, lovers, schoolmates and workmates top the list of the usual suspects. Witchcraft may be motivated by jealousy, or by unsolved conflicts between or among community members. People are particularly scared of the latter possibilities, since they may occur at random inside the community.

One of the motives for witchcraft is usually said to be jealousy, in situations of envy of emerging wealth. This is the reason why the ambiguity of witchcraft is often referred to as an "occult economy" (Geschiere, 1997). People say that someone desiring to become rich might go and ask for support from a 'bad' *nyàngà*, who would collect the support of all the ancestors, thus leaving the rest of the family unprotected by them.[19] Worse still, several medications can also be applied to protect and preserve wealth, while sometimes requiring the sacrifice of a relative or of non-kin.[20] People seek in witchcraft an explanation for events and circumstances for which they would otherwise have none. Thus witchcraft is believed to be at the root of many misfortunes, thanks to the actions of one's neighbors or kin. In this the inhabitants of Maputo city are no different from the inhabitants of urban and rural communities elsewhere in Africa. The examples available suggest a number of explanations for accusations of witchcraft in general, focusing on hardship and circumstances that cause tension, conflict, suffering, anxiety and uncertainty. As a person struggles to get by in a world where livelihoods depend almost entirely on earning an income, competition for jobs and other income-earning opportunities becomes intense. Those who succeed are prone to become the object of suspicion by those who do not. Suspicion may degenerate into actual accusations or even in an appointment with the traditional healer, so as to garner protection against a witch attack produced by a potentially envious or jealous community member.

In addition to being a malevolent force, witchcraft is also, paradoxically, believed to be a source of good fortune. There are reported cases in which political success is seen as the outcome of the possession of or an alliance with the powers of ancestors. In Cameroon, for example, as Geschiere and Nyamnjoh show (2000), rumors link witchcraft to the rich and powerful; here, witchcraft emerges as a central piece in the electoral process, since several of the powerful are described as allegedly owing their success to the use of varied occult sources and forces. In Maputo city, as we observed, the situation is similar. Businessmen and politicians, who have become wealthy in the urban centers, are easily suspected of having pursued their careers with the help of obscure methods, including the use of traditional medicine. The state elite is deeply rooted in these cultural practices, and resorts to this kind of protection whenever in need of access to special promotions, wealth, etc. The elite need special powers to fight off potential rivals, and vice versa: their impoverished relatives or neighbors, who have stayed in the villages, are also accused of witchcraft. Since they have not amounted to anything, one assumes that they watch the success of their affluent relatives with an evil eye, and – driven by envy and resentment – try to destroy them.

This explains the ambivalent relationship to witchcraft. Witchcraft is ambivalent in the sense that it is hard to establish a decision/action as being totally good or totally bad.

Research in urban and rural areas of Mozambique shows that social and economic inequality is firmly entrenched, and that communities, deep down, are socially heterogeneous. Wide gaps between the better-off and the worse-off cause social tensions, as the former try to avoid excessive demands by worse-off neighbors and kin, and as poorer members of the community increasingly perceive the better-off as selfish. As the better-off suspect deprived neighbors and as deprived neighbors gossip about and accuse the well-to-do of having prospered through witchcraft, the tensions erupt into suspicion and accusations of witchcraft.

The constant demand for traditional medicine is more visible today because there are many more individuals on whom fortune has not shone, and who are searching for success – through promotion, wealth, and social opportunities. Current means of coping with uncertainty involve seeking protection. As the Comaroffs have described for neighboring South Africa (1999: 283), in Mozambique the violence and insecurity that accompanied the rapid political and social transformations the country underwent over the last 10-15 years – under historical conditions that yielded an ambiguous mix of possibility and powerlessness, of desire and despair, of mass joblessness and hunger amidst the accumulation, by some, of great amounts of wealth associated with the introduction of a new liberal economic strategy – greatly exacerbated the fear of witchcraft, for people felt unprotected. Thus the appeal to traditional healers was an anticipated response in the search for protective and supportive actions against witchcraft and crime.

With time, the outcome of a clash of values leads to strains and tensions in social relationships and eventually to suspicion and accusations of witchcraft.

Accusations of witchcraft are a form of social control. Witchcraft acts as a 'leveling force' (Geschiere, 1999: 213) in that it undermines inequalities in wealth and power. It happens when, given the fear of attack by jealous mates, people desist from accumulating or displaying amounts of wealth that might elicit envy and jealousy from potential witches. It acts as a pacemaker, a means of setting and limiting the rhythm of social change. If this argument is to be accepted, then by arresting social differentiation, witchcraft prevents the growth of social tensions that might arise from it. Also, accusations are said to discourage socially unacceptable behavior, as sometimes it is people who behave in unusual or eccentric ways that become the target of accusations.[21]

As Santos points out (2003: 86), although culturally witchcraft affirms itself as being at the opposite pole of modernity, witchcraft is essentially an example of an alternative modernity, in which social change takes place without serious ruptures in the networks of social security and identity fixtures.

In sum, witchcraft and accusations of evil-doing may correspond to various situations of social unease, such as divine retribution or punishment by ancestors for breaking taboos or committing sins, or even as a spell cast by another person who caused harm under hypnosis, as we shall see further on. So the question that those afflicted must address in relation to this sort of misfortune is less what has caused this suffering than who is responsible for the suffering. To treat the malaise of witchcraft is to struggle with the witch by mystical or social means, or both. That is, either the malevolent powers are combated by occult or spiritual means or the individual deemed responsible is identified, induced to retract the evil powers, and punished (or cleansed and redeemed). Because the official means made available by the Mozambican state are usually unwholesome in situations of accusations of witchcraft, people believing themselves to be under attack at any one time may visit a traditional healer, seeking to establish the cause of their troubles, as well as who is behind them and how to take counter-measures (Green, 1994: 30).

The Tinyàngà and the Struggle against Social Illnesses

As we have just explained, witchcraft has a dual nature: on the one hand it seeks new means – apparently beyond human control – to achieve goals that would otherwise be impossible (such as the 'betterment of life' in situations of extreme social exclusion, which is a current reality in Mozambique); on the other hand it functions as a way to voice a desire for punishment of those who one envies and those who, for whatever reason, stand out. Since witchcraft deals with the 'occult', it becomes quite difficult to identify the 'modern' means, the sources and evidence to prove the presence of acts of witchcraft. The detection of the traces of witchcraft activity is normally left to the *tynyàngà*.[22]

Under the scientific model of rationality, the processes of fact-finding, guilt determination, the ritualized expressions of remorse and the demand for immediate, though often symbolic, reparation strike Western sensibilities as weak, irrational and unjust (Seidman, 1965; Horton, 1993; Nsereko, 1996).

The hegemony of modern science results in the local confinement of 'other' knowledges, which can be both the cause of its discrimination and the basis for its resistance to the singularity of knowledge. The finding of a *tinyàngà* appears both as a form of security and an affirmation of what is specific to them, of ways of knowing what belongs to them and which thus enables them to acquire room to maneuver, *i.e.* spaces of empowerment. The process of negation of knowledge and strength of the 'traditional field' of knowledge equated the image of this action with that of witchcraft. But these are in fact entirely different personages, as both patients and practitioners of traditional medicine attest. "There is a difference between a healer and a witch doctor. A healer cures and a witch doctor kills. A witch doctor knows potions that kill. But healers cure."[23]

In southern Mozambique, good health is a broad concept, requiring inner equilibrium within one's self, peace with one's ancestors, with one's neighbors, and with one's own body; adequate food (which in the present context includes having a job and therefore an income) and protection from evil – whether natural or 'sent' by a witch. If this situation is altered, either by the individual's failure to carry out necessary rituals or by greater forces at play, then the individual and/or the group become ill and everything must be done to identify not only the symptoms of social disorder, but moreover the origins of the evil and the contamination that results from it.

The *nyànga*'s power resides in his/her ability to identify existing social tensions, contradictions, and areas of distrust, as well as the latent antisocial grudges that could manifest themselves as an illness, or bad luck, or even bring death to the community. To expose a witch, to locate the person and lead her/him to confess is seen as a means of 'emptying themselves' of the burden of evil and restoring feelings of lightness and emptiness which signify balance, health and good relations.

The *nyànga* plays a dual role – divinatory and curative – based on a broader concept of illness, understood at two levels: as a social phenomenon, resulting in a deep alteration of everyday life, and as a physical phenomenon – a manifestation of something happening through pain in someone's body. The divinatory function seeks to identify the sources of the illness, prescribing several means to solve it. The curative function seeks to eliminate the physical symptoms. These two functions complement one another, and both help to cure. Thus the traditional healer knows best how to deal with these so-called 'traditional' illnesses, *i.e.* disorders with a heavy emotional component, because they deal with the body and the spirits which 'invade' the body and cause diverse problems to patients.

The healing process, aided by the *nyàga*, is two-fold: it fosters a return to physical equilibrium as well as a psychological and emotional balance by overcoming the sanctions that befell the individual as a result of his/her disregard for the established norms.

However, if in the past people accused of practicing witchcraft were condemned to death, expelled from the community, or ordered to seek a doctor to help him/her to 'remove' the evil, nowadays the problem is quite a bit more complex.

The *tinyàngà* hold the knowledge (and therefore the power) to diagnose people's problems and to identify their causes; they claim to be able to counter spells, find witches that are allegedly responsible for their clients' ills, and to find remedies to their supplicants' problems. In Maputo, consulting a traditional healer will result in a *séance* of divination, followed by the application of the *muavi* or ordeal. The ordeal is a form of divination that simultaneously exposes wrongdoers and punishes them.[24]

As we will explain below, nowadays, in cases in which the *régulos* or community courts cannot find a culprit for the act of witchcraft, they send the parties involved to seee a *nyàngà* (Meneses, 2000; Gomes *et al.*, 2003; Meneses *et al.*, 2003).[25] The selection of the *nyàngà* is normally carried out by Ametramo.[26] The association decides which *nyàngà* will carry out the divination and the application of the ordeal, so as to ensure the neutrality of the witch-finding process.

In the cases reported to us where the *muavi* was applied, suspects were made to ingest a beverage. Once ingested, it is supposed to run through the body looking for *witchcraft*: if it does not find any, it will be excreted or vomited, thus proving the innocence of the person falsely accused; in that case the accusers will compensate him. If *muavi* locates *witchcraft*, it will stop, and the accused will 'fall down' and even die. In the past the ones found 'guilty' used to be left to die; nowadays they are removed from the community.

I was told both that ordeals were forbidden since colonial times and that they could be authorized as part of the legal process nowadays (using dogs or roosters to symbolize people). The latter forms of ordeal were performed openly when we were carrying out our fieldwork, in early 2000.

Ordeals can also be a last resort for those made to feel vulnerable, when someone chooses to undergo them in order to show he/she is not guilty of witchcraft (Tonkin, 2000: 377, 381). Thus to investigate judicial ordeals involves analyzing different notions of guilt, innocence and the scope of human judgment – all part of a sociology of knowledge.

Witchcraft helps produce social balance within communities, a balance that is always precarious and in need of reconstruction. Both in an individual's life and in the life of the community, a continuous movement is present, oscillating between the moral ideal of community and the embarrassing reality of individual assertion. This contradiction is controlled through witchcraft. Witchcraft holds the balance of power relations: forces beyond one's power control the excessive success or power of a community leader – be it a traditional leader or a *nyàngà*. As a mechanism for controlling power, witchcraft is especially sensitive to changing patterns of social conflict, adapting rapidly to new situations.

When the state seems unable to resolve the conflicts and envy which arise from profound exclusion and social instability, the legitimacy of other forms of administering justice is greatly amplified. Traditional healers establish a very clear distinction between the limits and application of the official legal system and their possibilities of action. The process of locating the agent of evil by the *tinyàngà*, followed by the process of compelling the witches to confess their actions, should be analyzed as a way in which these persons are cleansed of the burden of evil, thereby opening the door for the restoration of equilibrium and good health of the community.

3. The Official Judicial System and the Problem of Witchcraft

In a recognized plurality of systems of conflict prevention and resolution, what does it mean to deal with witchcraft as part of this plurality?

In Mozambique, it is tantamount to saying that part of the normative, official system of justice rejects the possibility of the existence of witchcraft and, as a result, denies the potential for its practice. As noted by one *régulo*, "when they send cases of witchcraft to be resolved in the courts, they say that there is no basis [evidence]."[27] Consequently, witchcraft is not punishable as a crime. The failure to condemn witchcraft frequently leads to two paradoxical situations: on the one hand, the *nyàngà* can become a pernicioous actor because he produces invisible evidence that results in the social or physical exclusion of the subject of the accusations; on the other hand, because the definitions of good and evil and the concept of evidence are evaluated quite differently at the local level, the Mozambican state, by using the current penal code to continually uphold the accusations against the healers while dismissing those against the witchdoctors due to lack of evidence, risks turning away from being a defender of the community and turning into a defender of the evildoers – the *tinyàngà*.

After independence people expected the state to fight for them, to stand by them and free them from the long period of colonial exploitation. Traditional doctors expected greater openness "now that the country was finally ours,"[28] but that did not happen. In Mozambique, postcolonial legislators, following an approach that was also present in neighboring countries,[29] regarded witchcraft as a merely imaginary offense and tried to impose this view on the majority of the population. Frelimo's ruling elite looked at these practices as a shameful phenomenon that had to be overcome through modernization. Rather than punishing the witches, all those who tried to defend themselves against witches were threatened with prison sentences: the traditional doctors, who can 'smell out' culprits, as well as ordinary citizens, who accused others of witchcraft, in addition to everyone who used violence against alleged witches.[30] However, whereas in the colonial period some of the activities of traditional healers were tolerated, after independence and the prohibition of their trade, the healers were persecuted (even those who were able to deal with witchcraft issues and cure people). The healers came to be seen as old-fashioned defenders of 'obscure ideas' (Castanheira, 1979; Machel, 1981). In short, in the postcolonial period the presence of a plurality of legal systems continues to be ignored by the formal court system; people remain barred by official law from acting against the threat of witches in an open, legal, official manner.

The Absence of 'Facts' and the Testimony of the Nyàngà

As we have shown, the main available source for the analysis of witchcraft consists of accusations and rumors, which results in numerous problems in the evaluation of its efficacy. Thus, how can it be ascertained that it was exactly the accused person who caused the fatal lightning? And how does a plaintiff hope to prove that a malicious neighbor 'sent' him a disease or a serious accident? Given these difficulties, under the scope of official law it is basically impossible to prove witchcraft, since it cannot be witnessed by the naked eye.

From the perspective of the modern state in an era of human rights and the rule of law, there are unsurpassable problems involved in the judicial management of witchcraft.[31] Under official law it is impossible to prove witchcraft offenses, since there is usually no physical or tangible evidence, facts that 'prove' what the witch does. Therefore, witches cannot easily be brought to court for prosecution. Accusations of witchcraft can be presented as sworn testimony in courts of law easily enough. Witnesses can present evidence of motives that might plausibly be read as inclining a person toward witchcraft. They may also give precise testimony as to the opportunities that a person so inclined might have exploited in pursuit of their evil deeds. Such witnesses might be cross-examined and their veracity tested. But the evidentiary essence of culpability, such as an eyewitness account of the criminal act in cases of suspected witchcraft, is forever occluded from view. In cases of witchcraft, silence and discretion are the norm.[32] The forces at work are unseen, so an eyewitness is nowhere to be found, although when witchcraft is suspected herbs that might otherwise be acknowledged as innocent medicine can take on a harmful aspect (Ashforth, 2001: 15).

For the judicial court, it seems to be less difficult to make a fair judgment when judges do not have to deal with witches in a strict sense, but only with evidence of witchcraft practices, that is, apparent evidence of the aggression: *e.g.* fetishes buried under someone's door or hidden in a house. However, what those objects could prove is still questionable. Is a bunch of herbs a love incantation, aimed at regaining the affection of an unfaithful husband? Or is it intended to harm or kill him? (Schapera, 1975: 109) Ordinary judges would never be able to determine what power those fetishes possess; in case of doubt, evidence is sought in different forms. Because the official court cannot deal with these questions, if a case reaches the court, the judge usually sends it to be debated before community courts or directly by the *tinyàngà*.

As described above, traditional healers are called in since they do have the power to 'sniff out' the actions of a witch's craft; besides, their accounts of communication with ancestral spirits are taken as genuine forms of knowledge. But this knowledge is not open to direct corroboration in the manner typically required by modern jurisprudence (Peek, 1991; Meneses, 2000). The central proof provided by divination is directly accessible only by the *nyàngà*. Divination, especially when performed in a communal context where the 'predictions' of the diviner are legitimized by the response of an audience, can undoubtedly serve as a powerful means for unifying a community against a perception of internal threat. But such procedures are hardly consonant with the rituals of official court practice, due process, or doctrines of human rights. Within the witchcraft paradigm, it can be argued that requiring corroboration of accusations by independent *tinyàngà* can safeguard the veracity of divination as a form of evidence in judicial proceedings, as is the case in the procedures applied by Ametramo. By most accounts this was, and remains, the preferred practice in witch trials. But even independently corroborated narratives of the unseen worlds can leave questions of guilt unanswered. In order for justice to be perceived as being served in cases of witchcraft, the guilty party must ultimately confess. Given the inherent secrecy of the act, only the guilty can know what he/she has done.

Judicial Hybrids and Accusations of Witchcraft

According to Maciane Zimba,[33] in the first years after independence,[34] although *tinyàngà* were forbidden to carry out their medical activities, the popular courts would periodically turn to the *tinyàngà* to look for ways to resolve cases involving witchcraft. In vast areas of the country, rather than being persecuted by the state, they continued to perform their role as expert witnesses to help the judges solve the problem of how to establish evidence against witches. The solution found by the judiciary, still officially not acknowledging witchcraft as a criminal offense, was, as before, to solve these issues by using the customary rules.

During the early revolutionary years, and while searching for a symbiosis of the 'progressive' forms of the customary with more democratic principles of justice, some of the traditional practices were translated into newer institutions of popular justice – the people's courts – which worked both in urban townships and rural settings (Sachs and Honwana Welch, 1990). The post-colonial state knew that in order to be recognized as a legitimate authority, the new judicial structure had to be anchored, at least to some extent, in the everyday life of both rulers and subjects alike. People's courts meted out a sort of popular justice, allowing for accusations of witchcraft to be brought to these courts. People's courts – later transformed into community courts, an embryonic form of hybrid justice between the official justice and common law – can prosecute witches and seek support from traditional doctors to detect the culprit (Gomes *et al.*, 2003, and chapter 10 in this volume). Hence, ancient practices were transformed into new forms of community justice, operating both in rural and urban environments.

Traditional healers keep their role in administering justice: as intermediaries between community courts or traditional authorities and the local population, they take control over the final decision. Indeed, because the detection of the 'witch' has to happen *post factum*, the figure of the traditional healer, whose power and knowledge legitimize his/her decision regarding the responsibility of the culprit, remained central. Therefore, a large hybrid fringe of legal bodies, such as community courts and traditional authorities - representing non-state bodies before which traditional healers are recognized as key elements in 'detecting' traces of evil presence – continue to be the entities that can act against and punish witches.

The analysis of several accusations of witchcraft, as well as of other conflict situations, leads one to understand that the absence of formality in these types of community justice has the advantage of fomenting community participation. Once both parties to the dispute are heard, the issue is discussed in an open debate, thereby permitting various views to be aired and allowing the community members to question the parties on any aspect that may be considered relevant to the dispute. Any final solution, however, depends ultimately on a consensus between the conflicting parties, as the ultimate objective is to restore harmony within the community by reaching a compromise. In general, the appropriate sentence is determined in accordance with a majority vote of the 'court' and sentences are applied in the spirit of reconciliation and re-education.

Locally, the sanctions applied by the *régulo* on those accused of practicing witchcraft – physical punishment (shaving their heads, *chambocadas*,[35] money fines and even expulsion from the group) and fines – are seen as forms of sentencing (Meneses *et al.*, 2003). Community courts normally apply fines (Gomes *et al.*, 2003).

One of the great strengths of these institutions of community justice is that justice is immediate, public, collective, face-to-face, and relatively transparent, and is based on local knowledge which is flexible and always re-worked in the context of a debated and contested reality.[36] That is why traditional notions of justice[37] should be viewed as one way of evaluating individuals through their own eyes, where the power to discredit and defame function within traditional codes of honor and dignity. The *nyàngà* is therefore feared by what could be considered evil – he/she controls and oversees irregular actions, assists the powerless, upholds morals and disciplines the group. The *nyàngà* powerless the individual in an interplay of interests based on solidarity, seeking to keep pressure on emerging conflicts while acting as the 'knower' – the possessor of a knowledge that is continually expanding and changing – to assure the stability of the group.

Traditional healers, as part of the customary judicial process, are consulted because they 'talk' the language of the local culture, they are speedy in their intervention, informal, not intimidating (since the applied customary law consists of rules and customs of that particular group or community), and accessible. Many of the people interviewed stated that they would rather appear before these entities of conflict resolution than before a magistrate. But the role they play in the contemporary state system remains unclear.

In short, among the aspects which distinguish the practices of community justice from those of official, codified law, the following are particularly critical: while the former is normally consensual and seeks to avoid the escalation of situations of conflict, the latter is based on the individual and seeks to resolve situations of open dispute. This situation is associated with another important phenomenon: traditional justice does not operate in a unilineal way. Because it deals with a system that attempts to regulate and avoid problematic situations within a certain group, the traditional chief and the community court members cannot risk losing the support of the social base, the community. Hence the prominent members of the community act as counselors and the population as evaluators of the appropriateness of the final decision.

These hybrid legal community bodies – traditional authorities or community courts – have shown a clear willingness to depart from a closed conception of the interpretation of law (either official or customary), in order to afford believers in witchcraft some defense. As a result of this attitude, some form of defendants have been saved from the gallows. This has been accomplished by (*i*) using these non-state bodies of conflict resolution to comply with the findings of the traditional healers, and (*ii*) allowing such bodies to address the questions accordingly.

4. Different Views on Legitimacy

Notoriously difficult to define, legitimacy implies an acceptance of the 'right to rule' of the authority concerned, and a compliance that is more or less voluntary.

An analysis of the privileged role the state wants to play in the field of justice permits a better understanding of the ruptures and continuities in terms of the legal framework from the colonial to postcolonial times. By looking at who is authorized and/or favored by the state, what knowledge is tolerated or suppressed, recognized and even left unknown, it is possible to get a stronger and more profound idea of the logic of the state's action.

From the people's point of view, the picture is somehow distinct. People do legitimize the experts they consult, whether they are trained in the official or in the so-called traditional arena. In fact, in terms of problem solving, normally traditional legitimacy is spontaneously associated with the *nyàngà* and rational legitimacy with the modern lawyer, the latter as a result of his or her degrees. The acceptance of traditional healers depends on the loyalty and confidence of those who recognize them as the inheritors of wisdom. The legitimacy, the recognition of their competence, of their merit in that profession, is attested to by those who constantly consult them.

The paradox which many insist constitutes an impediment to development – the persistence of traditional values – deserves careful analysis. Traditionalism can only be that to the extent that it is distinguished from Western modernity by virtue of their differences, but in fact traditionalism is continuously fed by modernity. The crossover of various roles occurs at several levels: the state ignores traditional doctors, while its functionaries have frequent recourse to them; the Law Faculties do not recognize their knowledge while many lawyers do not hesitate to consult, or to send their clients to the *tinyàngà*. This paradox is only an apparent contradiction: the norm established and imposed by the state is based on a legal and rational model of legitimacy. The agents that make up these institutions, however, dispense with these principles when they behave as patients, obeying only practical rules. This is a phenomenon that Santos (2002b) describes as reactionary multiculturalism, when differences crystallize knowledge, compartmentalizing them as a means of recreating the traditional as immutable in time and space. What one observes from below is an active hybridization, an active meshwork which recognizes cultural differences but aims to construct a democratic interrelationship among them.

However, the *tinyàngà* may constitute a source of the problem, because they may prey on the ignorance of the people to extort gain for themselves, to accuse other people falsely of being witches, and to lead their clients to commit dastardly crimes against innocent people, usually close relatives. Accusations of involvement in witchcraft have become a convenient way of getting rid of opponents, rivals or unpopular people in the community. In a highly communal social setting, eroded by neo-liberal economic moves, witch-hunts often reflect the jealousy felt toward others who succeeded inside the group, or the envy aroused by successful individuals in the community.

Even in the case of trials by community courts or customary law, given that witch trials encourage arbitrary judgments, there is a danger of misusing them for personal vengeance. To denounce people as witches and drag them before a court may turn into a convenient means of intimidating one's political rivals or private foes. Also, due to the extreme ambiguity of witchcraft practices (in the sense that a person fighting to achieve a certain goal may leave the conflicting party totally unprotected by monopolizing, with the help of the traditional healer, the power of the spirits), in certain instances only plaintiffs who can gain the backing of a strong and influential witch-hunter (*i.e.*, someone who can fight a powerful traditional healer protecting the other party) will have a chance to succeed with their charges of witchcraft. Such backing, however, is not free. As a consequence, it is quite frequent for the wealthy to make use of witch trials to terrorize their opponents (Geschiere, 1997: 114, 170-72).

In any case, the competition for power and the overlapping of the spheres of intervention of the different structures in the resolution of conflicts on the ground is notorious. The landscape of justices in Mozambique is made up of a series of institutions whose performance depends on the fluidity of the connections between them. The better these relative roles are defined and the duties attributed to them by society in general and the communities in particular are fulfilled, the more efficient their performance will be and the more concrete citizens' rights and state interests will be.

The risk of involvement of traditional healers with the political and economic elite may lead to an increasing association of the state's representatives with traditional authorities, thus reinforcing the heterogeneous character of the state (s Santos, in this volume).[38] In a context of increased demand for community participation in the resolution of its problems, there needs to be a harmonization between constitutional principles and the administrative organization of the state, in terms of styles of action, cultural assumptions and the normative structures of traditional authorities, regardless of the form or guise that may have developed. The analysis undertaken corroborates the fact that a legal hybridization has long been developing in Mozambique; such hybridization even accepts the official modern legal model while creating the very space for its application. Seen from this perspective, the vitality of the justices in which the traditional authorities are located mirrors (albeit inversely) the difficulties faced by an official justice that appears more and more unable to meet its objectives, given the distance from its subjects.

Conclusion: Challenges for a Greater Democratization of Justice

Unofficial dispute resolution has been the norm in the urban areas in Mozambique for as long as these areas have existed. Official legal institutions have been regarded as secondary in importance, seemingly because of the inability to satisfy the community's sense of justice.

However, as the study on accusations of witchcraft and the role of community justices at work in Mozambique demonstrates, the most notable defect of the existing system of justice is that the majority of Mozambicans were (and still are) alienated from the court system due to the alien nature of the courts, based on an exogenous cultural system. Judicial systems have to be understood primarily in terms of their own dynamics, which are the product of the interplay of internal and external forces, whose legitimacy resides in the fact that they respond to the needs and perceptions of the local communities. Thus the reason for the presence of an immense display of alternative judicial systems is that "they are really ours, they are from here, and we see and know how they function [...] they understand the problems and know how to solve them."[39]

Witchcraft has not disappeared under the onslaught of modernity; instead, it has encroached itself in the very heart of modernity. In contemporary legal practice in Mozambique, witchcraft figures as a reality and as an actionable offense in its own right. In the region where this study took place, witchcraft operates as a privileged mirror which permits a greater manipulation of the traditional. Such a mirror suggests that one should perhaps be analyzing the mosaic of problems and solutions sought as examples of resistance towards the construction of another modernity, a situation which is not exclusive to Mozambique, or even to Africa.

Discourses concerning witchcraft do not express a resistance to modern development; rather they constitute reflections of a constant struggle for a better life. Because 'community justice' is an open system, formally delimited only in its practice, the possibilities to explain the problems of life are innumerable, allowing for an anthropophagic interaction with different elements and thus forming the cornerstone of projects of 'other forms of modernity', as several authors have pointed out. In this sense, accusations of witchcraft, far from reinforcing a radically different, alternative means of conflict resolution, constitute a discourse concerning the problems affecting the family, the community and society at large.

In Mozambique, as in most African countries, intellectuals, politicians and healers maintain that they, like all common citizens, share the belief that witchcraft is part of the cultural landscape, and that they act accordingly. Therefore there is a growing awareness that all efforts must be made to ensure that access to a broader conception of justice becomes a reality for the majority of the citizens. This is no small task, but the experience in Mozambique shows that it is possible to give established, distinct systems of dispute resolution the opportunity to be a part of this process. As with all alternative remedies for a problem, each should be carefully analyzed so as to formulate the best practical solution.

In short, the analysis of accusations of witchcraft and their trial constitutes a window that allows us to suggest that there are well-founded reasons for a 'Mozambicanization' of legislation. To the extent that the people's personal sense of justice and their state-imposed law diverge, nobody can expect them to have confidence in the institutions of a democratic state. If state authorities continue to avoid dealing with legal aspects of such facts of daily life as witchcraft, people will surmise that this is the result of the witches manipulating the state (Ashforth, 1998a; Niehaus, 2002). This probably helps to explain the recognition, in the 2004 CCConstitution (with the new Constitutional reforms), of Mozambican society as being characterized by legal plurality.[40]

The strengthening of local power presupposes the search for cohesive partnerships between local forces that, from below, can pressure the higher levels of the state to favor these changes (Ngugi, 2002). It introduces a dimension which lies far beyond the question of the search for a new strategy to respond to fears of witchcraft. Here lies perhaps – in the midst of tension and dialogue between communities, civil society and the basic structures of the state – the beginning of the uphill path to what Santos (1998b: 34) calls the "the state as a new social movement," a construct which envisages the building of a state in which the present emphasis on the Westernized approach to law and problems, and the lack of concern for the future, will be substituted with an emphasis on solidarity, social welfare and security for all Mozambicans.

Notes

1 Both terms were used, under the assumption of the presence of a common history, language and culture shared by specific, self-contained collectives. Customary law provided the prescriptive rules binding such units.

2 On this subject, see chapters 1 and 2.

3 The theme of legal pluralism and community justice in Mozambique is analysed in more detail in chapters 10 and 11.

4 Santos describes *inter-legality* as a dominant characteristic of our times. "We live in a time of porous legality or legal porosity, multiple networks of legal orders forcing us to constant transitions and trespassing. Our legal life is constituted by an intersection of different legal orders, that is, by *inter-legality*" (1995: 473).

5 I am aware of the unsatisfactory nature of 'witchcraft' as an analytical term. A detailed discussion of the concept and distinct definitions proposed in distinct contexts in Africa, as well as on the ambiguities of a transfer of Westernized concepts of magic and witchcraft in African societies can be seen in Douglas (1977: xiii-xxxviii); Last and Chavunduka (1986); Horton (1993); Geschiere (1997: 12-15, 215-24).

6 Even though the nationalist movement – Frelimo – was predominantly composed of natives of Mozambique.

7 See note 23 in chapter 1.

8 That is, the assumption of a country made of free and equal citizens.

9 In southern Mozambique, among the machangana, they were called *hosi*. In other parts of the country the designations differ – for example, they are called *mwene* in the northern, amakhuwa regions.

10 Indeed, whenever these traditional chiefs opposed the colonial authorities in one way or another, they were replaced with more prudent individuals.

11 And their assistants, the *cabos de terra*. To exercise their political power, traditional authorities had their own small police forces (and resorted to physical punishment).

Yet, the *régulo* did not act individually, but rather as a type of catalyst of opinions, such that a case was presented not only to the chief, but also to his counselors. The sentence was produced after hearing the opinion of the *b'andlha'*, i.e. the assembly of prominent members of the local community. Indeed, physical force was insufficient to guarantee the legitimacy of their actions. To that end, traditional authorities had to appeal to the support of the local lineages (to which they frequently did not belong, as mentioned above) to negotiate the demands of the colonial administration and find solutions to emerging conflicts.

12 This law criminalized both those who were regarded as practicing witchcraft and those who accused them of doing so, but 'witchcraft' itself was neither described nor defined. There was therefore considerable fluidity and room for interpretation as to what, exactly, constituted 'witchcraft', thus generating an ambivalent answer of the colonial state about the nature of witchcraft.

13 The failure of 'recognition' of the aims of local communities by the modern state was one of the main reasons that led Renamo (the National Movement of Resistance of Mozambique) to carry out a long civil war that ravaged the country for more than a decade. In 1992, Frelimo's government and Renamo signed a peace agreement, a fact that allowed for political and social stability in the country. Meanwhile Renamo transformed itself from a movement of resistance into a political party, thus becoming the second political force in the political landscape of Mozambique.

14 Plural of *nyàngà*. Although there are various designations for traditional therapists, this is the most commonly used designation in southern Mozambique. The *nyàngà* is the person who can smell out the evil person among the neighbors, who aims to bring disaster onto the community. The *nyàngà* has the knowledge and power to heal, counting on the help of ancestral spirits to protect the local community. Hence the healer is one of the pillars upon which the welfare of society rests and for this reason he is most highly respected (Krige, 1936: 297 ff).

15 In the sense that it will affect the entire community.

16 African healing traditions are generally described as holistic and do not recognize the Western distinction between medicine, justice and spirituality.

17 The *nòyì*, is a spirit with evil powers that can provoke trouble even from a distance, through the help of somebody whose body he/she uses. Usually the *valòyì* act at night, through the introduction of foreign pieces (bones, blood) into somebody's body; as a consequence, the person is poisoned and risks dying. During the day the evil spirit can act through elements he has previously contaminated. The *nòyì* can still use a person whose body he/she 'opened' and occupied, making that person his slave. These people can be transformed into animals, such as leopards, hyenas, serpents, as well as be forced to work in the fields for the spirit, or to steal goods to feed the spirit (Muthemba, 1970; Honwana, 2002).

18 P. Xavier. Personal interview. July 2000.

19 The crucial point is that the knowledge used by traditional healers is itself ambivalent. They can heal or kill. The distinction between good and evil in this struggle of knowledge powers is mainly a question of perspective. Everybody involved has to protect him/herself from the aggression of others, and, if possible, gain influence over the opponents, that is, to weaken and ultimately destroy them. Since this knowledge can be used for the most disparate purposes, it becomes almost impossible to draw a clear line between healers and witches.

20 This issue has been reported by the local and international media, and is usually described as cases of 'human organs trafficking'.

21 Besides, fear of accusation may enforce conformity, thereby preventing what might be perceived as anti-social behaviour (Marwick, 1965: 282).

22 Also known since colonial times as witchdoctors, given their power to fight witchcraft.

23 M. Suzana, traditional healer. Personal interview. February 2000.

24 Ordeals by fire or the administration of poisonous beverages, for instance – widely reported in time and space – burn the guilty or impure but leave the innocent or the genuine devotee unharmed. In other parts of Mozambique heated knives have been used as well.

25 The role of Ametramo in community courts is briefly addressed in chapter 11.

26 Ametramo stands for *Associação dos Médicos Tradicionais de Moçambique* (Mozambican Association of Traditional Healers). This association was formalized in the late 1990s.

27 *Régulo* Santaca. Personal interview. May 1995.

28 Zimba, M.F. Personal interview. March 2000.

29 In Tanzania, for example – though revised in 1958 to take into account changes in local government structure – the Witchcraft Ordinance of 1928, "declares both the practice of witchcraft and the accusation of another as a witch, unless before a local authority or a court of law, to be illegal" (Green, 1994: 23). Prescribed punishment, though not always applied, includes fines, imprisonment and house arrest under the supervision of district officials (*ibid*.: 24).

30 Zimba, M.F.; Tamele, C. Personal interviews. April 2000.

31 As Ashforth notes (2001: 16), another problem with the complex relationship between official, state justice and witchcraft, which we will be tackling only superficially, is of an ontological nature. No matter how culturally sensitive legal codes are, from the point of view of someone imbued with the Western human rights tradition it is impossible to understand the type of social exclusion and punishment to which traditional communities subject witches. Thus, anyone accused of witchcraft in an era of human rights can call upon these doctrines to trump the claims of their accusers. For people who live in a world populated with witches, however, the willingness of a person to practice witchcraft automatically cancels out his/her rights to membership in the 'human' community. From this perspective, if witches are something other than human, they can hardly claim

human rights to protect themselves from the righteous anger and justice of the community and of the society.

32 For many people, the identification and/or expulsion of an alleged witch represent the permanence, in the community, of a source of possible danger, since the witch may strike back, now that he/she has been exposed. Also, the 'official' detection of very few witchcraft cases is due to the fact that people like policemen, judges, etc. share the fears and beliefs that witches are a danger to well-being, and thus refuse to point them out and accuse them.

33 Personal interview with *nyàngà* F. Maciane Zimba. April 2001. See also Meneses, 2004.

34 In the early revolutionary years, when the *nyanga*'s therapeutic role was prohibited.

35 A form of physical punishment consisting of blows administered by a heavy wooden object, called *chamboco*.

36 In contrast to official, formal justice. Formal justice is extremely slow and removed from most of the population due to the hermetic nature of its design (Santos and Trindade, 2003). The language of the official courts is Portuguese, although less than 40% of the population is fluent in it; together with the 'foreign' court procedures, official justice is hardly accessible, user-friendly, or even fair to most people in the country.

37 Of course this, too, has many negative implications (including flagrant discrimination against and diminishment of women, physical punishment, etc., which are unconstitutional).

38 However, it may also have the opposite result, when important decisions are made in exclusive circles, to which one would only gain access by being a member of a restricted group or by possessing a specific knowledge, thus bringing up the question of legitimacy in a democratic state. Whoever rises to the highest political offices and knows how to defend himself against his rivals seems to have the necessary spiritual protection at his disposal.

39 V. Banze. Personal Interview. July 2000.

40 Article 4 of the Constitution states: "The State recognizes the various normative and conflict resolution systems that coexist in Mozambique, as far as they do not contradict the values and fundamental principles granted by the Constitution".

Part II

Intermezzo

4

Economic Development:
From the 1960s to 2000

António Alberto da Silva Francisco

Introduction

An understanding of the legal system and the administration of justice in Mozambique today must, of necessity, include a study of the nature, operations and performance of the formal and informal institutional bodies which are directly or indirectly involved in the resolution of litigation, as well as their contexts, backgrounds and main determining factors: geographical, political, social, cultural and economic.

Mozambique has the fourth largest population of the fourteen countries which form the Southern African Development Community (SADC). As figure 4.1 shows, in 2002 the four countries with the largest populations in the area (the Democratic Republic of Congo, South Africa, Tanzania and Mozambique) together made up over 70% of the approximately 208 million inhabitants of the member countries of the SADC (INE, 1999; UNDP, 2004).

However, in terms of the Human Development Index (HDI), Mozambique comes last in the SADC; on a worldwide scale it is one of the ten countries with the lowest level of human development.

This low level of human development is due to an average life expectancy at birth of 38.5 years, an adult literacy rate of 46.5%, an overall level of basic education of 41%, and a *per capita* GDP[2] of about US$ 195[3] (UNDP, 2004).

Figure 4.1: Population of Southern Africa[1] (left) and HDI (right) in 2002

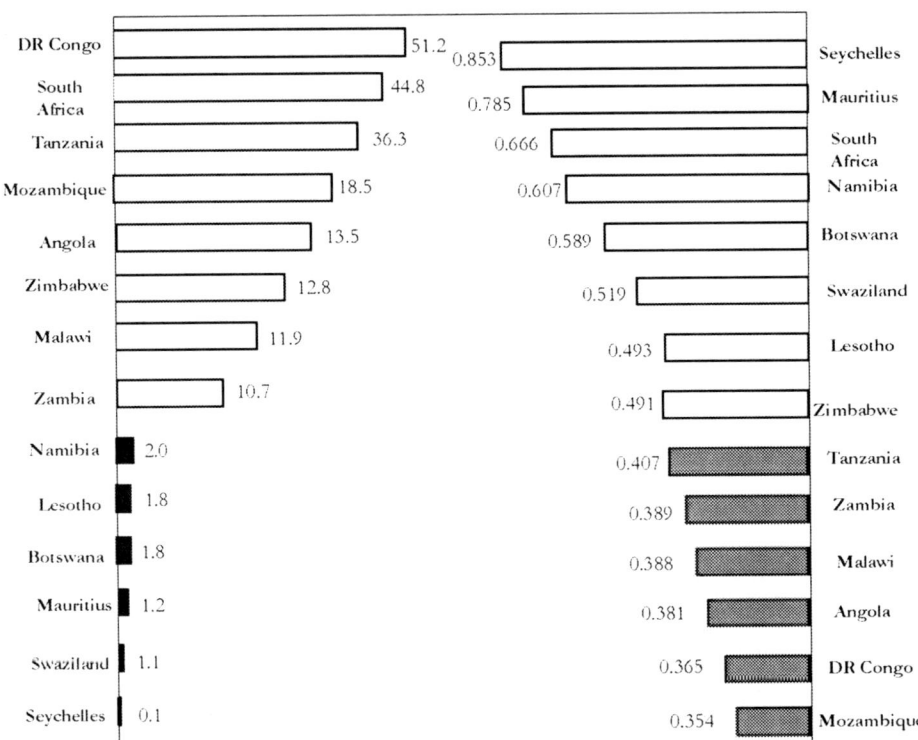

Regional Differentiation

Map 4.1 shows the distribution of the population within the three main regions – North, Central and South – and the subdivision of the country into 11 administrative provinces.

This subdivision into three main regions was used during the colonial period, as much for geographical as for historical and economic reasons. Recently, however, the so-called mega-projects and corridors of development have also followed this subdivision.[4] In political debates, regional imbalances have generated heated controversy, and the fact that the southern region is always favored in terms of investments is criticized.[5]

Each of the three regions has its own specific natural resources and potential, as well as differing cultural characteristics. It should be noted, however, that 38% of the population of the country is concentrated within two provinces – Zambézia and Nampula.

In the Northern zone there is the railway line between Nacala (Nampula province) and Malawi and the port of Nacala, which has the deepest waters on the eastern coast of Africa and offers access by sea to countries such as Malawi and Zambia. Before independence, the Northern zone was heavily defined by the compulsory production of cotton and the emigration of the labor force to the plantations in Tanganyika and Zanzibar.[6]

The Central region possesses the rich hydrographic basin of the Zambezi river, as well as the Beira Corridor (including the port of Beira, which has the capacity to handle 7.5 million tons per year, a 317km pipeline between Beira and Zimbabwe and two main road networks to Zimbabwe and the Tete province). In the colonial period this region developed an economy based mainly on the plantations, particularly in the Zambezi Valley.

Map 4.1: Percentage Distribution of Population (1997)

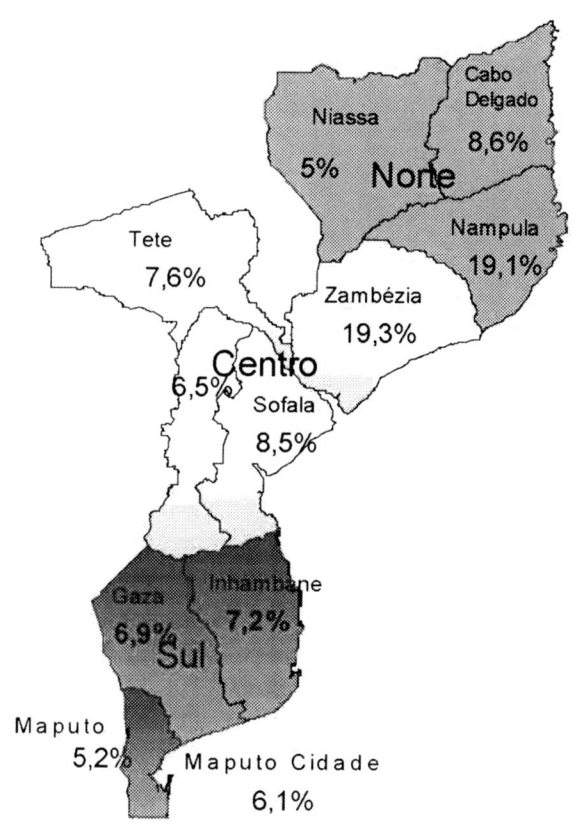

In the Southern region, the Maputo Corridor is an important feature which includes the port of Maputo (with the capacity to handle 14 million tons per year), three railway networks, two road networks (one to South Africa and another to Swaziland) and the promised economic projects in collaboration with South Africa. One of the factors that has had significant economic repercussions on the area was the fact that more than a century ago thousands of workers, originally from the Gaza and Inhambane provinces, emigrated to the mines of South Africa.

1. The Processes of Economic Restructuring

Three processes for restructuring the economy and developing the country are particularly relevant to an understanding of the present-day connections between economy, development and the justice system in Mozambique. The first – which was in fact the last under Portuguese colonial rule – relates to the period between 1960 and 1974, the second covers the first decade after independence (1975-1985) and the third corresponds to the period of 1985-1994 (setting the stage for the country's existing economic structure).

An analysis of the Mozambican economy shows the real *per capita* GDP was US$ 260 at the beginning of the 1960s, which rose to US$ 418 in 1973. Although 1973 had been the best economic year in the second half of the twentieth century, it was also the beginning of an unprecedented and dramatic crisis in Mozambique. Regardless of any temporary recovery, by 1993 the declining economy had reached its lowest level ever: 5.4% of the level of the real GDP and 3.6% of the real *per capita* level of the 1973 GDP. Since 1993 there has been a gradual recovery which is seemingly consistent with economic growth. In 1997 the real GDP surpassed the 10% limit of the 1973 level, but living conditions, measured by GDP *per capita*, only represented between 7% and 8% of the 1973 level.[7]

Table 4.1 presents the most important dates and indicates some of the most significant features of each period.

Since the mid 1960s, Mozambique has experienced colonial (1965-1974), socialist (1975-1984) and capitalist (1985-1994) economic restructuring. Although these periods encompass very different motivations, purposes, strategies and economic systems, they share many common aspects. Firstly, in all of them it was argued that the main failings of the economic strategies were due to unfavorable political, national and international factors, in particular external factors beyond the country's control. Curiously, the political and government leadership involved in each of the three restructuring processes reacted with a common rhetoric to justify the poor results and the failure of the economic models and development strategies they had introduced. In the first restructuring, the Portuguese colonial administration blamed the imperialistic aspirations of the then communist Soviet Union. In the second, the Mozambican government blamed military destabilization by the *apartheid* regime in South Africa and natural disasters. In the third restructuring, debt and the population's high incidence of poverty have been attributed to globalization. Secondly, the purpose and the ideals of modernization that inspired the three economic restructuring processes all manifested a strong disregard for the historical circumstances, socio-cultural diversity and human development challenges of Mozambique. They were all incapable of establishing strong, healthy and sustainable links and flows between economic growth and human development.

Table 4.1: Political Context of Main Economic Restructuring (1965-1999)

	Political-social regime	Types of political opposition	Strategic Plan	Economy
1960-74	Portuguese colonial rule	Frelimo – Armed struggle for liberation	Protectionist Plan	Service and export, but with accelerated industrial growth and internal demand
1975-84	Single party system	MNR – National resistance movement; armed resistance	PPI – Indicative Prospective Plan	State and cooperative, planned by administration
1985-92/94	Transition to multiparty system	Renamo – Mozambique National Resistance; civil war	PRE – Economic Rehabili-tation Programme PRES – Economic and Social Rehabilitation Programme	Emergency aid and debt
1995-99	Multiparty democracy	First multiparty legislature	Five-Year Plan 1995-99	Export economy

The Economic Structure under Colonial Rule

The first economic restructuring process, which was, in fact, the last under Portuguese colonial rule, failed because Portuguese colonial rule refused to promote any social progress amongst the population in general. In particular, it failed to promote a national bourgeoisie that would have been minimally capable of preventing the elimination of the colonial system which in turn led to the destruction of the capitalist market system, developed primarily to benefit the white minority.

The Socialist Experiment

The second economic restructuring, between 1975 and 1984, undertaken by the first independent Mozambican government, extended the experience and the development strategy designed by Frelimo in the course of its struggle for political independence to the whole of the country. The spirit and substance of this development strategy were explicitly laid down in the 1975 Constitution of the People's Republic and, in fact, anticipated by Mondlane[8] in the vision of the future he outlined in his book *Struggle for Mozambique* (1969). This was to promote broad-based economic and social progress, eliminating minority privileges and suppressing the socio-economic forces that favored minorities, (meaning not just racial minorities but the formation of privileged African groups capable of concentrating wealth and services in small areas of the country and in the hands of just a few) through strong central planning. This economic and development strategy failed, both in form and content. It failed in terms of content because the attempt to eliminate the socio-economic forces favoring minorities caused violent reactions, promoted both internally and externally, with tragic consequences for the majority of the Mozambican people. In terms of form, the system of top-down central planning proved to be economically inefficient and unsustainable.

Capitalist Economic Restructuring

The third economic restructuring, between 1985 and 1994, was based mainly on short-term objectives designed to reverse and overcome the immediate causes of the economic crisis and the war. Along with economic reform, far-reaching political, administrative and legislative reforms were also introduced, in particular the replacement of the single party system with a multiparty system.[9] Here, the Frelimo government not only survived the reforms, but in fact led them and sought to take advantage of them. Ironically, the process of appropriation and state control of the economy on behalf of the people did not lead to the socialization of the country but certainly concentrated sufficient power in the hands of the political and administrative class. By leading the reforms, the members of the political-administrative powers were able to build up their economic capabilities and ensure their survival and reproduction. In this context, top-down central planning gave way to outside-inside planning, in which institutions and representatives of the international donors began to play an active role in economic leadership and management.

2. An Assessment of Economic Development over the Last 50 Years

The three major economic restructurings attempted in Mozambique since the 1960s were incapable of establishing connections and strong, healthy and sustainable flows between economic growth and human development. The weaknesses associated with the three restructuring processes appear to be directly linked to the fact that the political and economic forces that implemented them were prisoners to ideas of modernity and institutional frameworks which did not favor any effective widening of choices and opportunities for the majority of the Mozambican people, i.e., within the context of development integrated into the socio-cultural diversity of the country. Such development implies the re-conversion of the structure, functioning, performance and results of economic activity into gradually increasing benefits for the Mozambican people themselves. There is a dual significance to these benefits. There is, on the one hand, the satisfaction of internal needs and, in a wider sense, an improvement in standards of living and the gradual satisfaction of the well-being of the population. On the other hand, there is also the progressive accumulation of both material and financial wealth on the part of Mozambicans, which may accumulate in quite unequal ways according to the dynamics of the leading social groups. In short, human development, rather than economic growth, is seen as the main goal of social actions. From the 1990s onwards, the definition of development as a process of widening individual choices with the aim of enabling people to live a longer and healthier life, have a better education and better access to the resources needed for a reasonable standard of living, has acquired widespread recognition (UNDP, 1990, 1994: 91, 199, 1996, 1997: 14-15). As Sen argues (1999), the idea of human development has triumphed as a result of a general discontent with the disparities between the lifestyles of the rich and the poor.

Rapid Economic Development – Low Human Development

This vision of human development in Mozambique is useful for two main reasons. Firstly, it helps us to understand the connections between the ends and means of the main aspects of progress. Assuming that the people themselves – including the satisfaction of their needs, aspirations and choices – must constitute the worthy target of all for development efforts, economic growth should be seen as an indispensable and decisive means for the fulfillment of this objective (UNDP, 1990, 1996; Ramirez *et al.*, 1998; Ranis and Stewart, 1999). Secondly, although human development and economic growth in Mozambique have figured among the main objectives of all the post-Independence governments, their materialization has remained far removed from the stated expectations and intentions.

Today Mozambique has accumulated three valuable public assets: positive economic growth, high market optimism, and peace and political stability. Yet Mozambique has also three extremely heavy liabilities: more than half the population living in absolute poverty, an unsustainable external debt and one of the lowest development indexes in the world.[10]

The fragility of the Mozambican economy will persist as long as the country continues to depend, as it does now, on loans and external aid to minimize the severe imbalances and the deficit in the balance of payments, sustain recent positive economic growth and improve the human development of the population. In the last instance, overcoming this fragility will depend on developing the socio-economic potential of the national minorities who are dominant at present and, in particular, on an ability to develop the economy in accordance with the diverse social and cultural needs of the country.

The type of economy developed in Mozambique over the next decades will be crucial to the long-term stability of the country. Will it be an economy aligned with an internal minority and predominantly aimed at the requirements of external demand, or a progressively structured economy aimed at satisfying the needs of the population and, in particular, the growth of the internal market and the gradual satisfaction of the internal demands of the population as a whole? Here, precisely, lies the great challenge faced by the governments emerging out of the context of the multiparty legislature.

Contrary to the ideological fantasy of the global free market, the country certainly needs more, rather than less, governing and state administration. The problem lies not in being in favor of active state and government intervention in the economy and in development, but rather in the nature, ends and methods of this intervention. In the long term, the stability of the national minorities that are currently the object of development efforts will, itself, be determined by two main factors. On the one hand, it will involve the real ability of these minorities to replace debt and external dependency with a strong internal market and full investment in increasing internal demand, production and national productivity. On the other hand, it will involve the strengthening of existing ties and strong, sustainable flows between economic growth and the human development of the Mozambican population in general.

Conclusion

Mozambique has several options, very much depending on the nature and type of institutions that will eventually prevail. It can move toward an economy which is not only open to the exterior but also, in fact, predominantly extractive and determined by external interests and priorities, in the hope that rapid economic growth will eventually improve the human development of the majority of the population. However, the implications of this option, which has already been tried in many parts of the world – including Mozambique – are notorious for their tragic consequences.

Over the past decade or so, the growing national elite has managed to establish relative political stability in Mozambique, although this stability is not necessarily efficient and sustainable as far as the overall well-being of the population is concerned. In this respect, it remains to be seen whether, or when, the growing Mozambican elite will become more virtuous and creative than the colonial and assimilated bourgeoisie that ruled the country until its independence in 1975. This statement is far from an expression of nostalgia for the past, or a suggestion that political independence is useless and unsustainable.

For the time being, the issue at stake is that one can simply hope, without any serious guarantee or confidence, that the existing political and economic elites (who at present control resources and institutions) will eventually make an effort to become more worthy than the national and foreign elites have been in the past. In the long run, this will depend not so much on the goodwill of political leaders but, most probably, on the nature and type of political and economic institutions to be developed and which will eventually prevail.

Notes

1   SADC, expressed in millions of inhabitants.
2   Gross Domestic Product.
3   The initial value was 1,050 US dollar PPP, where PPP stands for Purchasing Power Parity. The PPP is a method used to calculate an alternative exchange rate between the currencies of two countries, based on the principle that the exchange rates of their currencies are in equilibrium only when their purchasing power is the same. PPP exchange rates are used in international comparisons of standards of living.
4   In the Southern region, namely in the Maputo and Gaza provinces, for example, there are the aluminum foundry projects in Mozal, the iron and steel industry in Maputo, the construction industry in Ponta Dobela and the project for extracting heavy sands (titanium). In the Center region, namely in the Sofala province, there is an aluminum foundry project in Beira, iron projects and the Beira Free Zone.
5   For example, in a Mozambican newspaper Aloni (1999: 4) questioned the government's decision to build the Dobela port in the extreme south of the Maputo province. Aloni argued that Zambézia, one of the richest provinces in the country, was still facing serious problems in distributing its products. The columnist considered that this port was an example of a return to the colonialist projects of the 1960s, which mainly benefited the neighboring interests of the Southern African 'hinterland'.
6   In the 1960s, Tanganyika and Zanzibar formed the United Republic of Tanzania.
7   The internationally comparable Penn World Tables (PWD 6.1, 2002) depict a similar trend, although not so sharply, due to the conversion of US dollars to purchasing power parity (PPP).
8   Eduardo Mondlane was the first president of Frelimo – the Mozambique Liberation Front (*Frente de Libertação de Moçambique*). Mondlane was assassinated in 1969.
9   See chapters 1 and 2.
10 As part of the Indebted Poor Countries (HIPC) Initiative, Mozambique has benefited from the cancellation, in 2005, of its debt to the International Monetary Fund (IMF), the World Bank, and the African Development Fund.

Part III

The Administration of Justice:
Characteristics and Performance

5

Methodological Issues

**Boaventura de Sousa Santos, João Carlos Trindade,
Maria Manuel Leitão Marques, Conceição Gomes,
João Pedroso, André Cristiano José, Guilherme Mbilana,
Joaquim Fumo and Maria Paula Meneses**

When discussing the African state or African law, we run the risk of making false generalizations: it is assumed that, since they are in the same continent, the social and political practices of the different countries have more in common with each other than they do with countries in other continents. The situation of some of these countries is used as a reference point and identical characteristics are attributed to all other countries. Africa has been the object of abstract and homogenizing characterizations which have converted the differences and specificities of each country into unimportant details (Mudimbe, 1988, 1994). It is certainly true that almost all of the African countries have been subjected to the same historical experience: European colonialism. But there are also specific internal differentiations within this experience and a lack of attention to these also risks creating spurious generalizations in relation to colonialism. The truth is that eurocentric social sciences, by uncritically taking English and French colonialism as their reference points, have created a unit of continental analysis which is eventually imposed on smaller analytical units, whether state or local, as if they were miniatures of a broader picture. This analytical procedure is still employed today, and is often justified by the homogenizing pressures of hegemonic globalization. This is, however, only part of the story. The social sciences produced in Africa have also favored the continent as the privileged unit of analysis, even when only one given society or region is being studied. In recent years this analytical procedure has also been justified in terms of the processes of globalization, though viewed from a different perspective – that of resistance to hegemonic globalization. It is necessary to determine what the specific African characteristics are and what realities they contain, in order to produce emancipatory alternatives on a continental scale. These concepts, whatever their verisimilitude, do acquire a certain 'grain of truth' by transforming themselves into political and scientific common sense and, as such, they should be taken into consideration. The question of specific African characteristics and 'Africanness' is, to a great extent, a product of discourses that convert the description of certain African characteristics into uniquely African justifications of social practices and politics. The challenge we had to face, therefore, was to organize a research project whose analytical and methodological framework allowed for an understanding of the specific features of the multiple socio-legal realities at work in Mozambique.

The research conducted as part of this project enabled us to amass an enormous amount of new data, both on the official courts and on the unofficial mechanisms of conflict resolution in Mozambique. The theoretical and analytical frameworks underlying the research have already been discussed in previous chapters, but a short account of the difficulties the project faced allows for a broader understanding of the options that were favored and of the decisions we made.

Amongst the many other difficulties that the researchers involved in the project had to confront and overcome, the fact that the research team involved two nationalities should be emphasized. It was our aim to test out a new model of collective scientific work involving a team from two countries with two coordinators, one from each country, and a research team also consisting of researchers from both countries. This organizational model was more advanced than the conventional model of international research, and obviously it created new and more complex challenges. We felt that in this way the learning process would be richer, both for the Mozambican and the Portuguese researchers. It was also important to establish effective collaboration between the people and the institutions of both countries, which was to continue beyond the scope of the project.

Given the breadth of the field of analysis, the methodologies had to be adapted to the features of each of the subfields. Amongst the difficulties we had to confront and overcome, we would like to underline the following: the absence of official quantitative data that might give credibility to the exclusive reliance on quantitative methods; the chaos of the judicial archives, where they existed, and the consequent difficulties with the requisite documentary analysis; the enormous logistical difficulties and difficulties with access to the more remote areas of the country where we intended to carry out systematic observation and interviews. It should be added that the project did not restrict itself to simply coping with some of these difficulties but, on the contrary, attempted to overcome them, not only for the benefit of the project but also for the benefit of the country hosting it. Various seminars were held with magistrates, for example, with the aim of making them more aware of the importance of collecting statistical data and supplying them with the technical means to improve the process of record-keeping. In this and in other areas, the research was conducted according to the principles of action research, which constituted an additional and complex factor. As a result, the research contributed towards improving the quality of the statistical information currently being produced in Mozambique.

Given the model adopted, it was neither possible nor appropriate to define the analytical framework of the project in great detail at the time when the project was initially proposed and the funds were requested. Most of the theoretical and analytical concepts underlying the project were arrived at through teamwork as the research group started the preparation of the fieldwork. Some important guiding ideas were identified and later converted into the general working hypotheses presiding over the research work: the administration of the judiciary had to be analyzed, as part of the process of consolidating and deepening the transition to democracy; the fact that Mozambique is a plural society in terms of the legal and judicial systems that provide normative government of the daily life of the population and the fact that this sociological pluralism had to be central to the research, even when not officially recognized; the fact that the research had, at all costs, to maintain its independence in relation to the government and the existing political forces, whilst at the same time listening to all of them.

Accordingly, one of the central topics was the analysis of the relationship between the state and the plurality of systems of law which, whether officially recognized or not, regulate conflict and social order in Mozambique. The idea of the modern state assumes that each state has only one system of law and that the unity of the state is based on the unity of the legal system. Sociologically speaking, however, various legal systems operate within the same nation-state and the state legal system is not even always the most important in terms of governing the daily life of the great majority of citizens. Such disjuncture between political and legal forms on the one hand and political and legal practices on the other, is probably more visible in Africa nowadays than anywhere else and has cultural, political, legal, economic and social ramifications. Such disjuncture has multiple impacts on state action and legitimacy, on the operation of the official legal system, on the relationships between political and administrative control, on the mechanisms of conflict resolution operating in society, on the legal and institutional frameworks of economic life and on the social and cultural perceptions of politics and legality.

Contrary to one of the limitations of legal studies – the tendency to analyze law and justice in isolation, as if they existed hovering over society and untouched by it – , we sought to pay specific attention to socio-legal conditions in Mozambique. In fact, it was judged to be particularly important to increase the stock of information and macro-sociological characterization of the society to clarify the articulation between legislative law and the courts, on the one hand, and the normative needs and resolution of conflicts experienced by society, on the other. Therefore, the project embodied a broader concept of law that was not just limited to official, state law, but instead considered Mozambican society as legally and judicially plural.

We are living in a world of legal hybridizations, a condition which Mozambican state law itself cannot escape. The new hybrids are legal phenomena that mix heterogeneous entities, operating through a disintegration of forms and retrieval of fragments, giving rise to new constellations of meaning. The mixture involves not only heterogeneous legal elements and time-spaces, but also heterogeneous legal durations and degrees of embeddedness. This legal hybridization does not only exist on the structural or macro level of the relationship between the different legal orders. It also exists on a micro level, that is, on the level of the legal behavior and representations of citizens and social groups. The concrete 'legal personality' of citizens and social groups is increasingly composite and hybrid, incorporating several different representations. This new legal phenomenon is described by Santos as *interlegality* (1995: 473), meaning the multiplicity and combinations of legal 'layers' which characterize everyday legal life. As the phenomenological counterpart to legal pluralism, interlegality does not mean the mere juxtaposition of different legal orders and cultures but also the porosity between them, leading to constant transitions and trespassing, of which individuals and groups are often only vaguely aware, if at all. According to the situation and context, citizens and social groups organize their experiences around official state law, customary law, local community law – which may be guerrilla law or paramilitary law in countries under civil war – or different kinds of global law – from international human rights law to transnational labor contracts – and, in the majority of cases, according to complex combinations of these different legal orders.

In order to avoid uncritically importing models of analysis, the research was undertaken using several dichotomies that we sought out to help define the contours of our study. Situations involving hybridization and interlegality challenge conventional dichotomies to the extent that legal practices frequently combine the opposite poles of the variables and contain an infinite number of intermediary situations. Even so, on an analytical level, the dichotomies are a good starting point, as long as it is clear from the outset that they will not provide an end point.

The conventional dichotomies considered most relevant to an analysis of legal plurality in Mozambique are the following: official/unofficial, formal/informal, traditional/modern, monocultural/multicultural. In addition, there is the variable trichotomy: local/national/global.

In the modern state, it is up to the state to dictate the criteria to define what is official and what is not, and the criterion has been, in the overwhelming majority of cases, that of the state itself. In other words, official law and justice are those types of law and justice produced and/or controlled by the state. In this dichotomy, the unofficial is everything that is not recognized as being of state origin. It may be prohibited or tolerated; most of the time, however, it is ignored.

The formal/informal variable relates to the structural aspects of the legal orders in operation. A form of law and justice is informal when it is dominated by rhetoric and when, therefore, both bureaucracy and violence are absent or only marginal. The opposite configuration defines the formal. In the modern state, formality arises out of bureaucracy. In its ideal form, bureaucracy is a way of reducing the complexity of social reality by reducing the infinite variety of interactions and practices to a stylized set of models for actions and sequences. Historically, bureaucracy has not been the only source of formality. In pre-modern societies other methods of reducing complexity predominated, such as ordeals and ritual. Today religious formality and magical formality still exist in social fields not penetrated by bureaucratic formality. There are also hybrid types of formality in which the bureaucratic element blends with the religious or magical element.

The traditional/modern variable relates to the origins and historical duration of law and justice. The traditional is that which is believed to have existed since time immemorial, in which it is impossible to identify with any accuracy the moment or the agents of its creation. Conversely, what is called modern is believed to have existed for less time than the traditional and its creation can be identified in terms of time and/or author. This variable, as we shall see later, is the most complex of all. Contrary to the previous variables, the traditional/modern variable relates to social representations of time and origins, which are always difficult to identify. Moreover, according to the differences in power between the social groups which support each of the poles of the dichotomy, traditional power may be just as much a creation of modern power as modern power is a creation of traditional power.

The monocultural/multicultural variable relates to the cultural universes in which the different laws and systems of justice occur.[1] There is mono-cultural legal plurality whenever different laws and justices belong to the same culture and, conversely, there is multicultural legal plurality whenever the diversity of laws and justice correlates with important cultural differences.

Finally, there is the aforementioned trichotomy: local, national and global. This variable is seemingly obvious, as it refers to the spatial or territorial sphere of the laws or systems of justice in operation. In fact, however, these spheres are so defined because of the absolute priority granted to the national sphere by Western political and legal modernity.

As these definitions clearly show, the variables are partially superimposed. For example, the official tends to be formal, modern, monocultural and national, whereas the unofficial is often informal, traditional, multicultural and local. Yet these superimpositions are only partial and may occur more frequently in certain situations than in others. In addition, cultural or political contexts may determine that one particular socio-legal diversity is formulated in terms of one dichotomy or another. For example, in Latin America indigenous law and justice, although considered ancestral, is more commonly analyzed in terms of the monocultural/multicultural variable than the traditional/modern variable. In Africa, a diversity that differs only slightly from this – the existence of customary law and the traditional authorities side by side with the modern Western-centric legal system – is more often constructed, both academically and politically, within the sphere of the traditional/modern dichotomy.

Taking this set of variables or dimensions as starting points, we will briefly describe the three main topics around which the research was organized: the official judicial system, the community courts and the traditional authorities.

For this purpose, periods of extensive fieldwork took place in the city of Maputo, starting in 1997.[2] Fieldwork in the provinces was carried out between 1998 and early 2000.[3]

1. The Official Judicial System

In the domain of the official judicial system, quantitative methods prevailed although they were combined with qualitative methods. The methodology employed in this area of research was both intensive and extensive. It covered the extensive gathering of quantitative data from the lower courts (the district and provincial courts), the gathering and processing of legislation, a detailed analysis of case proceedings and other documents including press cuttings, the observation of trials, and interviews with specialist informants, legal actors (professional and lay/elected judges, lawyers, legal staff, representatives from the General Attorney's Office assisting the Public Prosecution Service, the justice officials, etc.) and non-legal actors (economists, business people, leaders of associations, administrators, etc.).

Inadequacies in the official statistics available (provided by the Department of Statistics of the Supreme Court) already identified by other researchers (Dagnino *et al.*, 1996), were one of the greatest difficulties we had to overcome. Faced with this situation, and taking into particular account the discrepancies in statistics recorded in certain years, it was necessary to gather samples of additional information that would enable us to confirm trends in the case flow and proceed with characterizing closed cases. This allowed us to obtain a profile of the different variables in civil and criminal justiceas well as in juvenile justice in the provincial courts and in some of the district courts.

Due to the timetable established for the completion of the project and the budget available, it was not possible to cover the entire geographical area of the country, except in terms of a broad characterization of provincial litigation, in collaboration with the provincial judges. It was therefore necessary to select the provinces and districts in which fieldwork could take place, which was done according to the following criteria: ethnic-cultural diversity; geographical location (particularly in terms of the coastal/interior variable); density of population; approximate volume of cases; existence/non-existence of courts; historical-political importance (see map 5.1).

2. Community Courts

In relation to the community courts, the combination of quantitative and qualitative methods was even more intense. For the first research project, the study on community justice included information relating to a total of 34 courts distributed over six provinces. The fieldwork took place between February 1998 and March 2000.[4]

Map 5.1: Regions Covered by Research (1997-2004)

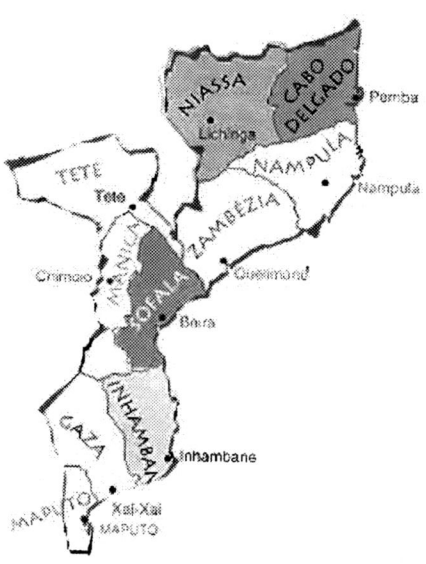

North – the province of Cabo Delgado (the districts of Mueda, Chiúre, Mocímboa da Praia and Pemba-Metuge); Nampula province (Nampula city and Angoche district);
Center – the province of Tete (the districts of Cahora Bassa, Angónia and Moatize); the province of Sofala (the district of Dondo); the province of Manica (Macossa district); the province of Zambézia (the district of Alto Molócuè, Pebane and the city of Quelimane);
South – the province of Maputo (the districts of Namaacha and Moamba); Maputo city (which holds the status of province) and the province of Inhambane (the district of Zavala, Homoíne, Maxixe and Vilankulo).

Given the number and distribution of the community courts, it was necessary to limit the number of courts observed to one or two per district and also to reduce the number in which the most detailed observations took place. Therefore, from amongst the courts observed, it was only possible to prolong the observation period and gather the information which would enable us to understand their structural and functional characteristics with some degree of certainty in 13 of them. These were the community courts of the neighborhoods of Mafalala, Xipamanine, Minkadjuíne, Inhagóia A (Maputo city), Liberdade (Inhambane city), Munhava Central (Beira city), Cerema, Inguri A, Angoche sede, Johar and Mussoriri (Angoche city) and Boila-Nametória (Angoche district, Nampula) and Maimio (Mueda district, Cabo Delgado).[5]
During the course of the fieldwork we came up against two great difficulties. The first was the fact that the central administration held no records of either the numbers or the names of the community courts in operation. The information received from

the Ministry of Justice mentions the presence, early in 2004, of about 1,740 community courts functioning in Mozambique, 15.4% of which were created after 2000. There are about 8,300 judges assigned to these courts, if the statistics from the Ministry of Justice are correct[6]. Even at a local level we were faced with a serious lack of information on the part of the judicial and administrative authorities in relation to the community courts.

The second difficulty had to do with the problem of communication, since the researchers were not always fluent in the national languages of Mozambique. To overcome this difficulty translators had to be used, which required some preliminary preparation.

In order to determine which community courts were active in each district, it was first necessary to gather information from specialist informants. The following methods were used to collect this data: systematic observation, unstructured interviews and documental analysis. So far, in total, over seventy trials have been observed using systematic observation.

In the courts where systematic observation was employed, the presiding judges and the majority of other judges and participants in the court were interviewed. In these community courts it was also possible to interview the parties involved. In addition, we held interviews with the social actors who were most involved in the activities of the community courts, as well as with members of the *grupos dinamizadores*,[7] the heads of administrative sections, police stations and members of Ametramo,[8] and with specialist informants, namely religious leaders and presidents of community associations.

In terms of documentary data, there was an effort to create the most representative sample possible of case proceedings. In order to do this, we relied on the help of the presiding judges of the community courts, who made sets of proceedings available to us for random selection, photocopying or, when there were no other technical means available, copying them in their entirety. The information was collected by filling in a form that identified the cases, which was specifically designed for this purpose.

3. Traditional Authorities

Because Mozambique is a multicultural society where several bodies are involved in the process of conflict resolution, we observed and conducted interviews with multiple social actors who were considered pivotal in maintaining the social fabric of communities through their mediation. Although the research was centered on the *régulados* (chiefdoms and chieftainships), we always started off with a broad concept of the traditional authorities which, in addition to these, included religious authorities, traditional therapists, *grupos dinamizadores*, presidents of community associations, etc.[9]

Generally speaking, research into the traditional authorities as bodies intervening in the resolution of litigation faced the same constraints and difficulties as those already mentioned in relation to the community courts: the difficulty in identifying the number and location of the *régulados* or local leaders and the lack of up-to-date bibliographical information on lineage or genealogical origins; criteria for establishing legitimacy; relationships with the state administration, etc.

In the study of traditional authorities, qualitative methods predominated. The methodology employed was based preferentially on systematic observation and interviews. Observation took place in different parts of the country (the provinces of Cabo Delgado, Tete, Zambézia, Nampula, Manica, Sofala, Inhambane and Maputo). The method most frequently used was that of unstructured interviews of varying duration, due to the fact that the traditional authorities, like the other informal bodies for resolving conflicts, have particular days for *mab'andla* (public meetings to hear cases and deal with various matters of interest to the community). Due to this difficulty, very often the researchers could only use interviews as a research method. In some *régulados* (*e.g.* the régulado Luís, the régulado Cumbana) it was also possible to collect a variety of documentation which is not normally easy to obtain, not only because of the lack of a tradition of written records, but also because of an almost universal unwillingness to disclose information considered to be restricted.

In addition, several branches of *grupos dinamizadores* (including neighborhood secretaries) actively involved in conflict mediation were also studied, including the observation of several cases. The *grupos dinamizadores* were mostly studied in the 'caniço' areas of Maputo city (the neighborhoods of Minkadjuíne, Mafalala, Xipamanine, Jorge Dimitrov/Benfica) and Horta, in Angoche city.

Traditional healers, mostly organized around Ametramo, are normally called upon by the *régulos* and community courts and even by the police to solve cases involving suspicion of practicing witchcraft. During the research project, seven cases involving accusations of witchcraft solved by traditional healers were observed (cases referred by other bodies, such as the community courts, or cases where the litigants sought the assistance of the traditional healers directly).

Finally, religious leaders, such as xéhès, were also interviewed.[10]

In addition to the difficulties listed above, the fieldwork also faced other methodological and epistemological complexities: the precarious guarantee of objectivity afforded by the research methods; the relationships, which were always political in the broadest sense of the word, between the researchers and the populations being studied; team research work as a social process in itself — and one which was experienced intensely by the research team.

It was a very complex and rich learning process that allowed us to build up a complex map of the legal orders active in the country by avoiding the temptation to transplant foreign models — produced to analyze other situations — in order to interpret the situation in Mozambique.

Notes

1   For a more detailed analysis of the debate on multiculturalism and the law see Santos, 2002c.

2   The initial research project ran from 1996 to 2000. A new project, aimed at preparing the legal reform, was initiated in 2003.

3   For the second research project, field work was carried out in the Nampula and Manica provinces (2003-2004).

4   To date (2005) the project has studied over 40 community courts; 34 during the first project and 8 during the second project. Some chapters already refer to data gathered during the second phase of the research.

5   These courts were chosen taking the following factors into consideration: (i) proximity to the district capital; (ii) the institutional context, especially the networking between the community courts, *grupos dinamizadores* and traditional authorities.

6   Ministério da Justiça (2004). *Relatório ao X Conselho Coordenador.* Tete, 13-15 July 2004.

7   See note 34 in chapter 1.

8   *Associação Moçambicana de Médicos Tradicionais* – Mozambican Association of Traditional Healers.

9   A word of caution is needed here, since, following the colonial example, most of the studies conducted on the subject tend to emphasize the role of the *régulos*, forgetting the enormous array of other entities who are considered legitimate and are legitimized from below by the communities that recognize their authority.

10 The above-mentioned report from the Ministry of Justice states that in Mozambique there are 592 officially registered religions, structured around 125 religious organizations.

6

The Judicial System: Structure, Legal Education and Legal Training

João Carlos Trindade and João Pedroso

Introduction

A characterization of the judicial system and the so-called 'Mozambican legal sector' is necessary in order to contextualize the litigation patterns and the performance of the official courts in Mozambique. This chapter presents a brief, purely descriptive account of the Mozambican judicial system. We do not propose an exhaustive approach to the subject but instead prefer to focus on the organization of the courts, their constitutional framework, their powers, etc. It is impossible, however, to avoid other questions relevant to the characterization of the judicial system of the country and the work of the courts. Special attention will be paid to the Supreme Court, the General Attorney's Office[1] and the particular institutions involved in legal education and training.[2]

1. The Evolution of the Judiciary (1975-1999)

The evolution of the organization of the judicial system from independence to the present is a reflection of the development of the political system and the legal-constitutional order of Mozambique. It is therefore possible to identify three periods in the evolution of the organization of the judicial system, which can be defined as:

a) post-independence (1975-1978);
b) the judicial organization of the 'new legality' (1978-1992);
c) the new judicial organization within the context of peace, political pluralism and a market economy, following the 1990 Constitution in which the separation

of powers and the independence of the judicial system are enshrined (since 1992).[3]

The Period from 1975 to 1978

The first period identified (from 1975 to 1978) represents the evolution of the colonial system into the construction of a new legal order. On 25 June 1975 the Constitution of the People's Republic of Mozambique was published, as the almost natural consequence of the declaration of independence. In it a new (political, economic, social, etc.) national order was proclaimed – popular power – which aimed to break with all the old operational frameworks of the colonial state. Expressly enshrined in the Constitution as one of the fundamental objectives of the Republic was "the elimination of structures of oppression and colonial exploitation [...] and the mentality which underlies them" (Article 4 of the Constitution). Based on this political line, the 1975 Constitution envisaged, in abstract, the fundamental rules for the organization of the judicial system, referring them to statutory law for concretization.[4] In general terms, it consigned the basis of the judicial function to the courts (Article 62), with the Supreme Popular Court as the highest organ in the hierarchy of the system, responsible for promoting the uniform application of the law by all the courts and ensuring that the Constitution and all the legal norms of the Republic (Article 63) were implemented. In addition to this, particular attention was paid to the principle of the independence of courts in the exercise of their functions (Article 65).

The building of a new 'legal order' and a new judicial system was one of the objectives to be fulfilled. The Directive of the Third Frelimo Congress on Justice is particularly illustrative in this context, emphasizing urgency in the "destruction of the existing judicial structure, as part of the destruction of the colonial-capitalist apparatus" (*Justiça Popular*, 1980: 3). The goal was to construct a system of popular justice inspired by the experiences of the people, especially those in the liberated zones,[5] since "they show just how profoundly incompatible colonial and capitalist legislation is with the traditions, way of life and characteristics of our society and our people." It was in this context that the draft bill of the Law on the Organization of the Judiciary was discussed widely, at a national level. This experience constituted a high point in the history of Mozambican justice, with the establishment of a legal and judicial system that was intended to be unitary and based on the country's very reality.

The Judicial Organization of the New Legal Order (1978-1992)[6]

Three years after independence, the Law on the Organization of the Judiciary of Mozambique (Law no. 12/78 of 2 December) was approved.

After establishing some general principles to guide the activity of the courts (such as the guarantee and defense of the legal order and constitutional principles, the equal right of all citizens to have recourse to the courts, the independence of the courts, etc.), the law defined the division of the judicial system. This had "whenever possible, and bearing in mind the needs of the system of judicial organization, to coincide with the division of the administration, with any alteration to the latter implying corresponding changes to the division of the judicial system" (Article 9). As a rule, a court was to be in operation in each administrative division. Therefore, in descending order of the hierarchy of the courts, the functions of the judiciary would be exercised by the Supreme Popular Court, the provincial popular courts, the district popular courts, and the local popular courts. Neighborhood popular courts could also be created "in cities where this was justified by the density of the population or by other circumstances" (Article 10). The fundamental right to have verdicts reconsidered – wherein each of the courts had to review, on appeal, the decision of the court immediately below them – was guaranteed.

In accordance with the Law on the Organization of the Judiciary of Mozambique, popular courts began to be created at all levels of the country's administrative divisions: locality, community village, neighborhood, district, province, right up to the Supreme Court.

The popular courts (with the exception of the local ones – the community village, locality and neighborhood courts, which functioned only with elected judges[7]) were composed of professional judges appointed by the Ministry of Justice and judges elected by the Popular Assemblies at the appropriate level.[8] Although Law no. 12/78 envisaged the creation of the Supreme Popular Court, the former Court of Appeals of the Portuguese judicial system remained in operation until 1979, when it was replaced by the High Court of Appeals. The Supreme Court only began to function after 1988, when the Chief Justice, the Deputy Chief Justice and the Justices were appointed.

One of the most striking characteristics of the Mozambican judicial system is that at all levels, including the Supreme Court, the exercise of judicial activity is not the sole prerogative of professional judges. Up to the new Constitutional reforms (2004), the law also required that elected judges should take part in judicial proceedings alongside them (see below).

Elected judges were lay citizens who were presented as candidates to the popular assemblies and elected by them to carry out judicial duties. Elected judges who had the confidence of citizens and the Frelimo party sat alongside professional judges and applied official law.

Elected judges, who still serve today, exercise authentic jurisdictional functions and intervene in decisions on matters of fact and matters of law in criminal cases.[9] They work in shifts, ensuring that there is a certain amount of circulation among them. During the time they are involved in working for the courts, they are given leave of absence from their regular employment.[10]

The Locality and Neighborhood Popular Courts

The locality and neighborhood popular courts formed the base of the judicial system. These courts were the only ones made up exclusively of elected judges and had to number a minimum of three and a maximum of five judges (Articles 36 and 37 of Law no. 12/78).

In criminal matters, these courts only dealt with minor infractions liable to lead to sanctions such as a public warning, community service for no more than thirty days, payment of a fine not exceeding $ 1,000 or even compensation for the injured party. In terms of civil litigation, they could deal with cases involving amounts not exceeding $10,000.[11]

At local and neighborhood level all judges were elected and resolved the cases presented to them by reconciling the parties concerned. When this was not possible they made decisions on the basis of common sense and justice (Article 38) and could only apply measures that did not entail deprivation of liberty (such as fines, temporary suspension of a right, and community service).[12]

The District Popular Courts

In addition to the elected judges, the district popular courts included a judge appointed by the Ministry of Justice, on the advice of the Governor of the Province (Article 30). Both the appointed and the elected judges (a minimum of two and a maximum of four) had to participate in decisions (no. 1 of Article 31).

In terms of civil jurisdiction, they dealt with cases pertaining to family matters and all others in which the financial sum involved did not exceed $50,000 (Article 32, no. 1, a). If there was no special law delegating powers to any other court, they also dealt with all criminal cases liable to a prison sentence of no more than two years and with infractions committed by judges from the locality, community village and neighborhood popular courts involving criminal acts committed during the exercise of their duties (Article 32, no. 2, a and b). Finally, they also functioned as an appeals court for all decisions made by the locality, community village and neighborhood popular courts, which represented the base of the court system (Article 33, no. 2, c).

The Provincial Popular Courts[13]

The provincial popular courts consisted of a judge appointed by the Ministry of Justice (who acted as the chief judge of the court) and four elected judges. The presence of the appointed judge and at least two of the elected judges was required for the court to hear any case or trial (Article 22, no. 1).

These judicial courts had residual powers both in civil and in criminal matters. They heard all the cases which had not been previously attributed to other courts (Article 23, no. 1, a and no. 2, a). They also judged magistrates from the district courts for crimes committed during the exercise of their duties. In addition, they were empowered to reconsider, as appeals, all the decisions of the district courts (Article 23, no. 1, b and no. 2, b). However, in relation to civil jurisdiction, the law only allowed appeals on decisions made by the district courts in which the amount involved was in excess of $5,000 (Article 34 to the contrary). By decree the Ministry of Justice, special sections (civil, criminal, labor, etc.) could be created in the provincial courts when justified by the amount of work. In this case, judges were nominated to preside over the various sections.

The Supreme Popular Court

The Supreme Popular Court was the highest body of the judicial system and had jurisdiction over the entire country. It was responsible for directing the entire organization of the judicial system, and could "issue instructions or directives of a general and mandatory nature" to the various courts, "in order to ensure uniformity in the application of the law." These directives assumed the status of laws.

The court had to consist of at least six justices appointed by the Ministry of Justice and a minimum of eighteen elected judges, nine of whom were substitutes. The appointed justices had to have a law degree and be over 25 years of age.

The court functioned in sections, as a higher court (reconsidering the decisions of the provincial courts), and as a lower court to – amongst other cases – judge magistrates from the provincial courts who had committed criminal acts during the exercise of their duties. In this case, each section could only deliberate if two elected judges and one appointed judge (the sentencing magistrate) were present.

Decisions made by sections, when operating as a lower judicial court, were heard as appeals at a Plenary Sitting of the Supreme Court. The Court was also authorized to standardize jurisprudence, settle disputes relating to jurisdiction between the courts and other authorities, judge criminal proceedings in which the accused were particular categories of people with an important position in the state or the Frelimo party (for example, the President of the Republic, the Popular Assembly deputies and the members of the Central Committee of Frelimo party),[14] etc. In order for the Plenary Sitting to deliberate on questions concerning its own powers, at least three appointed Justices and five elected judges had to be present, in addition to the Chief Justice.

In general, the popular court system as a whole (including the prosecutors who were an integral part of the system) played a double role: the courts contributed to the countrywide presence of the new independent state institutions, whilst promoting the transition from one legal system to another. Popular courts were perceived as part of a social laboratory where the 'old' and the 'new' characteristics of Mozambican society could find forms of coexistence and compromise that could be reflected in the creation of a new legal framework. However, a note of caution is required. In fact, genuine popular participation in the administration of justice did not really suit the centralized, authoritarian nature of the single party state of the time, meaning that, in many instances, the people's courts became vehicles for the imposition of state power, thus delegitimizing their own essence.

The New Judicial Organization in a Period of Peace, Pluralism and Market Economy

The political and economic reforms introduced in the country at the end of the eighties, following the change from a single party socialist regime to a multiparty regime defending a market economy, had immediate repercussions on the judicial system.

The 1990 Constitution gave ample recognition to political and human rights, such as equality (Article 66), freedom of expression and information (Article 74) and the right to freedom of movement, as well as the right to reside in any part of the country or abroad (Article 83). It established the right to strike – except in the essential services – (Article 91) and freedom of religion and worship (Article 78). It also established the principle of strict legality to be observed in detentions and trials, the principle of the presumption of innocence (Article 98), the principle of non-retroactivity in penal law (Article 99), the right to resort to *habeas corpus* (Article 102) and the right to defense and to legal assistance and aid, regardless of financial status (Article 100).

This new Fundamental Law gave the country access to the global economy and established various types of ownership: state, cooperative, private-state joint ownership, and private (Article 41). While the land remained the exclusive property of the state, the Constitution established conditions for using and benefiting from the land which could be conferred upon individuals or collectives (Articles 46 and 47).

The 1990 Constitution, in proclaiming that "the courts shall penalize violations of the legal order and shall adjudicate disputes in accordance with the law" (Article161, no. 3) came, in the opinion of many, to reinforce a state monopoly over the production and application of the law and, consequently, the professionalization of the judicial function. Subsequent regulatory legislation, by producing a significant turnabout in the principles and practice of previous judicial practices – which had attributed great importance to the participation of citizens and communities in the entire process of the administration of justice – managed, among other things, to define the disintegration of the courts that had constituted the base of the judicial system (and which subsequently became known as the Community Courts).[15] In the same way, it altered the hierarchy of the judicial courts[16] by creating new courts with special powers[17] and established the Institute for Legal Assistance and Representation [18] and the Bar Association.[19] It became necessary, therefore, to formulate certain new rules for the organization of the judicial system. In addition to those laid down by the former 1975 Constitution, some general principles were announced which, in modern constitutions, are enshrined in the democratic rule of law. These include the principles of the general obligation to comply with judicial rulings (Article 162), the impartiality and independence of judges (Article 164), exclusivity in the exercise of judicial functions (Article 166), etc. The creation of special courts was also forbidden: "Other than the courts specified in the Constitution, no other court may be established with jurisdiction over specific categories of crimes" (no. 2 of Article 167).[20]

The new Law on the Organization of the Judiciary – or Organic Law of the Judicial Courts (Law no. 10/92 of 6 May) introduced profound alterations to the judicial system, in compliance with the political and constitutional philosophy which had been adopted, based on the separation of powers and the principles of independence, impartiality and autonomy of judges and their exclusive obedience to the law. The elected judges became eligible to participate only in decisions on matters of fact, assisting the professional judges (Article 71 of the 1990 Constitution).

The 1990 Constitution defined the courts as sovereign bodies which guaranteed and reinforced the legal order, securing the rights and freedoms of citizens and the legal interests of the different bodies and entities officially in existence (Article 169 and 161). This constitutional innovation made judicial, executive and legislative powers independent, with the Minister of Justice no longer directing the judicial system.[21] The courts were no longer accountable to the Popular Assembly.[22] Since then, judges have had their own statutes, which establish basic principles such as their independence and tenure, define their career structure and establish their rights and duties (Law no. 10/91 of 30 July). The autonomy of the judicial system also had budgetary repercussions: the national budget has separate sections for the Supreme Court and the courts at provincial level.[23]

The Organic Law of the Judicial Courts establishes that "the courts are sovereign organs which administer justice in the name of the people" and regulates the organization, competence and functioning of the courts in the light of the new constitutional principles. The same law also stipulates new general principles (for example, citizens' access to justice guaranteed by the state, the presumption of the innocence of the accused, public hearings), thus complementing the constitutional guarantees.

One of the important changes in the new judicial organization was to limit formal jurisdiction to district level, by adopting the then-dominant interpretation of Article 161, no. 3 of the Constitution. As they did not apply purely legal criteria (written law), the grassroots (locality and neighborhood) courts created under the previous judicial organization were excluded from the official judicial system. At the same time, a new law was passed (Law no. 4/92) creating the Community Courts as bodies for conciliation and the resolution of minor conflicts under what could be defined as the informal administration of justice. The Community Courts continued to be ruled by the principles previously applied to the local and neighborhood courts and remained under the direction of the Ministry of Justice.

The separation of the executive, a fundamental step towards the construction of the rule of law, was established to the extent that the government had no responsibility for the management of the judicial system. This had collateral effects, for which the system was not prepared. Executive and management tasks increased substantially, without a corresponding increase in human resources. On the one hand, the courts, namely the Supreme Court, are currently responsible for the effective functioning and management of all levels of the official judicial system. On the other hand, the autonomy of the courts and the General Attorney's Office has had the parallel effect of making the attorneys 'guests' of the judicial courts, since they are now no longer an integral part of them. Consequently, the organization of the judicial system is no longer dependent on the Ministry of Justice,[24] the courts no longer use the term 'popular' and the elected judges can now only take part in lower court trials and deliberate only in matters of fact.

The Composition, Powers and Structure of the Courts

As had been the case under the previous systems, the current court structure was intended to make the organization of the judicial system correspond, as closely as possible, to the administrative divisions in the country.[25]

The system included the Supreme Court and the provincial and district courts (Article 19, no. 1), with the potential to create specialist courts and district judicial courts in the capitals of the provinces whenever justified by circumstances (Article 19, no. 2). In its internal order, the power of a court is established in terms of subject matter, hierarchy, value and territory (Article 22, no. 1). Whenever the circumstances justify it, specialist judicial courts and district judicial courts can be established in the provincial capitals. Some specialist courts have already been created – such as the Juvenile Court in Maputo city,[26] the Police Court in Maputo city and the Labor Courts. Although created by law in 1992 with competence in labor matters and constituting a specialist court system, the Labor Courts have not yet been formally established.

The hierarchical structure of the courts guarantees the right to appeal the court's decision. Appeals are allowed on matters of law and matters of fact, although in the latter case this is allowed only once. This means that, as far as matters of law are concerned, there can be two levels of appeal (from the district court to the provincial court and from there to the Supreme Court), depending on the requirements established in the Civil Procedure Code.

In accordance with the changes brought about by the Organic Law of the Judicial Courts under Decree no. 24/98 of 2 June, the first and second class district courts hear cases in which the sums involved do not exceed 30,000,000 *meticais* and 15,000,000 *meticais*, respectively.[27] The provincial courts are responsible for judging cases involving amounts of over 30,000,000 *meticais*. In criminal matters, the district courts are responsible for judging crimes punishable by sentences of not more than eight years in prison. The provincial courts, as lower courts, judge civil and criminal cases which do not fall within the responsibility of the district courts (see figure 6.1).

The District Judicial Courts: The Country, the Courts Created and the Courts in Operation

Given the exclusion of the base courts from the judicial system, the district judicial courts act as lower judicial courts. The law envisages the existence of first and second class district courts and establishes the powers of each. In practice, however, this distinction is not preserved.

Each of these courts is composed of a Chief Judge, who is a professional judge, and elected judges (Article 57).[28] If justified by the volume of work, they can be organized into sections, which must, in this case, include a Chief Judge. They function as a collective and at least two elected judges must be present, in addition to the Chief Judge when a case is to be decided (Article 58).

Figure 6.1: The Organization of the Judicial System

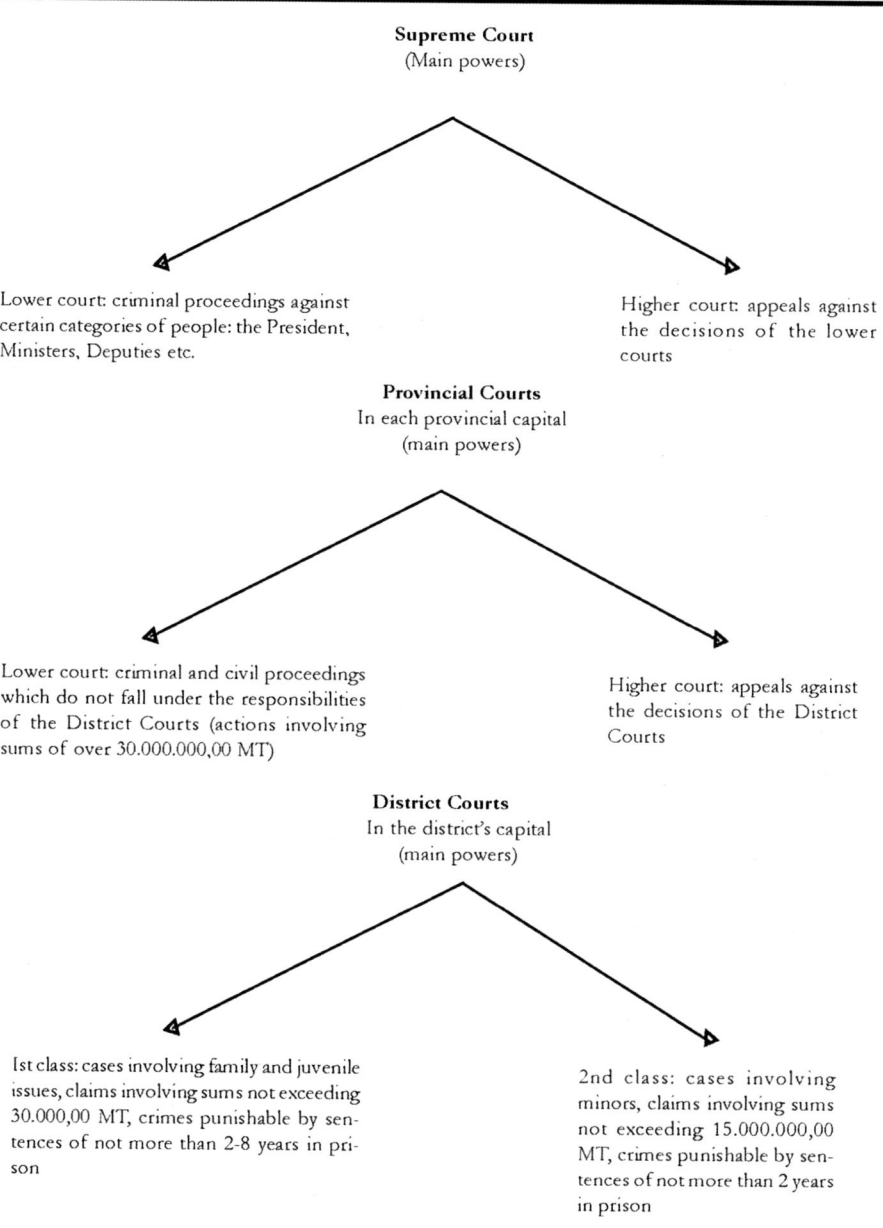

Supreme Court
(Main powers)

Lower court: criminal proceedings against
certain categories of people: the President,
Ministers, Deputies etc.

Higher court: appeals against
the decisions of the lower
courts

Provincial Courts
In each provincial capital
(main powers)

Lower court: criminal and civil proceedings
which do not fall under the responsibilities
of the District Courts (actions involving
sums of over 30.000.000,00 MT)

Higher court: appeals against
the decisions of the District
Courts

District Courts
In the district's capital
(main powers)

1st class: cases involving family and juvenile
issues, claims involving sums not exceeding
30.000,00 MT, crimes punishable by sentences of not more than 2-8 years in prison

2nd class: cases involving
minors, claims involving sums
not exceeding 15.000.000,00
MT, crimes punishable by sentences of not more than 2 years
in prison

Source: Law no. 10/92 of 6 May and Decree no. 24/98 of 2 June.

Law no. 10/92 of 6 May presents a map of the judicial organization in which the administration of justice covers the whole country. As we have already indicated, this objective is far from having been achieved.

District judicial courts have limited competence in both criminal matters (crimes punishable by up to two years in prison) and civil matters. In civil matters, in addition to cases involving the aforementioned sums, they also hear cases involving the jurisdiction of minors (Article 60, no. 1, a). In relation to criminal litigation, they deal initially with infractions punishable with a prison sentence of not more than two years, but their powers were widened by Decree no. 24/98 2 June so as to include crimes punishable by a prison sentence of up to eight years.

In terms of the administrative division of Mozambique, the district courts must be created by legislation, but this has not happened in the case of 35 of the 143 district courts.[29]

An analysis of the districts where the district judicial courts have not been created by legal decree enables us to detect two kinds of rationale underlying their selection. The first is that they correspond to the districts which are farthest away from the capital and have increasingly smaller populations, which the state and the official administration have difficulty in reaching, or do not reach at all. The second logic is that of not creating district courts in cities in which provincial judicial courts are functioning or where other municipal district courts exist, as in the case of Maputo city.[30]

Among the courts that have been created, there are six municipal district courts in operation: three in the city of Maputo (six court offices), two in the province of Maputo (the city of Matola and Machava) and one in Gaza (the city of Xai-Xai). Of the 128 rural districts which exist in Mozambique, according to Dagnino *et al.* (1996) the appropriate judicial courts are only in operation in 80 of them. According to the Ministry of Justice, there were about 90 district courts functioning in rural districts in 2000.[31]

The situation observed in the field enables us to state that, of the 90 courts officially understood to be in operation according to the table above, at least four had not yet been legally created in 2000 (Chemba and Chibabava, in Sofala, and Mabote and Funhalouro, in Inhambane). In relation to Chibabava, the research team visited the district at the time of the first project (1996-2000) and found that the administration of justice was carried out by a 'Municipal Court' from the colonial period which was still in operation and was directed by an assistant district administrator and three 'elected' judges.[32] Also, the more recently created districts are not expected to have district judicial courts, this being the case in the Macossa district, in this Manica province.[33]

As we have already stated, in Mozambique the total number of both rural district and municipal district (urban) judicial courts with powers at district level is 143.[34] With only about 90 in operation, this means that over 50 districts still lack a judicial court. Thus, the judicial system ends at district level and barely covers 62% of the districts in existence.

Table 6.1: Judicial Courts in 'Rural' Districts

CABO DELGADO
1. Ancuabe
2. Chiúre
3. Macomia
4. Mocímboa da Praia
5. Montepe
6. Mueda
7. Namuno
8. Palma

NIASSA
1. Cuamba
2. Madimba
3. Maúa
4. Marrupa
5. Mecanhelas
6. Metangula
7. Unango
8. Mavago

NAMPULA
1. angoshe
2. Eráti (Namapa)
3. Malema
4. Meconta
5. Mecuburi
6. Moma
7. Monapo
8. Mossuril
9. Murrupula
10. Nacala (Porto)
11. Ribáuè
12. Ilha de Mocambique
13. Rapale
14. Muecate
15. Nametil
16. Liupo (Mogincual)
17. Memba

ZAMBEZIA
1. Chinde
2. Gurué
3. Ile
4. Alto--Molócuè
5. Mocuba
6. Pebane
7. Milange
8. Maganja da Costa
9. Morrumbala (to open)

MAPUTO
1. Boane
2. Manhica
3. Namaacha
4. Marracuene
5. Magude
6. Matutuine (Bela Vista)
7. Moamba

MANICA
1. Gondola
2. Guro
3. Machaze
4. Manica
5. Espungabera
6. Catandica

SOFALA
1. Buzi
2. Caia
3. Dondo
4. Gorongoza
5. Marromeu
6. Nhamatanda
7. Chibabava
8. Chemba
9. Inhaminga

Table 6.1: Judicial Courts in 'Rural' Districts (contd.)

INHAMBANE
1.   Maxixe
2.   Massinga
3.   Morrumbene
4.   Homoíne
5.   Vilankulo
6.   Zavala (Quissico)
7.   Inharrime
8.   Funhalouro
9.   Panda
10. Inhassoro
11. Mabote
12. Nova Mambone
13. Langano (proposed)

GAZA
1.   Bilene-Macia
2.   Chibuto

3.   Chicualacuala
4.   Chokwé
5.   Guijá
6.   Mabalane
7.   Mandlakazi
8.   Massingir

TETE
1.   Angónia
2.   Chnagara
3.   Marávia (to open)
4.   Moatiza
5.   Mutarara
6.   Cahora Bassa
7.   Magoé
8.   Macanga (to open)
9.   Zumbo (to open)
Total 90+5 (to open)

Source: Information from the Supreme Court 11/07/2000

The Provincial Courts

Provincial courts exist in all of the country's eleven provinces (including the city of Maputo, which has the status of a province), with one or more court offices. They are presided over by a Chief Judge and are divided into criminal sections and civil sections. All the provincial judges have a law degree. They can function as lower or higher courts. In the case of the former, they are competent to hear all civil or penal cases which are not the responsibility of the other courts, while still retaining their own residual powers. The provincial court also considers all crimes or illicit civil acts practiced by lower-ranking magistrates which are related to the exercise of their duties (Article 51). When it functions as a lower court, there must be a minimum of two elected judges and one professional judge present for it to be able to deliberate.

As a higher court hearing appeals against the decisions of the district courts, it consists of three professional judges, two of whom are required for any deliberations. As previously mentioned, the Constitution limits the elected judges to hearing cases in the lower court.

In the provincial courts sections can be created as required to deal with the demands of the workload.

In the city of Maputo, the provincial court has four criminal sections, three civil sections, two labor sections and one criminal instruction section. There are also two courts with special jurisdiction, the Juvenile Court (two sections) and the Police Court.

Between 30 December 1978 and 19 December 1979, legislation was produced to create today's provincial judicial courts (then known as the provincial popular courts). Later on, the Judicial Court of Maputo city (2 November 1983), the city of Maputo Juvenile Court (13 November 1980) and the city of Maputo Police Court were created. This meant separate jurisdiction for the city and the province of Maputo and an answer to the concentration, quantity and specific nature of litigation in the capital of the country.

Between independence and the creation of these courts, the former area judicial courts (*tribunais de comarca*) – dating from colonial times – remained in operation.

The process of specialization in the provincial judicial courts took place in two complementary ways. On the one hand, this occurred through the creation of courts with special jurisdiction (the Juvenile Court and the Police Court in Maputo) and, on the other hand, through the creation of both civil and criminal specialized sections and, in recent years, the creation of labor sections (in the city of Maputo, the province of Maputo and Sofala) and criminal instruction sections (the Court of Maputo city).[35]

2. The Supreme Court: The Guardian of the Judicial System

Judicial and Administrative Structure

In accordance with Law no. 10/92, the Supreme Court is the highest judicial court and is composed of the Chief Justice, Deputy Chief Justice, Justices and elected judges. It consists of a minimum of seven Justices and 17 elected judges, eight of whom are substitutes (Article 30).[36] As already noted, since 1992 the judiciary is no longer dependent on the Ministry of Justice and the personnel within it have become dependent on the Supreme Court.[37]

The Justices are nominated by the President of the Republic, on the advice of the Superior Council of the Judicial System (Article 226, no. 2 and 3 of the 2004 Constitution).

The Supreme Court is organized both as a plenary and in sections. Specializations are established by the internal regulations of the Supreme Court. The Chief Justice presides over the plenary sittings. He or she can also preside, when necessary, over the sectional closed sessions. In this case, the Chief Justice does not have the right to vote, unless there is a hung verdict (Article 41, no. 1, d and 36, no. 4). The Deputy Chief Justice replaces the Chief Justice whenever the latter is absent or sick. A plenary sitting can function as a lower or higher court. In the former case, it consists of the Chief Justice, Deputy Chief Justice, Justices and elected judges. To deliberate, the presence of at least two thirds of its members is required (Article 32). Just like the other attributes which may be conferred, by law, upon the plenary sittings as a unique body, it can judge crimes and illicit civil acts practiced by a particular category of people (for example, the President of the Republic, the President of the Assembly of the Republic, the Prime Minister and the Justices of the Supreme Court – Article 34).

As a higher court, amongst its other duties, the plenary sitting is responsible for standardizing jurisprudence, hearing conflicts of jurisdiction between the courts and other authorities, judge (as the highest body and in matters of law) appeals against rulings made by the various jurisdictions and reconsidering (on appeal) the decisions of the sections of the Supreme Court as lower courts (Article 33). With regard to the sections, when they function as higher courts they are composed of a minimum of two professional judges. When they rule as a lower court, they also include two elected judges. The sections, as lower courts, are responsible for judging criminal cases in which the accused are deputies of the Assembly of the Republic, members of the Council of Ministers, magistrates and professional judges from the provincial judicial courts, etc. As higher courts, they judge appeals on matters of fact and matters of law against decisions which – under the terms of the law on civil proceedings – must be brought before the Supreme Court; rule on conflicts of duty in the provincial district courts, hear requests for *habeas corpus*, etc.

Figure 6.2: The Supreme Court – Judicial Structure

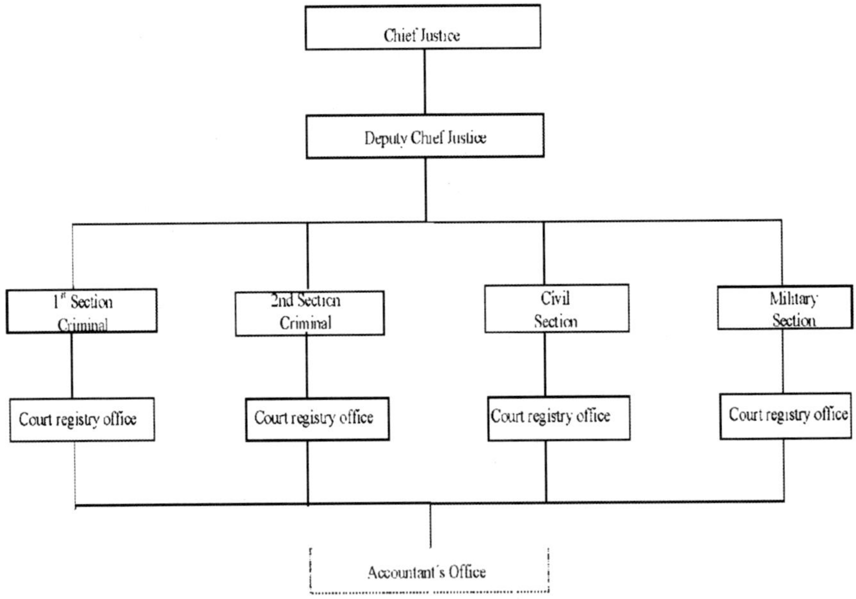

Source: Law n.o 10/92 and adapted from Dagnino *et al.*, 1996.

The Supreme Court still assumes the powers of a higher appeals court in labor and military matters. The Constitution envisages the creation of labor and military jurisdiction, but this has not yet been implemented.[38] In fact, since 1992 – the year in which the justice and labor commissions were abolished and before the labor courts were created – jurisdiction has been exercised on a lower level by the civil sections of the provincial courts and in appeal by the Supreme Court. The Supreme Court also rules – as a higher court – in military cases, with the provincial military courts acting as the lower court. Additionally, it acts as a lower court when dealing with the trials of higher-ranking officers. Finally, as established by the 1990 Constitution, the Constitutional Council was formed in 2003. Since then, the responsibilities previously assumed by the Supreme Court in relation to constitutional and electoral matters have ended.[39]

At present (2005), the Supreme Court has a Chief Justice, a Deputy Chief Justice and six Justices.[40] It has two criminal sections, one civil (and labor) section and a military section, each possessing its own court offices. The court also has an accountant's office (see figure 6.2).

In addition to its jurisdictional function, the Supreme Court is responsible for the general administration of the court system, including its human, financial and patrimonial resources. Thus, the Supreme Court is internally organized with the aim of carrying out various managerial and technical support functions for the judicial apparatus: the Department of Administration, Patrimony and Finance (DAPF), the Department of Human Resources (DHR), the Department of Information and Legal Statistics (DILS) and the Library.[41]

The Supreme Court: Functions, Independence and the Credibility of the Courts

The political and symbolic functions of the Supreme Court are of particular importance in Mozambique, because it is responsible for directing and supervising the organization of the judicial system. This encompasses internal control and discipline, management of the system, litigation resolution and social control, as well as jurisdictional functions, through its decisions. When it exercises its competence to judge cases of major social and political interest or those of a political nature, the Supreme Court also takes on the function of guaranteeing the stability and maintenance of the political system.

We will pay particular attention, in this chapter, to some of the decisions relating to the functioning of the political system. When the Supreme Court was entitled to exercise constitutional competence (up to the introduction of the Constitutional Council in 2003), its decisions (such as the decision on the unconstitutionality of the law that decided that Muslim holy days were to be national holidays, as well as its decisions on electoral matters) functioned as a guarantee of the stability and independence of the court system.

South Africa, Russia, Hungary or Colombia also provide examples of constitutional courts (or courts carrying out such functions) which can judicialize politics whilst maintaining (or constructing) their independence in relation to other bodies of political power, thus providing credibility for the judicial system. Heinz Klug (1996, 2000), however, notes that in the construction of the South African judicial system, there is a gap between the credibility of justice and the credibility of the Constitutional Court.

The Supreme Court in Mozambique has given credibility to the courts by deciding, in an impartial and independent manner, to acquit a general accused by the party in power of treason and attempting a coup d'etat, as well as by penalizing and even dismissing judges involved in illegal activities.

In an analysis of the Mozambican judicial system, it may be seen that its credibility can be evaluated from four perspectives: 1) its distance from citizens, *i.e.* in relation to citizen access to the law and to justice; 2) the excessive length of cases; 3) the civil and criminal alegality and illegality of certain corrupt practices; 4) the independence of the judicial system.

In terms of the Supreme Court, we have to take into account that, at the moment, one source to its discredit is the excessive slowness of the proceedings, which requires us to analyze whether this is attenuated, compensated for or even overcome by the level of political independence which its decisions reveal.

The ability of the judicial courts to judge and sentence crimes of corruption committed by those who exercise political, economic and social power and/or by members of the judicial system is also a challenge to their own external and internal independence. On the one hand, there is an almost total absence in the courts of cases of corrupt practices imputed to citizens who exercise political, economic and social power. On the other hand, in cases of corruption practiced by magistrates and state officials who stand trial, the defendants are usually condemned.

Like the courts in the countries previously mentioned, an analysis of the Supreme Court's performance shows that it has been a guarantor of the consolidation of independent judicial power in this transitional period in the political system and that, through its supervisory and managerial functions, it has also established the credibility of the legal system. Nevertheless, in the opinion of many people we interviewed, the Supreme Court should be more active in tackling the evils of the system, namely delays, corruption, inadequate legislation and the poor qualifications of its human resources.

3. The Organization and Recent Activities of the General Attorney's Office

Since 1975, the Constitutions have defined the General Attorney's Office (the body of state attorneys) as a hierarchical magistracy that functions in parallel with the court judges, under the Attorney General.[42] As stated by the 1978 Law on the Organization of the Judiciary, its functions essentially consist of inspecting and controlling legality, promoting compliance with the law and participating in the defense of the established legal order. Together with the courts, it is its mission to file cases, that is, to present the state's case against the defendant in a criminal prosecution, to supervise criminal investigation, to control legality and periods of detention, to guarantee the protection of minors, absentees and the disabled, and to defend and represent the interests of the state.

However, in spite of the new functional model, the General Attorney's Office as an institution continued to operate, to a large extent, under colonial legislation.

Law no. 6/89 – approved on 19 September – created the General Attorney's Office as a central body of the state. The General Attorney's Office enjoys autonomy in relation to both the Ministry of Justice and the official court system and is bound only by the criteria of legality, objectivity and exemplary behavior. As this law – granting the General Attorney's Office a much wider range of powers than before – was only passed one year before the 1990 Constitution, it does not completely embody contemporary constitutional principles. For example, it states that the body of state attorneys represents and defends the property of the Frelimo party, that the Superior Council of the General Attorney's Office studies party and state decisions on the law, justice and legality with a view to their implementation and that the General Attorney's Office presents an annual report on its activities to the People's Assembly.

Both the 1990 and 2004 Constitutions did not include the General Attorney's Office among its sovereign bodies.

The General Attorney's Office has a dual nature. On the one hand, it is a central body of the state for controlling legality, promoting observance of the law and defending the legal order. As such, the Attorney-General and the Deputy Attorneys-General are appointed, released and dismissed by the President of the Republic. On the other hand it is the highest body of attorneyship in the country, being independent and accountable exclusively to the law. The General Attorney's Office therefore constitutes a parallel body to the judicial magistracy and has as its primary function the defense and control of legality. The attorneys are bound by the criteria of legality, objectivity, impartiality and subjection to the law. However, the current Organic Law of the General Attorney's Office – which was the first sign of a change in the judicial system – although advanced for its time, now needs to be adapted to the *status quo* created by the new constitutions.

The provincial and district attorney offices are peripheral bodies of the General Attorneys' Office. At a central level there is the Consultative Council (a counseling body comprising the Attorney-General, the Deputy Attorney-General and the Assistant Attorneys General) and the Superior Council of the General Attorney's Office, a management body comprising the leadership of the institution and the Provincial State Attorneys (still inactive).

The law envisages the creation of specialized departments and a secretariat with technical and administrative duties. The General Attorney's Office consists of specialized departments (the Department of Legal Control; the Department of Criminal Affairs; the Department of Civil Affairs, Juveniles, Labor and the Family and the Department of Administrative Affairs), a General Secretariat, a Judicial Registry Office, and the Library and technical infrastructure.

In recent years some of the functions attributed to the Attorney-General have been carried out by entities within civil society, as is the case with actions aimed at raising the legal awareness of citizens. Others, such as the control of legality, the issuing of legal opinions and the inspection of prison establishments, have been partially attributed to them, or else are being exercised by other institutions, namely the Administrative Court, the Constitutional Council and the Ministry of Justice.

According to the annual report of the General Attorney's Office for the year 1999,[43] the Consultative Council issued legal opinions and analyzed enquiries arising out of denunciations against deputies in the Assembly of the Republic and the non-governmental organizations (NGOs). The same document stated that, in the period under analysis, the Department of Legal Control received and acted on denunciations through public institutions and bodies of the state in order to achieve legality. The departments of Criminal Affairs and Civil Affairs, Juveniles, Labor and the Family helped meet needs and fill internal gaps, working together with civil society and other state bodies in order to fulfill their mission. The Department of Administrative Affairs took charge of personnel problems – particularly training – and oversaw actions brought against the Mozambican state. The General Secretary initiated a process of administrative and financial restructuring, replacement of personnel, the computerization of services and the standardization of statistics from judicial proceedings.[44]

The General Attorney's Office: Problems, Crises and Opportunities

The General Attorney's Office, like the Mozambican courts, has serious shortcomings in relation to human resources (in terms of recruitment, selection and training), insufficient financial resources, inadequate premises (offices and housing for state attorneys) and equipment. This situation is made worse,, on the one hand, by the autonomy of the General Attorney's Office and its separation from the judicial courts, which has made the state attorneys tolerated 'guests' of the court system, and on the other hand because 15 years after the autonomy of the General Attorney's Office was legally established (Law no. 6/89), legislation has still not been issued to approve the statutes of its magistrates.

Since the early nineties the rise in non-legal, illegal and criminal corruption, violent crime and urban insecurity have placed the General Attorney's Office at the center of controversy in Mozambican society.

Paradoxically, rather than increased support for the idea of consolidating the General Attorney's Office, support has frequently been given to the creation of new bodies to carry out functions within the areas of responsibility of the General Attorney's Office.

First of all there were the 'external' and 'internal' supporters of the Higher Authority to Combat Corruption within the state, which has not yet been created. The Superior Council of the General Attorney's Office was obviously, against the establishment of such an authority. Secondly, and more recently, the 2004 Constitution created the legal figure of an Ombudsman, "as an office established to guarantee the rights of citizens and to uphold legality and justice in the actions of the Public Administration" (Article 256). So far, however, the new bodies competing with the

Attorney-General have not begun to operate, although the latter has neither reinforced nor improved its performance.

Figure 6.3: The Organization of the General Attorney's Office

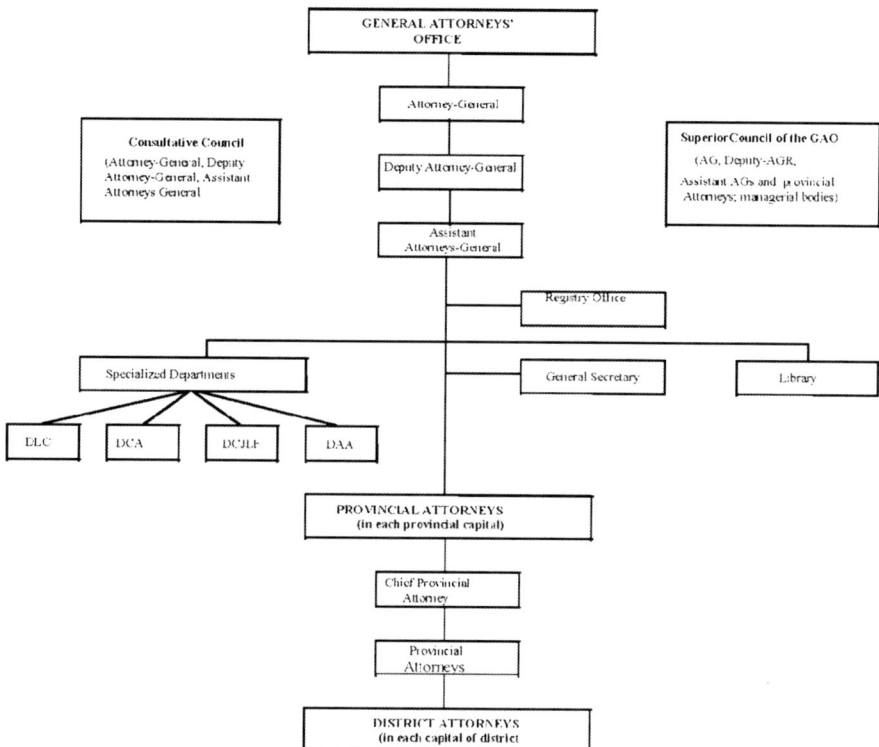

In short, the General Attorney's Office is repeatedly accused of a lack of action and of apathy. There have been several successive crises involving the Assembly of the Republic, which has echoed these criticisms, and which led to the President of the Republic, in 1997 and again in 2000, to relieve the General-Attorney from office. It is to be hoped that the solution to the crisis will open up a window of opportunity for the General Attorney's Office to establish itself within the landscape of justices in Mozambique.

4. The Institutional Structure of the Administration of Official Justice

The administration of official justice is not limited to the judicial courts, the community courts or even the various modes of legal representation (lawyers, legal technicians and legal assistants)[45] and their organizations (the Bar Association and the IPAJ). We therefore need to summarize the basic institutional structure of the administration of justice, with some notes on the following categories of institutions: a) the managerial and consultative institutions of the judicial courts; b) the Ministry of Justice; c) the Administrative Court; and d) the Constitutional Council.

Table 6.2: The Main Institutional Structures of the Administration of Justice

Ministry of Justice	Responsible for the Prison Services, Registries and Notary Public services, Religious Affairs, Investigation and Legislation, inter-institutional legal advice to the Government, technical supervision of legislation drafted by other Ministries, awarding legal recognition to associations, foundations and political parties, articulation between the State and religious organizations. Responsible for the Law Reform Commission recently transformed into a Technical Unit for Law Reform (UTREL), the Centre for Legal and Judicial Training (CFJJ), and the IPAJ.
Judicial Courts	Consisting of a Supreme Court based in Maputo which began operating after 1989, 11 provincial judicial courts – including the City of Maputo Court – and about 90 of the 147 district judicial courts throughout the country. The judicial magistrates are appointed, promoted, removed or dismissed by the Superior Council of the Judiciary – the self-governing body of the judges – under the direction of the Chief Justice of the Supreme Court.
Constitutional Council	Responsible for weighing the constitutionality of laws and the illegality of other normative acts of state offices, assessing electoral complaints and appeals in the last instance and validating and proclaiming electoral results.
Administrative Court	Responsible for judging actions which have, as their aim, litigation resulting from administrative fiscal and customs matters and controlling the legality of administrative acts, in addition to inspecting the legality of the State Budget and public expenditure (the Court of Accounts).

Table 6.2: The Main Institutional Structures of the Administration of Justice (contd.)

General Attorney's Office	Responsible for initiating and carrying out legal actions, especially criminal proceedings; controls the legality of detentions, guarantees the protection of minors, absentees and the disabled, and defends and represents the interests of the state at central, provincial and district level.
Institute of Legal Assistance and Representation (IPAJ)	Guarantees access to justice and free legal assistance and defense to economically disadvantaged citizens. Dependent on the Ministry of Justice.
Bar Association	Created in September 1996, consisting only of law graduates (around 300 lawyers, the vast majority of whom are based in the city of Maputo).
Faculties of Law[46]	Currently under the guardianship of the Ministry of Education and Culture. Since the early 1990s several private universities have been offering law courses. The main Law Faculty, however, remains the one at Eduardo Mondlane University. In 2002 it had 947 students enrolled in daytime and evening courses (the Faculty also has a branch in Beira city). The undergraduate course lasts 4 years. In October 2002 a Masters course was also introduced,
Community Courts	Fully integrated into the Judicial System (as the local popular courts) until 1992. Since then, considered bodies for the extra-judicial resolution of minor disputes. Although supervision of the Community Courts has been assigned to the Ministry of Justice, these courts remain separate from the official justice bodies.

Source: Dagnino *et al.*, 1996; 1990 and 2004 Constitution; CFJJ/CES, 2004

The Management and Consultative Institutions of the Judicial Courts

In accordance with Law no. 10/92 of 6 May, management of the judicial organization is exercised by the Chief Justice of the Supreme Court and by the Judicial Council. This body – which normally meets once a year or else extraordinarily, whenever justified by circumstances and convened by the Chief Justice – includes the Deputy Chief Justice, the Justices and General Secretary of the Supreme Court and the Chief Judges of the provincial courts. It is their responsibility, amongst other important matters, to establish the guiding principles of judicial activity, assess their efficiency and consider and approve the plans, programs, and annual budget proposals of the courts. In addition to this body, a Consultative Council also operates at the level of the Supreme Court, consisting of the Chief Justice, Deputy Chief Justice, General Secretary and four other senior judicial individuals appointed by the Chief Justice. Its function is to analyze and issue opinions on matters submitted for its consideration.

In turn, the statutes of the Judicial Magistrates instituted the Superior Council of the Judiciary as a self-governing magistrates' organization, responsible for nominating, appointing, transferring, promoting and dismissing members, as well as evaluating professional merit and exercising disciplinary action.[47] It is composed of the Supreme Court Chief Justice, the Deputy Chief Justice, two members appointed by the President of the Republic, five elected by the Assembly of the Republic and seven members of the judicial system elected by their peers.[48]

The Ministry of Justice

After the courts and the General Attorney's Office became autonomous, the Ministry of Justice suffered a substantial reduction of its powers. It is responsible for legal reform, the community courts, the Prison Services (a responsibility which it shares with the Ministry of the Interior), the IPAJ, the Registry and Notary Public services, the editing of legislative texts and the supervision of legislation from other Ministries. Recently the Centre for Legal and Judicial Training was created within the Ministry and put in charge of training for all the legal professions and for socio-legal research into law and justice in Mozambique.

The Ministry of Justice Department of Research and Legislation is responsible for developing research into legal matters as well as compiling and publishing the main legislation of the country. Nevertheless, this Department has been practically inoperative in this respect for some years.

The Administrative Court

After the new 1990 Constitution came into force, the Administrative Court was revitalized. It decides on administrative litigation in a single instance (conflicts arising from administrative acts, mainly between the citizen and the state) and decides on appeals in fiscal and customs litigation. In addition to its jurisdictional competence, the Administrative Court is responsible for controlling the legality of administrative acts and inspecting the legality of public expenditure, thereby assuming the function of a Court of Accounts. This has, to date, been its main activity, giving the Administrative Court functions similar to those of the General State Auditor.

Having emerged from a period of stagnation and almost complete inaction, the Administrative Court is still in a phase of replenishing its human (magistrates and functionaries) and material resources. Some legislative measures have been taken in order to update its methods of operation and help it adjust to the new situation in the country. There still remains, however, an urgent need to reform the Administrative Code.[49]

The Administrative Court is not yet represented at provincial level, but three 'regional' administrative courts are planned (with competence for the provinces in the north, center and south of the country, respectively) when enough appropriately trained auditors are available.

5. University Law Education and Legal and Judicial Training Institutions

Universities Law Schools

An analysis of education and legal training is essential to an understanding of the performance of the courts and the reform agenda for the legal system. Having opened in 1975, shortly before independence, the Law Faculty at Eduardo Mondlane University was closed between 1983 and 1987, following a review of its academic curriculum. Now it offers daytime and evening law courses, the latter attended mainly by student-workers. Both courses last four years. In 2002, 947 students were enrolled in the Faculty of Law. The data available indicates that there is a growing demand for admission (in 2002 about 2,000 candidates applied for the 100 available daytime vacancies). Recently, this School – the oldest in the country – opened a branch in Beira city.

Whilst in the late 1990s one of the strongest criticisms of this Faculty was the low number of graduates (amounting to 32 in 1999), conditions have since improved, with a significant increase in the number of students graduating since 2002 (see below).

The curriculum, like others in the country, is very similar to the curricula of the European Law Faculties in the Roman-Germanic tradition. In other words, there is a strong emphasis on legal dogma and specialist legal-technical knowledge, with little emphasis on subjects or areas of study that provide an understanding of the plurality of legal orders in Mozambican society and the need for articulation between oral and written law, so that the social and cultural contexts in which each of these operates can be understood. The teaching of state criminal law is based on sanctions, yet the cultural practices of the people of Mozambique are based on reconciliation. The teaching of law must free itself from the strict formalist limits of a curriculum structure that is excessively dogmatic, reconciling expert legal knowledge with a general understanding of the production, function and conditions for the application of positive law. A multidisciplinary approach to the teaching of law which is able to reveal the social contexts underlying the norms and legal relations entails providing students with new working methods, encouraging active participation in teaching, teamwork, seminars, applied research or legal aid wherever needed. It also requires the introduction of new subjects which focus more on areas such as the History of Law, the Sociology of Law, the Anthropology of Law or the Philosophy of Law.

Very recently, the Eduardo Mondlane University's Law Faculty initiated a pilot legal clinic (the Law Practice Centre) in Maputo, so that students could put the knowledge they had acquired into practice, whilst granting legal aid to the more needy citizens.

Since the mid-nineties new Law Schools have opened, all in private universities. For example, the ISPU,[50] ISCTEM[51] and the Catholic University of Mozambique[52] – in various regions of the country – all offer law degrees. Therefore, in addition to students graduating in foreign countries, there has been a substantial increase in the number of law graduates in recent years, generating a wealth of lawyers for the private sector and a greater possibility of integrating law graduates into all levels of the state apparatus, namely the courts and state attorney offices.

As a result, there has been a dramatic increase in the number of law graduates. In 2003, 353 students graduated from the various Law Schools, 42% (147) of whom were from the Eduardo Mondlane University. In the same year over 2,300 students were enrolled in Law Schools (Ministério do Ensino Superior, Ciência e Tecnologia, 2004: 5-6, 10).[53]

The Center for Legal and Judicial Training

The scarcity, quality and fragmented nature of legal training created the need to establish a central entity responsible for the legal training of magistrates: the Centre for Legal and Judicial Training (CFJJ).[54] With the CFJJ, the coordination of training activities – previously undertaken separately by each judicial institution – was achieved, thereby contributing to the creation of a common legal culture for the various actors in the justice sector.

Created by Decree no. 34/97 of 21 October, the CFJJ provides initial, continuous and specific training for judges, prosecutors, justice officials, public defenders and other sector employees (for example, court registry office and public notary staff).

In order to complement the professional training that should be adapted to the country's circumstances, the CFJJ seeks to create a new profile for the magistrate, in which the normative and technical-bureaucratic culture is replaced with a legal, political and democratic culture – a culture that has justice as its strategy and, on this basis, makes it possible to handle legal cases and legal judicial activity advantageously. Justice is, therefore, strategically in the service of social cohesion and the deepening of democracy, which means effective respect for human rights.

The general principles behind this new training, selection and recruitment correspond, first and foremost, to an initial training that cannot be obtained within the Law Faculties alone.

The CFJJ also provides for the possibility of having magistrates whose initial training is not in law. This will be tried out in pilot projects, for example in the area of family, juvenile or labor law, and the profile of the judge must emerge from this intervention.

In short, this means that in-service and complementary training are becoming increasingly important.

Training must also be specialized, or contain periods of specialization within it. The number and quality of trained judges is inadequate. Whilst almost all the judges and prosecutors at provincial level are law graduates and have entered their professions after a period of specific training at the Centre for Judicial Studies in Lisbon or, more recently, at the CFJJ, there are very few graduate judges at district level; the rest have only received basic training. Hence, the CFJJ also offers improvement courses, moving away from the dogmatic and formalistic legal education provided by the Law Faculties and seeking to discuss with the trainees the real problems faced by citizens, for which they demand justice.

Increasingly, courts with specialized competence must also have specific forms of training, with specific entry conditions and specific exams – which is the case in the criminal instruction courts, the sentencing courts and the administrative, maritime, commercial, arbitration and fiscal courts.

The Centre was therefore designed to serve a new judicial, political and democratic culture. It is structured according to the following principles:

a) the CFJJ teachers are, as far as possible, people with a wide range of professional experience – internship should not just take place in the courts;

b) with regard to formal law, the judicial courts are not the only instances for settling conflicts in Mozambique; it is deemed important to acknowledge the complex legal reality that characterizes Mozambican society;

c) the computerization of the judicial system is a crucial process and it is therefore necessary to acquire some basic knowledge of information technology;

d) recruitment and selection have to be pluralistic;

e) evaluation and disciplinary systems must be strict, but always contain two phases: firstly, pedagogical evaluation, followed by corrective evaluation.

In addition, in order to complement a professional training that should reflect the country's circumstances, the Centre also undertakes research into the administration of formal and informal justice. Although it is one of the most recent institutions in the justice sector, the Centre already enjoys considerable prestige, has held many courses and training activities for a variety of judicial actors (including criminal investigation officers) and has assembled a group of highly qualified Mozambican trainers and researchers (including lawyers, anthropologists and sociologists).

Conclusion

The evolution of the organization of the judicial system from independence to the present mirrors the development of the political system and the legal-constitutional order of Mozambique. It is therefore possible to identify three periods in the evolution of the organization of the judicial system which can be defined as: a) post-independence (1975-1978); b) the judicial organization of the 'new legality' (1978-1992); c) the new judicial organization within the context of peace, political pluralism and a market economy, following the 1990 Constitution in which the separation of powers and the independence of the judicial system are enshrined (since 1992). After 2004 a new period began, based on the new constitutional principle of recognizing legal pluralism (Article 4).

In contemporary Mozambique, the Supreme Court manages the administration of the court system, including the lower district courts, as well as the provincial courts. The district courts suffer from a lack of human resources, as well as from insufficient financial and material resources. In addition, not all districts have a formally established and/or functioning official court.

The intermediate-level or provincial courts also suffer from a serious lack of both human and financial resources, although the judges who serve in them do have law degrees. Nonetheless, some of these courts are already operating with general and more specialized sections (civil, labor, and criminal instruction). Specialized courts also operate in Maputo city (Police and Juvenile courts).

The administration of official justice is not limited to the judicial courts, the community courts or even the various forms of legal representation (lawyers, legal technicians and legal assistants) and their organizations (the Bar Association and the IPAJ). The main institutional structure of the administration of justice is divided into the following categories of institutions: a) the managerial and consultative institutions of the judicial courts; b) the Ministry of Justice; c) the Administrative Court; d) the Constitutional Council.

In conclusion, it should also be noted that two important changes have taken place in recent years that are central to the development of the justice system in Mozambique. Firstly, new private and state Law Faculties have been opened (in Maputo, Beira, Quelimane and Nampula). Secondly, the Centre for Legal and Judicial Training has been established and is responsible for training judges and state attorneys, as well as other judicial officials. In the near future, this will provide more and better qualified human resources for the courts.

Notes

1   *Procuradoria Geral da República*, in Portuguese.
2   See also chapter 2, which presents an overview of the main political and legal changes in Mozambique.
3   Recently a new period was initiated, following the approval of new constitutional reforms (2004) which led to the recognition of legal pluralism in the country. Since the necessary – and long-awaited – reform of the judiciary is still in progress, this period will not be analyzed in this chapter.
4   The option was to build a unitary legal system within a unitary state, prompting a transitional process in which the new Law had to be constructed from the concrete

experience of conflict resolution at the local level. Although the 1975 Constitution did not contain any specific reference to customary law, several Frelimo directives on law reform pointed to the need to gather and study local customs for conflict resolution, as well as to the experience of the liberated areas during the struggle for independence.

5 Regions of Mozambique controlled by Frelimo during the struggle for independence. There, the nationalist leaders devised the entire strategy for future political and social development of the country.

6 On this period of popular justice, see Sachs and Welsh (1990); Gundersen and Berg (1991); Gundersen (1992).

7 These judges were elected directly, by the community.

8 See also note 27 in chapter 2.

9 This situation was to change with the 1990 Constitution and with the present Organic Law of the Judicial Courts (Law no. 10/92 of 6 May), as we shall see later. After the constitutional reforms of the early 1990s, elected judges could only intervene in decisions on matters of fact and lower court trials. The 2004 Constitution reaffirms, in Article 216, the principle of the participation of elected judges in court, maintaining their intervention in lower court hearings and decisions on matters of fact (no. 2). This article imposes some conditions on their participation, by affirming that their presence will "be compulsory in cases where procedural law requires it, or when the trial judge so decides, when the Attorney's office recommends it or when the parties request it" (no. 3).

10 This system of using lay judges elected by assemblies representing the people to exercise judicial functions is not unique to the Republic of Mozambique. There is also, for example, the case of the former Soviet Union, in Terebilov (1978), or even the social judges which Portuguese legislation admits in jurisdiction relating to Labor, the Family and Minors; in the latter case, the jury can intervene, at the request of the interested parties, in penal judgments.

11 The colonial *escudo* was replaced by the *metical* – the new Mozambican currency – in 1980.

12 In this section of the chapter, legal references without further specification belong to Law no. 12/78 of 2 December.

13 The equivalent of the High Court.

14 Until the beginning of the 1990s, Mozambique had a single party political system.

15 See Law no. 4/92 of 6 May, which created the community courts. This topic is analyzed in detail in chapter 10.

16 The base of the formal judicial system became the district courts, with the creation of 1st and 2nd class district courts envisaged, in addition to the provincial courts and the Supreme Court (Law no. 10/92 of 6 May).

17 For example the labor courts, which replaced the former Labor Commissions of Justice (Law no. 18/92 of 14 October).

18 *Instituto de Patrocínio e Assistência Jurídica* – IPAJ, in Portuguese. On this subject see chapters 2 and 9.

19 See Laws no. 6 and 7/94 of 13 and 14 September, respectively.

20 This constitutional guarantee becomes extremely important when we look at the history of post-independence Mozambique. The 1975 Constitution, incomplete in terms of basic rights, allowed the creation of the Revolutionary Military Court. This aimed to combat crimes which threatened the political, social and economic order of the country. It is known that this Court, albeit in another political context, eventually threatened some guarantees which nowadays are considered inalienable (for example, the right to defense and protest, the right to a retrial by appeal, etc.) and sanctioned the death penalty.

21 The scenario of law and justice during the period from independence to the end of the eighties was dominated by extreme institutional simplicity and strong centrality. The Ministry of Justice was in control and was responsible for the courts, public prosecution, the defense and representation service and the prison system. There was a single line of command and a unitary policy on building justice, dominated by a concern to create popular courts as bodies for the administration of justice. The goal was both to resolve conflict and to educate citizens in the new values that needed to be affirmed and imposed.

22 Now the Assembly of the Republic.

23 Since then, the Supreme Court proposes a budget to the Ministry of Finance, which draws up the final budget.

24 But the President of the Republic appoints the Chief Justice and the Deputy-Chief Justice of the Supreme Court, and the Chief Justice of the Supreme Tribunal then proceeds with the investiture of the President of the Republic. The appointment of the Chief Justice and Deputy-Chief Justice is ratified by the Assembly of the Republic. The other professional Justices in the Supreme Court are appointed by the President of the Republic on the advice of the Superior Council of the Judiciary (which, apart from the automatic inclusion of the Chief Justice and Deputy-Chief Justice of the Supreme Court, also consists of two members designated by the President of the Republic, five elected by the Assembly of the Republic and seven members of the judiciary elected by their peers – Article 221 of the 2004 Constitution).

25 At this point, citations from legal norms which are otherwise unspeccified belong to Law no. 10/92 of 6 May.

26 The Juvenile Court only functions in Maputo city, with competence in civil matters (maintenance, attribution of paternal power, recognition of paternity, among other matters). In 2000, the criminal section, which was to deal with juveniles below the age of criminal responsibility (under 16 years of age), was not operating.

27 At the time, the exchange rate for 1 US$ was about 12,000 *meticais*. Nowadays, it is about 24,000 *meticais*.

28 Most of the district judges however, have only had an *ad hoc* training lasting six months to one year, initially organized by the Supreme Court and later by the Centre for Legal and Judicial Training (CFJJ). Only a few district courts have judges with a law degree, although the number is on the increase.

29 In 2000, the districts which did not have courts were: eight in the province of Cabo Delgado (Ibo, Mecúfi, Meluco, Quissanga, Balama, Muidumbe, Nangade and Pemba-Cidade); seven in Niassa (Majube, Mecula, Muembe, N'gauma, Metarica, Nipepe and Lichinga-cidade); one in Nampula (Nacaroa); three in Tete (Chiúta, Tsangano and Chifunda); three in Manica (Tambara, Macossa and Chimoio-cidade); four in Sofala (Chemba, Chibabava, Maringuè and Muanza); four in Inhambane (Mabote, Jangamo, Funhalouro and Inhambane city); three in Gaza (Xai-Xai, Chigubo and Massangena) and two in the city of Maputo (municipal districts 2 and 3).

30 The court in the city of Beira (with district powers) functions as the 3rd Criminal Section of the judicial court of the province of Sofala (Law no. 12/78). According to information provided by the Chief Judges of the judicial courts of Zambezi and Nampula provinces, the 2nd Criminal sections of the provincial judicial courts function as judicial courts with district powers (information from February 1998).

31 In 2003, besides the 11 provincial courts, the Supreme Court Statistics Department reported the existence of 105 district courts (including city courts). However, during the research carried out in 2004 we observed that some of the district courts were not operating.

32 These judges were not elected according to the principles established in the Organic Law of the Judicial Courts, but appointed from amongst worthy local candidates.

33 This information was obtained during the second part of the research project. See José *et al.*, 2004.

34 Dagnino *et al.*, (1996) refers to the existence of 147 district courts.

35 The creation of labor sections fulfills a legal requirement and is also part of Law no. 18/92, of 14 October. The criminal instruction sections derive from Law no. 2/93, of 24 June.

36 The 2004 Constitution does not refer to the possibility of incorporating elected judges into the Supreme Court (Article 226), as opposed to the earlier 1990 constitution. The latter specifically stated, in article 170 no. 1, that "the Supreme Court shall be composed of professional judges and elected judges". The participation of elected judges may occur in lower trial court hearings, and upon request, as determined by law.

37 Personnel from the Justice Department now come under the General Attorney's Office.

38 In addition to judicial courts, Article 167 of the 1990 Constitution envisaged administrative, military, customs, fiscal, maritime and labor courts, the majority of which are still not in operation. Article 223 of the 2004 Constitution defines the existence of several categories of courts: the Supreme Court, the Administrative

Court, and the courts of justice. It also recognizes the possibility of administrative, labor, fiscal, customs, admiralty, arbitration and community courts.

39 As the Council began operating in 2003, it was not included in our initial research and therefore we only comment briefly on its activities.

40 In August 2000, after one of the Judges was appointed Attorney-General, only six Justices remained in the Supreme Court. In 2003 two new Justices were nominated, including the first woman Justice in Mozambique.

41 Those responsible for the departments are ordinary-ranking functionaries but, in fact, up to 2000 only the DAPF had an appointed head. The organization of the Supreme Court establishes two more divisions, both under the DAPF: General Administration, and Patrimony and Finance, which, however, are still not in operation. The DHR is basically responsible for managing the non-specialist personnel working in the courts. In relation to magistrates, all matters are now the responsibility of the Superior Council of the Judiciary, which has its own individual procedures. As far as justice officials are concerned (notaries and bailiffs), responsibilities are shared between the Superior Council itself, which "evaluates professional merit and exercises disciplinary actions" over justice officials, and the DHR/DRH of the Supreme Court, which is responsible for appointing them. The DAPF has similar duties to those existing in other state departments, particularly in the Ministries. However, in the case of the Supreme Court, it shares some responsibilities with the Treasury. The DILS compiles the statistical data received from the provincial judicial courts and the sections of the Supreme Tribunal itself and publishes them annually as Legal Statistics. This department, however, operates under great difficulty, due to the fact that it has no specialized staff and there are no reliable controls on the trustworthiness of the data received from the provinces. It may be said that this has been a neglected area to date, which is only occasionally revitalized, usually around the beginning of the judicial year (Dagnino *et al.*, 1996).

42 The Provincial Attorney's Offices and the District Attorney's Offices are peripheral bodies of the General Attorney's Office.

43 The Attorney-General informs the Assembly of the Republic annually on the activities of the body of state attorneys, the crime situation in the country and initiatives to prevent and fight crime.

44 The report also stated that the registry office had received 525 cases and decided over 448 cases from the Supreme Court, provincial and district attorneys.

45 The bill for the Decree which will create a new system for access to justice and to the law recognizes paralegal staff – whether professionals or volunteers without a university degree – who will "be especially trained to work in the future 'Centers for access to justice'".

46 This subject is covered in more detail below.

47 Articles 220 and 222 of the 2004 Constitution.

48 Article 221 of the 2004 Constitution.

49 It is not our intention here to go into the full details of the functions of the Ministry of Justice, since those that are of interest to this study (the IPAJ and the Community Courts) will be covered in greater detail elsewhere. Administrative justice is not the object of this study, and for this reason we have limited ourselves to a few brief observations.

50 The *Instituto Superior Politécnico e Universitário*, which offers a four-year law course. It awarded its first bachelor degrees in 2000.

51 The *Instituto Superior de Ciências e Tecnologia de Moçambique*, which offers a four-year law course.

52 The UCM law course lasts five years, including an introductory year of general studies. The UCM Law Faculty awarded its first bachelor degrees in 2000.

53 Early in 2002, Masters courses were also introduced into some of the Law Faculties, including at Eduardo Mondlane University.

54 *Centro de Formação Jurídica e Judiciária*, in Portuguese. The CFJJ depends on the Ministry of Justice, although it holds administrative autonomy. Most of its activities are funded by international organizations (on the subject of foreign aid to the justice system, see also chapter 7).

7

The Courts in Action:
Functions, Resources, Case Flow
and Characterization of Litigation

João Pedroso, João Carlos Trindade,
Maria Manuel Leitão Marques and André Cristiano José

Introduction

The Functions of the Court in Contemporary Societies

In contemporary societies courts have different types of functions. Three main functions may be distinguished: instrumental, political and symbolic. In complex and functionally differentiated societies, the instrumental functions are those which are specifically attributed to a given sphere of social action and which are said to be fulfilled when the said sphere operates effectively within its own functional limits. The political functions are those through which the sector-based spheres of social action contribute towards maintaining the political system. Finally, the symbolic functions are the set of social orientations which the different spheres of social action use to contribute towards the maintenance or destruction of the social system, as a whole.

The instrumental functions of the courts are as follows: the resolution of conflict, social control, administrative acts and the creation of law. Resolution of individual or collective conflicts is the aim of court activity. Social control is the set of measures – internalized or imposed – that are adopted within a given society in order to prevent individual actions from deviating significantly from the overall pattern of sociability, which, for this reason, is called the social order. The social control function of the courts relates to their specific contribution in maintaining the social order and restoring it when it is violated (Santos *et al.*, 1996: 51-52).

The administrative functions refer to a series of actions which involve neither the resolution of conflict nor social control (processes which merely involve certification in situations in which there is no litigation or non-judicial functions are carried out by magistrates).

An analysis of the performance of the courts in terms of penal justice corresponds therefore to an analysis of the effectiveness of the judicial system within the area of social control. This becomes more problematic when the pace of social change becomes increasingly rapid. The judicial system – with its institutional, normative and bureaucratic weight – has always experienced difficulties in adapting to new situations involving deviant behavior. Control of corruption and transnational crime are good examples of the difficulties in adaptation faced by judicial systems.

Political systems can live with high levels of so-called common criminality, but not with organized crime, political crime and crimes committed by politicians during or as a result of the exercise of their functions, as in the case of corruption. The impunity of this type of criminality, beyond certain limits, threatens the system's own conditions for reproduction. In exercising social control, the courts – as sovereign bodies – are also exercising an eminently political function, either through repression or through the selective way in which they act.

Besides being instrumental and political, the control function is also symbolic, since it acts on values recognized as being particularly important to the normal reproduction of a society (the values of life, physical integrity, honor, ownership, etc.). Effective action in this domain has the effect of confirming the values that have been violated. Since citizens' rights, when internalized, tend to become the basis for concepts of retributive and distributive justice, the guarantee that the courts protect these rights usually tends to have the powerful effect of a symbolic confirmation (Santos *et al.*, 1996: 52 and ff.).

The political functions of the courts do not only extend to social control. Recourse to the courts by citizens for civil, labor, administrative matters, etc. always implies exercising an awareness of rights and, in this sense, it is a means of exercising citizenship and political participation. In democratic societies the extent of the legitimacy of the political system also depends on the quality of the courts' performance and, consequently, whether they function independently and are accessible, quick and effective.

In this, and the following chapter, our analysis of the human, material and financial resources of the judicial system, litigation (*i.e.* the conflicts that are brought before the courts) and the main constraints on the system will enable us to assess the performance of the courts in exercising their functions and in relation to the exercise of citizenship in Mozambique.

1. A Characterization of the Resources of the Judicial System

Human Resources in the Courts

It is generally accepted that human resources – the judges, state attorneys, functionaries and justice officials – are insufficient and that they are not adequately qualified. In addition, the staffing is inappropriate for the situation in Mozambique, with an 'unrealistic' number of professional posts and categories. With the exception of those commanded by the Supreme Court Justices, salaries are demoralizingly low, and frequently are not paid on time. In addition, elected judges spend long periods of time without receiving any compensation and their fees are very low.

According to Dagnino *et al.* (1996), in 1996 the Supreme Court considered that Mozambique needed more than 200 judges with academic training to get the judicial organization into good working order. In 1996 there were scarcely more than 120 judges in existence; in 2003 this number had risen to 159.[1] Of these (including the eight Justices in the Supreme Court), only a small number (27) were law graduates in 1996; in 2003 the figure had doubled (56).[2]

Table 7.1: Provisional Analysis of Judges (from official courts)

Courts	Estimate
Supreme Court (6 Court Registry Offices: 2 Civil, 2 Criminal, 1 Labor, 1 Military)	14
Provincial Courts (Civil, Criminal, Juvenile, Police and Criminal Instruction)	56
Provincial Labor Courts	12
District Courts (160 Court Registry Offices, Civil and Criminal)	160
District Courts (147 sections, Criminal Instruction)	147
Total	389

Source: Decree no. 40/93 of 31/12; Law no.18/92 of 14 October and Dagnino *et al.*, 1996.

The first question we should pose in relation to the provincial courts is whether at this stage in the development of the Mozambican judicial system it is necessary to have a criminal instruction judge (*i.e.*, a judge in charge of pre-sentence investigation) and a labor judge in all the provincial judicial courts. In light of the analysis of the movement of cases which we are about to present, it is certainly not a priority that all these positions should be filled.

In the mid 1990s, of the 39 provincial judges appointed, only 20 were law graduates. This number includes those who had finished the academic part of their course in the Law Faculty at Eduardo Mondlane University and were waiting to defend their final dissertation. Of the rest, some had only attended a one- or two-year course, whilst the others were judges who had had no higher education but had attended *ad hoc* courses organized by the district magistrate training program.

As far as the district magistrates were concerned, they supplied around 47% of the total number needed. This figure is reached by considering that 147 district courts should have been in existence, with a total of 160 court offices or sections. It does not take into account the labor courts and criminal instruction judges at district level (Dagnino *et al.*, 1996). A strict application of Decree no. 40/93 of 31 December and Law no. 18/92 of 14 October would imply a labor court and criminal instruction section in each district court, which would mean that 454 judges would be needed to serve in the total number of existing and planned district courts. Direct observations from our case study revealed, on the one hand, a conviction that this number of judges was not necessary and was even absurd and, on the other hand, that we are not sure of the needs of the district courts in all districts.[3]

In fact, from the point of view of training, the picture has changed over the last decade. In 1996 most judges had only had an *ad hoc* training, acquired through courses organized either at a central or provincial level, with some having benefited from additional training programs. More recently, after the Centre for Legal and Judicial Training was created, many district judges benefited from more specific training. In 1996, in addition to the existing 76 district judges, there were also eight substitute judges who carried out their duties without possessing the status of a magistrate and without any specific legal training. They were very experienced elected judges or court clerks. In 2003, the data available suggested that the number of judges with *ad hoc* training had been reduced to about one hundred.

The number of judges trained in law is still far from ideal to ensure the functioning of the judicial sector under the terms envisaged by the law, with citizens' rights guaranteed and defended. It is therefore imperative to establish a plan for recruiting or contracting judicial magistrates in accordance with particular priorities, which will have to be defined.[4]

This aspect will have to merit special attention, since it will have to be balanced against many other factors such as the availability of funds to pay the magistrates and justice officials who have been contracted, the availability of the officials themselves, and the existence of premises for courts and residences for magistrates, court clerks and other court officials (Dagnino *et al.*, 1996).

However, recruiting magistrates is not easy, bearing in mind the unattractive salaries.[5] In 1998, magistrates' salaries varied from between a maximum of 8 to10 million *meticais* at the top of the scale, to around 1,700,0.00 *meticais* for first class judges and a minimum of 650,000,00 *meticais* for district judges. To this basic salary were added the emoluments derived from the income of the courts (on average a few hundred thousand *meticais*) and the extra benefits established in the Statute of Judicial Magistrates: housing, water, electricity, telephone (up to a certain limit) and a vehicle. However, due to the scarcity of resources, these benefits very often did not materialize, which prevented judges from being assured of a standard of living which, if not equal to, was at least sufficiently competitive with what they could obtain in other professions with the same or equivalent training.

Although by 2004 the picture had significantly improved, much more still needs to be done. It would not be an exaggeration to state that if decent conditions are not created for judicial magistrates at all levels of the profession – as well as for the magistrates in the General Attorney's Office – the country runs the risk of having weaker magistrates and jurists who are less well prepared academically, intellectually and culturally and who lack the solid moral training that will prevent them from incorrectly exercising the immense power they wield.

The number of judicial employees is still clearly insufficient and they are not adequately trained.

According to statements made by the Chief Judges and the court clerks in the respective provincial courts, the main bottlenecks in terms of personnel concern bailiffs and court clerks or assistant court clerks — the posts which demand greater knowledge of civil and criminal proceedings in general.

Moreover, the staff requirements established in Decree no. 40/93 of 31 December impose levels of specialization and specific qualifications that are unrealistic considering the overall administrative situation in the country.

The salaries, privileges and general working conditions established by law for justice officials and functionaries are clearly inadequate to guarantee quality professional work and, consequently, the correct, effective and transparent implementation of justice.

Material Resources in the Judicial System (Infrastructures and Equipment)

In addition to the aforementioned problems pertaining to the human resources allocated to justice in Mozambique, there are other serious problems related to the infrastructure, support equipment and materials needed for the work of magistrates and justice officials.

The management of justice administration premises is an issue that has been resolved in various ways over time. From the proclamation of independence in 1975 until the end of the 1980s, the courts and attorneyships were subordinate to the Ministry of Justice. When these institutions were declared independent of the Government in 1989, it was subsequently decided that assets should be shared. In practice, and with the exception of some residences belonging to the Courts' Fund (the revenue from the courts) which were retained by some magistrates from the General Attorney's Office, all assets went to the courts (the working premises) and to the respective magistrates (the housing). It is, however, important to mention that, with the nationalization of real estate in 1976, the Courts' Fund lost many residences which were transferred to APIE[6] management. Some of these have already been recovered, while others are still in the process of being reclaimed.

The Supreme Court is installed in the state building where the highest body of judicial power in Mozambique has always functioned – including the former Courts of Appeals from the colonial period and, in the immediate post-independence era, the Appeals High Court (from 1979 to 1988).[7] In the 1990s, with financing from the General State Budget (GSB), a new building was constructed next to the old one, where the Supreme Court now operates. In the provinces, the courts usually operate in premises separate from the attorneyships, although at the district level the two institutions quite often share the same building. Of the eleven provincial courts, only the Zambézia Provincial Court has its own premises, rented from the *Banco Comercial de Moçambique*.[8] Similarly, in the late 1990s, of the 92 district judicial courts, 50 rented premises from the APIE, which serve as courts and magistrates' residences.

The management of property assets relating to the Supreme Court and the other courts is undertaken by the Courts' Fund, which also manages the revenue from judicial services. It should be mentioned, however, that the creation of a Property Assets Management Office is envisaged within the structure of the Supreme Court, which we feel is laudable. This structure is to be entrusted with managing investments established as part of a project financed by DANIDA,[9] which basically consisted of building courts and residences for judges in 20 districts in the country. It remains to be seen whether the management of the current assets will continue to be the responsibility of the Courts' Fund or whether this will also be transferred to the Office that is to be created.[10]

It is also important to look at property that is connected to the services, either at central or peripheral level. Although in 1996 there was no Supreme Court inventory (Dagnino *et al.*, 1996), the Court does possess, in addition to furniture, reasonable office equipment, including a certain number of computers which are used by the Justices, among others, for writing up their decisions. The provincial courts possess at least one computer, a printer and a fax machine, whilst the district courts do not possess any of this type of equipment, apart from some ancient manual typewriters.[11] The most distant courts are centrally supplied with cars and office equipment. However, in general, resources are bought locally.

The Financial Resources of the Judicial System

The judicial system is financed by the current and investment budgets of the Supreme Court and the Ministry of Justice (GSB), revenue from the courts (the Courts' Fund) and foreign aid (DANIDA,[12] UNDP,[13] the World Bank,[14] USAID,[15] etc.).[16]

With the 1990 Constitution – establishing the separation of powers and the independence of the courts – the judicial system started to attract substantial attention from external donors. The subsequent peace process and its consolidation through the first multiparty elections made it clear that the stability desired by the country also required the strengthening of public institutions, including the justice institutions. 'Good governance' and 'strengthening democratic institutions' became the new banners for international assistance, which considered them a prerequisite and guarantee of the success of other initiatives carried out in the more traditional development aid sectors. Consequently, the 1980s tendency to see the state and its institutions as an obstacle to the liberalization of the economy began to change, and the 1990s were generally characterized by the incorporation of international aid measures aimed at institutional capacity building, since institutions had seen a consistent reduction in their operating capacity during the previous period.

Additionally, at the same time the judicial institutions themselves became more open to international cooperation. One of the reasons for this lies in the serious crisis the sector was experiencing during the 1990s. Human resources in the provincial courts had become increasingly weaker, both in terms of numbers and quality and the district courts were largely paralyzed or left to their own devices as a consequence of the war. There was a situation of almost total collapse that the State budget could not resolve on its own.

In recent years, despite a gradual rise in public expenditure on the justice sector, it is still an open question whether the judiciary is a high priority for the state. In fact, in real terms, GSB funding for the sector has remained almost unaltered, thus blocking any real perspectives for the growth and expansion of the judicial network in the country.

In 1996, the Salaries and Operational Fund which the GSB attributed to the Supreme Court and the General Attorney's Office amounted to 1.9% and 1.3% respectively of the total state budget. In relation to the provinces, the percentage of the provincial budget attributed to the courts (including the district courts) ranged from a minimum of 1.1% in the Zambézia province to a maximum of 2.9% in the Manica province, while that of the Attorney's Offices varied from between 0.6% in Zambézia to 1.7% in the Cabo Delgado province.

In 1996, 26.2% of the Supreme Court's budget was for salaries and 73.8% for expenses such as equipment and services. In the same year, the investments budget amounted to 23,728,000,000,000 *meticais*, designated for the renovation of the Maputo City Court, equipment for the Supreme Court, renovation of the old Supreme Court building and the beginning of construction work on the new provincial courts of Maputo, Inhambane, Zambézia and Niassa, with the construction of a district court also envisaged (Dagnino *et al.*, 1996).

Between 1996 and 1998, the allocation of public funds established by the GSB for the Supreme Court continued to grow, especially the funds designated for salaries, which increased by approximately 100% between 1996 and 1997. Between 1996 and 1997 there was also a significant increase in funds for the acquisition of goods and services, amounting to nearly 30%.

The Courts' Fund

In addition to the revenue from the GSB, the biggest source of income for the courts is from judicial costs and from the fines levied in civil cases (court costs) and infringements of the law (punished by fines), respectively. Of these, 40% of the respective amount goes to the state (via the Ministry of Finance), while the remaining 60% is allocated to the payment of functionaries and to cover other costs related to building maintenance and the current expenses of the courts, since the GSB funds are not sufficient to cover this. This income is managed by the Courts' Fund,[17] an institution considered a self-governing body of the judiciary, although its independence has proved damaging to the sector, as the majority of its income came from court registry offices. Housed in a small office in the Maputo City Court, the Courts' Fund is managed by an Administrative Council which should consist of two Justices from the Supreme Court (one acting as President and the other as First Spokesperson) and one representative from the General Attorney's Office, acting as Second Spokesperson. In reality, since 1992 the Administrative Council has functioned solely with a President, who is a Justice from the Supreme Court. Outside the Supreme Court, each duly constituted Court has a Treasury delegation that functions under the same criteria.

In 1994, the total revenue of the Courts' Fund was around 391 million *meticais*, whilst in 1995 it was close to 400 million *meticais*. Due to the fact that the amounts charged in the Code of Courts' Costs are completely out of date, this income cannot approach the levels which in previous times had enabled the Justice Treasury to make important investments, even if productivity increased in the courts.[18]

It is therefore through the income of the Courts' Fund that the magistrates and functionaries supplement their (meager) salaries. In the Supreme Court, as there is a common fund the magistrates received a fixed emolument of 100,000 *meticais* per month in the late 1990s. In the provinces, on the contrary, emoluments are linked to the income of each section and magistrates and functionaries therefore receive an 'addition' to their salary according to their productivity. Additionally, current expenses are always covered by this income when GSB funding runs out (Dagnino *et al.*, 1996).

Under these circumstances, external aid and loans are one of the conditions that allow for a more rapid development of the judicial system.

2. The Case Flow: Cases filed and closed by the courts

Case flow is understood to mean the variation in the number of cases filed, pending and closed. The cases filed correspond to the effective demand for the judicial system. The cases closed show the supply of judicial protection. The pending cases are a measure of unsatisfied judicial demand. An analysis of the evolution of the case flow must take into account two sets of factors: endogenous and exogenous factors. Endogenous factors are those inherent to the system, namely legislative, substantive or procedural legal changes, and institutional or technical changes. Exogenous factors are those outside the system, such as social, economic, political and cultural changes and their impact on the administration of justice in general and on the case flow in particular.

Due to a variety of statistical incoherencies and inconsistencies, the statistics on justice prepared by the Supreme Court initially only allowed for an indicative analysis of the period between 1992 and 1998. Later, more recent data was obtained (extending up to 2003), which is used here for the purposes of comparison. In addition, the data is limited to case flows in the Supreme Court and in the provincial courts (cases filed, pending and closed).

An Overview of the Procedural Case Flow in the Provincial Courts

Between 1992 and 1998 there was a reduction in the number of cases brought before the provincial courts. A rise in cases filed since 1994 occurred in the provincial courts of Tete, Manica, Sofala, Gaza and the city of Maputo, particularly in the Maputo Juvenile and Police courts, with the latter having been in operation since 1996. Between 2002 and 2003 we observed a decrease of 7.3% in the number of cases filed in provincial courts, from 23,618 cases in 2002, to 21,884 cases filed the following year.

Between 1992 and 1998 there was a significant rise in the number of cases pending, from 83,932 to 115,369. This increase occurred both in civil and criminal litigation, and reveals the declining efficiency of the provincial courts, where, in 1992, 14,451 cases were closed, as opposed to 12,368 in 1998. This situation is particularly evident in the Maputo City Court, where the cases pending accounted for over half the total number of cases pending in the provincial courts.[19] By contrast, in 2002 and 2003 the situation had changed radically, with the vast majority of cases pending being from the Police Court (about 26%). The next provincial courts with significant percentages of cases pending were Zambézia (14.3%) and Maputo city (14.1%).

It should also be noted in this context that there are qualitative differences in court performance in relation to cases pending, filed and closed, with some courts closing relatively larger numbers of cases than others.

The Case Flow of Criminal Jurisdiction in the Provincial Courts

More than half of the litigation handled by the provincial courts involves criminal complaints. For example, in 1998, 18,981 criminal proceedings were brought before these courts, corresponding to 80.9% of the total number of cases filed in the judicial system. In 2003 this figure dropped to 57%, due to a marked increase in civil and labor actions brought before the courts.

Between 1992 and 1998, the number of criminal proceedings filed decreased (from 20,210 to 18,981) but an increase was registered in cases pending (from 70,249 to 92,130). The amount of cases closed varied, in some instances registering a significant increase and sometimes a reduction.

Between 1992 and 1996 the amount of criminal proceedings filed decreased markedly and only approached the initial (1992) level in 1998. The period between 2002 and 2003 witnessed a continuing reduction in the number of criminal proceedings filed, with 13,560 cased filed in 2002 and 12,637 the following year. One possible explanation is the deteriorating performance of the Police and the General Attorney's Office following changes to the state and in society (the peace process, the market economy, the destabilization of the administration), as it is highly unlikely that crime fell sharply during this period.

Between 1992 and 1998 an increase was registered in the number of proceedings involving serious crimes,[20] which became more marked after 1996. The largest number of cases filed was at the Maputo City Court. However, the numbers were also significant in the provinces of Nampula, Manica, Zambézia and Tete which, in 1998, together represented 40.9% of the total number of cases filed. The data available indicates that in 2003 the situation remained the same.

In general, the number of felony cases[21] filed and closed decreased, whilst pending cases increased significantly. In fact, in 1992, there were around 2,453 cases pending and in 1998 this figure had almost doubled to 4,065. Contrary to the other forms of criminal litigation, relatively few cases were brought before the Maputo City Court, with the Provincial Court of Sofala having the largest number of cases. Ten years later the picture was quite different: in 2002 there were 1,026 cases pending and, a year later, the figure had fallen to 1,161 cases, the heaviest concentrations occurring with the provincial courts of Manica, Zambézia, Niassa and Nampula.[22]

The Case Flow for Civil Jurisdiction in the Provincial Courts

Civil jurisdiction, which includes civil litigation *per se* together with labor litigation, also accounts for a substantial proportion of the cases heard in the Maputo City Court. Together with Maputo, the provinces witnessing a rise in the general movement of cases filed were Sofala and Nampula.

In short, an analysis of case flows reveals an increase in civil demand between 1992 and 1998 and the rise in this type of litigation is, in itself, enough to explain the huge increase in the number of cases pending. It means that procedural delay has become one of the problems affecting the legitimacy of the judicial system in Mozambique today, in addition to the other problems that have intensified during the same period of time.

The ratio between the number of cases closed and the number of cases pending and filed provides an index of the system's efficiency. Thus, in 1992, the index was 7.49, and in 1998, 11.22, although in 2003 the index had lowered to 6.50. This suggests that whilst inefficiency was on the rise in the provincial courts in the late 1990s, it seems to be improving in the early twenty-first century.

The Case Flow of the Supreme Court

The performance of the Supreme Court has been characterized by a singular inability to respond to solicitations. Less than 300 cases are brought before the Supreme Court every year. Although the cases filed have registered varying figures – 102 in 1992, 213 in 1996, 218 in 2002 and 171 in 2003 – over the same period the number of cases pending has increased steadily (524 in 1992, 934 in 1998, 1,121 in 2002 and 1,013 in 2003). The number of cases closed is quite low, even insignificant. In 1996 only 52 cases were closed, although this figure rose to 123 in 2002, only to drop dramatically to 43 in 2003. The number of cases pending has risen in all areas of litigation.

Unlike the provincial courts, where most proceedings are criminal, most of the appeals heard in the Supreme Court are related to civil and labor matters. Thus, in 1998, 25 criminal appeals and 160 civil and labor appeals were filed in the Supreme Court, with 450 criminal proceedings and 477 civil and labor proceedings pending. In 2003, the pattern remained similar: the majority of appeals were civil (368 proceedings, corresponding to 32.8%) and labor (327 proceedings, corresponding to 29.2%) cases.

This is obviously due to a demand for the Supreme Court by litigants with economic interests who lodge appeals against civil and labor actions of significant economic status. Despite a few highly publicized cases of social, economic and political significance, on the whole criminal litigation involves crimes committed by ordinary citizens, or situations of social or virtual exclusion. The Supreme Court is unable to satisfy the demand – more than 50% of which comes from the Maputo City Court. The increase in the number of cases pending is in line with the general opinion amongst judges and lawyers that the Supreme Court is a 'burial ground for cases'.

3. The Characterization of Judicial Litigation in Mozambique

As mentioned earlier in chapter 5, the research team created a form for gathering data that was used to categorize the conflicts brought before the courts, as well as the people who used the courts. This form was used for the Supreme Court and the provincial and district courts in order to gather a sample of the cases, whose analysis helped to characterize the litigation and the litigants who made use of the courts.

Civil Justice in the Provincial Courts

Civil justice in Mozambique, together with other systems of justice, benefits from great structural stability. Despite differences in procedural and substantive law and in levels of development, the different systems of civil justice tend to present very similar configurations in relation to their essential features, both in terms of the types of users and most frequent types of litigation, and in their operational problems.[23]

This relative homogeneity, however, masks important differences in degree which reveal themselves in almost all the variables usually used to characterize civil justice and which can be detected in a more detailed analysis of the litigation and the organization of the judicial system in its proper context.

In the vast majority of civil judicial systems the major types of litigation consist of payment of debts, family litigation (particularly divorce cases), labor litigation and litigation involving property. However, the relative weight of each of these types of litigation varies greatly and the extent of this variation can significantly modify the characterization of civil justice.

If the payment of debts is dominant, justice serves regular, collective users, whereas if family or leasing issues predominate – as is the case in Mozambique – the majority of litigants are individual and occasional users. Although in all systems, lawyers prefer civil cases or drafting contracts to being involved in criminal cases, the results of this preference can be very different: either the latter cases are usually not defended by professionals or they are dealt with by the least well-known or experienced lawyers.[24]

Civil Justice and Economic Development

The true profile of civil justice in each country is also marked by differences in degree which are registered in other problems – usually considered common to almost all systems – such as excessive slowness and delays in proceedings, the frequency and magnitude of corruption cases, the lack of resources or the high cost of access to justice. The greater or lesser availability of either formal or informal alternative means of resolving litigation is another relevant factor in the analysis of similarities and differences and, above all, in the study of reforms which could improve the resolution of litigation in the different areas in which they occur.

Only a study of this type enables us to accurately define the common and specific problems in each system and find adequate solutions for them, which may combine those already used in other countries – with all the necessary adjustments – with solutions of our own, forged out of local experiences and resources, or purposely designed in response to very specific problems.

The table which follows (table 7.2) is the result of an exercise comparing the main characteristics of civil justice in the more developed market economies and consumer societies with market economies in a phase of consolidation (including any possible reforms which may be aimed at them), known respectively as cases A and B. For case B, we have taken civil justice in Mozambique as our example.[25]

Some differences are enduring and difficult to overcome in the short term, which confers a structural quality on them. Others are only transitory and evidence shows that they will diminish or disappear in the short or medium term.

Among the structural differences, the context of the judicial system should be singled out. In the first example (case A), this context is characterized by weak legal plurality (Santos, 1995; Castrillo, 1997), since the official judicial system clearly predominates in the resolution of litigation. In the second example (case B), legal plurality is strong, with different laws and means of resolution – particularly those of an informal nature – competing with each other.

Equally hard to overcome in the short term is the difficulty in increasing resources, particularly financial, for public service. This problem is common to both cases, but is much more serious in the second. The persistent lack of resources will make it difficult to extend access to justice, particularly in terms of the potential rural demand in case B.

Above all, these two differences – the context of the legal system and its resources – end up by consolidating the merely formal centrality of the judicial system in B, which is valued more from the top-down (in the organization of political power, in the constitutional text and in the hierarchy of the state) than from the bottom-up (in the culture and experience of the majority of the population). However, we cannot ignore the fact that the development of a market economy tends to favor greater affirmation of the system of civil justice.

Table 7.2: Characteristics of Civil Justice in Relation to Economic Development

Characteristics of civil justice	More developed market economies and consumer societies	Market economies in consolidation (e.g. Mozambique)
Context of judicial system	Weak plurality	Strong plurality
Resources for the official system	Substantial but always subject to limits	Insubstantial and insufficient
Magistrates	High pay, average legitimization	Low pay, legitimization badly affected
Legal services market	Excess supply / corporate organization	Incipient supply / corporate organization
Cost of access	Variable	Generally high
Access	Differentiated	Very limited and selective
Origin of effective demand	Urban/ rural	Urban
Main type of use in most common types of litigation	Collective and frequent (consumer and production)	Individual and sporadic (family, property, employment)
Large-scale economic litigation	Absent	Absent
Official defense by professionals	Usual / poor quality	Rare / poor quality

Table 7.2: Characteristics of Civil Justice in Relation to Economic
Development (contd.)

Private legal defense	Usual/quality average-high /costs high	Rare/ quality very variable / costs very high
Delays	High, in general	High
Type of resolution	Low intensity, in general	High intensity/ withdrawals
Quality of decision	Average/good	Very variable/ unpredictable
Weight of judicial system	Substantive centrality for non-self-composed litigation	Formal centrality for non self-composed litigation
Perspectives	Lowering of ability to respond to continued rise in demand	Lowering of quality and ability to respond, even to very moderate rise in demand
Consequences and possible reforms	• Development of new ADRM[26] procedures for different litigation and litigants • Procedural reforms and reformsto judiciary • Modernization of the management of the courts	• Development of new ADRM procedures and reinforcement of formal and informal types • Resources for the base of the judicial system • Procedural reforms and reforms to the judiciary • Modernization of the management of the courts

With regard to the transitory differences, the one which stands out most is the situation in the legal services market, where the offer which is at the moment incipient in case B will tend to increase when new law graduates enter the market. The predictable consequences of this increase will be a lowering of fees and an increase both in the number of cases involving private legal defense and those in which the official defense is undertaken by professionals (although the quality will remain low). In addition, depending on the type of legal education and supplementary training given, this increasing number of professionals may contribute towards an increase in the quality of judicial decisions. The differences between the dominant type of users in the system and the means of resolving litigation in the courts are equally transitory, although these differences will decrease much more slowly than those previously discussed. The time that this takes will depend on the process of consolidating the market economy and the rate of expansion of consumer society. These are the changes that will most influence the increase in demand by frequent litigants as well as demand relating to minor disputes such as the payment of debts, which will tend to superimpose themselves onto inter-individual litigation.

In terms of similarities, the absence of large-scale economic litigation and the increasing delays in providing the protection of the law should be emphasized as two characteristics that still persist in most civil systems.

When we consider the evolutionary perspectives of cases A and B, we can observe a common difficulty in responding to the increase in effective demand for civil judicial protection, which enables us to anticipate common points in the reforms that need to be adopted. These concern what will happen in terms of procedural material, of modernizing the managements of courts and of developing new procedures for the resolution of litigation (for example, 'arbitration'). Nevertheless, the aforementioned structural differences between cases A and B should demand that specific responses be found which make use of the potential characteristics of the local context.[27] For example, in case B, the context of strong legal plurality is a recommendation for strengthening interaction between the official judicial system and the traditional and alternative means of resolving litigation already in existence, without precluding the incorporation of new forms. In fact, alternative means of resolving litigation are being sought out and even reinvented today in all judicial systems, as these systems find themselves unable to deal with the large-scale demand in particular areas of litigation.

It is equally admissible that, in situations in which resources are scarce, the base of the system, rather than the top, should be favored in order to increase access and influence.

In spite of the existing differences that are liable to remain in the coming years — namely those which require the large-scale mobilization of qualified human resources and increased financial resources — there may be points in common in terms of the strategic orientation of some reforms. This is the case with the management of the courts, the increasing transparency of procedures, the development of a justice of proximity (a very fashionable concept in the reform of judicial systems) and the diversification of the means of resolving litigation by making it proportional to the seriousness of the litigation involved.

An Overview of Civil Justice in Mozambique

Main Litigation

A closer analysis of civil justice in Mozambique confirms that, like the economy and the civil society of which it is a part, civil justice in Mozambique is going through a period of transition.[28] In addition to divorce cases, in recent years civil justice has, above all, been used to manage the privatization of the housing market[29] and the loss of jobs resulting from the restructuring of businesses in the wake of structural adjustment policies.

An overview of the profile of plaintiffs and defendants shows that inter-individual litigation still predominates, with a particularly heavy emphasis on family and labor conflicts and those associated with housing (possession or ownership). The complexity and variety of the latter reflect the difficulties encountered as part of the shift from a publicly administered system to one based on private interests.

In fact, in recent years, we have observed an increase in the relative weight of civil cases in the judicial system. For example, between 2002 and 2003, the number of civil cases filed rose by 6.3% (whilst the criminal cases filed fell by 6.8%)

There was very little economic litigation up to the mid 1990s, but this has been rising steadily since then. This situation encompasses not only large-scale litigation, which is common to most market economies, but also debt collection, the most frequent litigation in these economies. What we are witnessing is a moderate increase in demand, to which, nevertheless, the civil court system has great difficulty in responding. As mentioned earlier, between 2002 and 2003 the provincial courts witnessed an increase in economic cases especially in the Maputo City Court and the Maputo, Sofala and Nampula provincial courts.

The Users

The users of the system reside in the most developed urban areas, particularly Maputo city, which clearly stands out from the rest of the provinces in terms of the number of cases filed, closed and pending, even taking into account their smaller population.

Rural areas are virtually beyond the reach of the civil judicial system, partly because they use a different type of law and partly because there is no court or it is geographically, financially and culturally removed from them. The predominantly urban nature of civil justice, which is restricted to the main urban centers, means that it is less affected by the inter-penetration of the various different legalities than the other forms of justice analyzed in this book. Even so, some local cultural practices and habits do stand out in the litigation brought before the judicial court, above all in family conflicts.[30]

In urban centers it is mainly people with low and/or moderate incomes who resort to the courts. Access remains very difficult for the poorest, and the wealthiest exclude themselves from the courts because they distrust the quality of the court's decision and its independence. For these reasons they try at all cost to prevent conflict or else resort to various forms of negotiation to resolve it.

Those who do resort to the justice system often find themselves 'unprotected' in terms of legal defense and sometimes in a very unfair position, due to the high cost of the services of a lawyer.[31]

In order to reach a final verdict, most civil actions have to go through all the phases of the judicial proceedings. Cases are usually decided in court, and an increasing number of appeals are being brought before the Supreme Court. In recent years, the Supreme Court has heard an increasing number of economic cases in appeal, thus reflecting the structural changes that the society is experiencing.

Criminal Justice in the Provincial Courts

Social control through criminal justice is a specific contribution towards maintaining the social order. However, it becomes difficult and complex to exercise this control when the communities'culture is based on reconciliation within the community and not on the application of punishments and sanctions.[32]

In Mozambique, it is not possible, at the moment, to determine the volume of undenounced crimes[33] and therefore only denounced, accused and sentenced cases of criminality have been analyzed.

The number of cases denounced has not increased (in the period between 1997 and 1999) in the attorneyships and for this reason it has to be accepted that there is an accumulation of cases at the Criminal Investigation Police (PIC).

The rate of accusations is very high. Only 12.2% of the cases have been shelved or ordered free by acquittal. According to the General Attorney's Office, 50% of cases involving accusations that are brought to trial fill the lists of cases pending. Denounced and accused crimes concentrate on crimes against property (in its broadest sense), followed by crimes against people. With the privatization of state companies there has been a reduction in embezzlement. In the mid 1990s, the almost total absence of crimes involving the use and trafficking of drugs was explained by the inability of the police to tackle such crimes; an image that has seen some changes over the years. The reduction in car thefts may signify better coordination between the regional police forces (both at national and international level, especially in relation to South Africa).

There was a reduction in the average number of defendants held in custody, which may have been caused by various factors: increased awareness of the law on the part of law enforcement agents and a consequent increase in compliance with the law with respect to the regulatory norms for custody; a decrease in crimes against assets not subject to bail; the action of the judges in charge of pre-sentence investigation; possible leniency on the part of law enforcement agents as a result of being bribed by delinquents. Consequently, there was also a reduction in the number of suspects held in custody by order of the court.

According to a report by the Attorney General (1999), the judicial system's capacity for investigation has been reduced. In 1998, the PIC handled 42,106 cases, but only 9,637 of these reached the General Attorney's Office.

The Characterization of Serious Crimes and Felonies

The proceedings for serious crimes and felonies analyzed in the courts indicate that denunciations made by the victims (predominantly male) are, as a rule, made through the police.

In general, cases that are denounced, presented to court and sentenced relate to crimes against property and physical integrity (bodily harm and attempts on life). In 1987 there were still many crimes of embezzlement. The defendants are usually men, as are the victims, which gives criminal justice a predominately masculine character. The defendants are either salaried employees or unemployed, with little education or illiterate and are not members of the victims' families. As a rule, the defendant is immediately detained and awaits trial in custody. The intervention of the criminal instruction judges in the first hearings and in the validation of preventive detention has increased in recent years (70%, in 1997). Sometimes the legal validation of detention is very slow.

There is also a very high rate of conviction (78%, in 1997), with the courts usually opting for imprisonment. Fact-finding procedures for this 'common criminality' usually involve gathering evidence on how the crime was committed. The Provincial Attorney's Office does not appear at the trials and the defense is normally undertaken by a public defender without a law degree (a legal technician or legal assistant).

Due to the extent of the burden facing the courts, most trials have been delayed at least once. However, from the time when a case reaches the court until the sentence is pronounced, the case proceeds rapidly, due to the fact that 80% of the defendants await trial in custody.

Proceedings for Misdemeanor

In criminal cases which follow the proceedings for misdemeanor[34] and are judged in the provincial courts, the victim is usually male. Usually it is the victim who files the complaint with the police (in most cases they are security agents or soldiers). In general, proceedings for misdemeanors involving bodily harm or car accidents predominate; they are committed by both salaried employees and unemployed people, not related to the family of the victim. A legal technician or assistant from the IPAJ[35] usually defends the defendant. Despite the growing presence of the Attorney's Office, it was still absent in about 40% of the cases; as a result, a citizen was usually appointed as an *ad-hoc* substitute for the attorney. In about 80% of the cases the defendant was convicted and fined or sent to prison, although the latter sentence was normally converted into a fine later. An analysis of the duration of the proceedings for misdemeanor indicates that they are normally quick, with only a small number lasting a long time.

The Absence of Criminal Litigation in the Provincial Courts

The absence of criminal litigation in the provincial courts is due in part to two factors: the 'refusal' of the judicial courts to judge certain crimes and the fact that there are institutional, social and economic structures which 'filter out' criminal litigation involving political or judicial bodies, so that these 'types of crime' do not reach the formal institutions of control. In the case of the former, there are situations in which judicial courts do not accept certain cases, namely those relating to family matters, and refer them back to the family and the community (the community courts, traditional authorities, etc.). In the case of the latter, there are the crimes which harm the state and society, namely crimes against public health, speculation, the illegal exchange of currency, the illegal exportation of money, unauthorized foreign trade, corruption, theft of energy cables, vagrancy, prostitution, illegal hunting, environmental crimes, sexual crimes, domestic violence, international trafficking and money-laundering.

The General Attorney's Office is an institutional means of addressing absent litigation, but in practice it takes very few proactive measures to enable this discourse to materialize.

4. Justice in the District Courts

The current Law on the Organization of the Judiciary establishes that the district courts are the first formal instance in the judicial system.[36] However, from the information gathered, it can be concluded that, as previously mentioned (see chapter 6), around one third of the districts in Mozambique still do not have a district court, and that the function of resolving litigation is undertaken by the community courts, the police and other formal or informal bodies.[37]

In addition, all the judicial courts face enormous difficulties in complying with the requirements of the Organic Law (Law no. 10/92) with regard to the *quorum* needed for them to function. There have been no elections for lay judges at any level in the court system since 1987. Many of the judges elected at that time have now given up, moved away or simply died. The few who remain are not motivated to continue with their activities, as they receive very little, and sometimes no, financial compensation for their work.

A Brief Characterization of the District Courts

From the direct observation of 16 district courts[38] we can, in spite of their differences, establish a certain pattern in relation to human resources, material resources, the movement of cases and performance.

Resources and Working Conditions

In the courts studied during the first research project (1996-2000), human resources were considered inadequate. However, given the volume of cases registered it appears to us that the fundamental issue is that of the training and technical upgrading of the functionaries, clerks, bailiffs and other justice officials already employed in the courts.

The level of professional training for justice officials is, as a rule, extremely low. Despite their great willingness to learn and improve the quality of their work, most officials never have access to adequate training programs and their links with the court administration are precarious, involving interim or provisional nominations.[39]

With the exception of the Maxixe District Court, whose premises had already been renovated by DANIDA at the time of our study, all the others were located in precarious premises and suffered from a lack of equipment and supplies.

In terms of the condition of the premises, most buildings used by the courts are rented from other entities and are, in general, severely run-down, with no electricity or mains water supply, sanitation, archives or adequate furniture. The courts also face enormous difficulties due to a lack of – or an insufficient amount of – transportation (even bicycles), equipment (typewriters, calculators, photocopiers, telephones and fax machines, etc.), paper and other consumables. Not infrequently, they receive assistance from private individuals or through the goodwill of entities outside the judicial system.

It is imperative that efforts to renovate district courts' premises should continue, so that dignified working conditions can be provided. The district courts need a courtroom, offices for the judge and the attorney and a room where court files can be kept.

The district courts do not have their own budget. They operate on the basis of funds made available to them by the provincial courts. Even paying salaries to the serving magistrates and justice officials (clerks, bailiffs, etc.) requires a courier to go to the provincial capital each month to withdraw the funds needed to pay the salaries of the judges, attorneys and other court staff. This creates serious problems with delayed payments and even embezzlement.

The efforts to renovate district courts and improve interaction with provincial courts with regard to budgets and the supply of materials must continue. In addition, it is necessary for the courts to stop being dependent in terms of premises, equipment and materials needed in order to implement the resolution of litigation and preserve their own legitimacy, independence and impartiality.

The Self-Transformation of a Community Court into a District Court

During our research, we encountered one district court (Pemba-Metuge, in the Cabo Delgado province) that is not official but acts as if it were, having built its own court headquarters with local materials. This court, which started off as a community court, is now recognized by the local inhabitants, local authorities and the provincial court as a district court and it aspires to formal recognition by the Supreme Court, which recognizes it *de facto*.

Litigation in the District Courts

Civil Litigation

As a rule, the 16 district judicial courts visited by our research team[40] and subjected to direct observation have witnessed a fall in the number of cases presented to them between 1987 and 1997 in eight courts, and an increase in only six.[41] With the exception of two of the district courts in which wide-ranging civil litigation is emerging and has been registered (payment of debts, alimony, leasing, etc.), the demand in the district courts centers on criminal litigation. From the interviews carried out during our research we detected that many district courts frequently refuse to handle family litigation, claiming that the conflict should be solved by the community courts or even within the family.

From the data analyzed and in light of the current socio-economic development in the country, it seems likely to us that the demand for penal cases is on the rise and that civil cases are beginning to appear in the district courts. This being the case, these courts need to prepare themselves for the situation which is likely to occur in the coming years.

Criminal Litigation

In the proceedings for serious crimes and for felonies that were analyzed,[42] offenses were reported to the police by the victims. Most cases filed concerned property (petty theft or medium-scale burglary – 49.5% in 1987 and 64.4% in 1997) or bodily harm.[43] Most of the plaintiffs were male (over 80% during 1987-1997). This information, together with the fact that most of them were also the victims of the crime, leads us to conclude that there is a gender bias in the criminal justice system, as men seem to be the ones who have been able to overcome the barriers that stand in their way when filing a case (both at the police headquarters or in court). Women remain the silent victims.[44] In terms of age, most of the plaintiffs are between 20 and 50 years of age, although we identified an increasing number of younger people (between 18 and 25) in the most recent years of our sample.

In terms of occupation, in the mid-1990s most of the plaintiffs were salaried employees, workers or unemployed (30.1%), as well as security agents and soldiers (26.5%). Towards the end of the 1990s we observed a wider variety of occupations, the majority being fishermen, peasants, (19.6%) housewives, self-employed citizens, security agents and soldiers (13% altogether). The greater 'democratization' of criminal justice can clearly be observed.

Finally, it should be pointed out that after a case was filed, in most situations the defendant did not hire a lawyer, either for financial reasons, a lack of awareness of their rights or a shortage of lawyers and legal technicians or assistants.

Most of the offenses reported were committed by single individuals, indicating the predominance of a small-scale, non-organized criminal activity. The defendants were also mostly men, confirming the male character of criminal justice in Mozambique (94.8% in 1997 and 95.1% in 1997). The age range of the defendants was quite wide, although most of them were between 25 and 35 years old (36.8% in 1987 and 32.6% in 1997).[45]

The defendants were either salaried employees (workers, service sector employees) or unemployed,[46] with little education or illiterate, and were not members of the victims' families. The defendants were usually held in custody – which, in the majority of cases in 1997 (75%) was authorized by one judge – and defended by legal assistants or legal technicians from the IPAJ or by a defender appointed on an *ad-hoc* basis. In 1997, in 35% of cases, the District Attorney's Office was not present at the trial or was represented by an *ad-hoc* attorney. Cases were tried quickly, as the accused was held in custody.

In the proceedings for misdemeanors judged in the district courts the defendants shared the same characteristics previously described, except that in terms of occupation they were mainly farmers, fishermen or unemployed. In this type of case, the order of importance of the crimes practiced is reversed, with crimes involving bodily harm appearing first, followed by crimes against property.

The vast majority of the trials were postponed at least once (84.2% in 1997). This occurred both for reasons internal to the court (absence of the judge, court inspection) or because the parties had not been notified.

In a significant number of trials, the state attorney was absent (54.2% of the cases in 1987 and 36.9% in 1997). We also identified a significant number of cases in which a citizen was appointed as an *ad-hoc* substitute *for* the attorney.

Most of cases lasted less than a year (92.2% in 1987 and 82.3% in 1997). The sentence was either a fine or a prison sentence converted into a fine. Fines varied from 500,00 to 700,000,00 *meticais*.[47]

The main reason why criminal litigation reaches the court is that in cases of bodily harm a hospital or health center does not provide treatment unless the police are present, and when they intervene the case is subsequently sent to the district court. In addition, most plaintiffs report crimes against property directly to the police. In 90% of the cases analyzed in our sample, the police had initially filed the cases. The number of cases directly filed by the attorney's office or at court was extremely small.

The District Courts: the Crossroads between Community Justice and the Judicial Courts

The district courts face various constraints, amongst which the following should be emphasized: budgeting and finance to prevent dependency; motivation of the elected judges; the recruitment and training of magistrates and judicial functionaries; working conditions.

The district courts lie at the crossroads between community justice and the judicial courts, establishing both complementary and competitive relationships between them. On the one hand, the district courts make use of the community courts and the traditional authorities in order to ensure that court summons are complied with.[48] In addition, they establish a special relationship with these entities, by ruling that questions relating to family matters are their responsibility. In the district courts the police function as the distributor of litigation to the instances that can resolve it, sending the more serious cases to the district or the provincial courts.

5. Courts: the Illusion of Centrality

As already stated, the administration of official justice is not limited to the judicial courts. The community courts form the base of the system for the resolution of conflict and, in practice, continue informally to be the lower instance in the judicial system. Simultaneously, new legislation on arbitration, conciliation and mediation as alternative means of resolving litigation (Law no. 10/99 of 7 June) aims to create 'new' means of resolving litigation to meet the demand that the judicial courts cannot satisfy. Mozambican state justice thus finds itself squeezed between two waves of non-judicial or de-judicial processes: one at the top of the social hierarchy (arbitration or negotiation with lawyers, transnational actors or private actors who act on the margins of the state and settle business suits or cases where state intervention is not desired), and another at the base (the community courts and the whole set of authorities who are designated traditional and who resolve local suits affecting the life of the society).

The judicial system therefore has an illusion of centrality, but the state and official justice penetrate neither the bottom nor the top. Moreover, public and private are merged so that, for the time being, justice follows the trend towards the 'privatization' of political power.

Figure 7.3: The Resolution of Litigation in Mozambique and the Social Pyramid

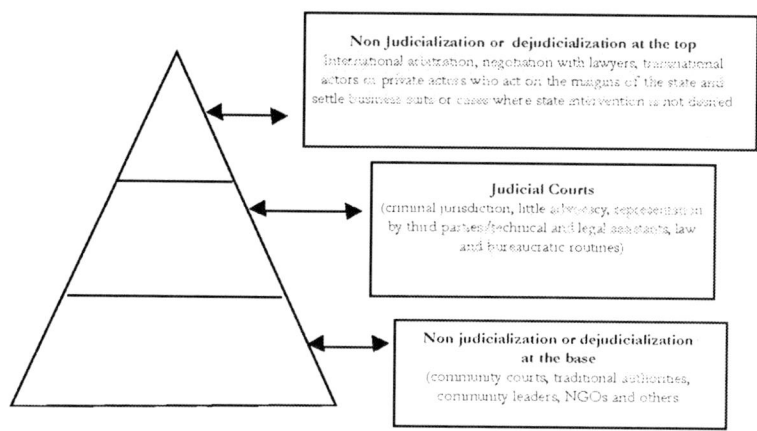

Conclusion

Human resources – judges, state attorneys, functionaries and justice officials – are insufficient and not adequately qualified. In addition, the staffing is inappropriate for the situation in Mozambique, with an 'unrealistic' number of professional posts and categories. With the exception of those commanded by the Supreme Court Justices, in general salaries are demoralizingly low and are frequently not paid on time. In addition, elected judges spend long periods of time without receiving any compensation and their fees are very low.

The Government budget and Court's Fund are inadequate for the needs of the system and consequently external aid and loans are one way of securing the more rapid development of the judicial system.

More than half of the litigation handled by the provincial courts involves criminal complaints corresponding, in 1998, to 80.9% of the total number of cases filed in the judicial system. In 2003, however, this figure fell to 57%, due to a marked increase in civil and labor actions brought before courts.

To sum up, in Mozambique provincial criminal justice is characterized by litigation centering on crimes against property and involving bodily harm. The defendants are predominantly men, who are normally held in custody, have no lawyer and are, in almost all cases, found guilty. There are also some cases of misappropriation and several high profile cases of crimes against human life or economic crimes which have a great public impact and receive extensive media coverage. However, there are also types of litigation that are almost absent from the criminal justice system, such as most economic crimes, domestic violence and violence against children.

Civil justice in Mozambique is facing the problems inherent to an emerging judicial system operating under both new and old concepts of the rule of law. It suffers from a lack of resources and competences, which lowers its quality and makes the judicial system susceptible to corruption. At the same time, it is already experiencing the problems of the more structured judicial systems, such as high costs and excessive delays. The reforms that have been initiated seek to combine the successful measures tried out in other countries with a process of taking carefully measured advantage of the potential within its own mechanisms and specific local features.

The district courts lie at the crossroads between community justice and the judicial courts, establishing both complementary and competitive relationships between them. The judicial system therefore has an illusion of centrality, but the state and official justice penetrate neither the bottom nor the top (revealing an absence of judicial litigation). Justice is following the trend towards the 'privatization' of political power.

Notes

1 This figure refers to judges both with and without a degree. It does not include, however, the judges temporarily transferred to other areas of the administration of justice (information kindly provided by the Supreme Court's Statistical Department).

2 All the 11 provincial chief judges have a law degree, while law graduates have gradually been appointed to several district courts over the last years. In mid 2002 the first district judges who were law graduates were appointed, for example, in the law courts of the districts of Chókwè and Macia, in the Gaza province. See also chapter 6 for an analysis of some of the changes in legal education and training in Mozambique over the last few years.

3 This also depends upon the future status of the community courts (see chapter 10).The new law of the community courts is currently being discussed.

4 Although the situation has changed significantly since 2000, as some of the figures in this chapter illustrate, the justice system still needs many more law graduates.

5 Recently (2004), the salaries of the Mozambican magistrates (judges and state attorneys) were increased.

6 See note 40 in chapter 2.

7 On this subject, see chapter 2.

8 Commercial Bank of Mozambique – CBM.

9 Danish Agency for International Development Assistance.

10 For further details, see Dagnino *et al.*, 1996, the source of the above information.

11 Information from the Supreme Court, obtained in July 2000.

12 DANIDA has been the most important donor in the justice sector. Over the 1990-1995 period DANIDA implemented a US$ 2.8 million project involving the Eduardo Mondlane University Law Faculty, the INAJ and the Supreme Court; this project was followed by another (1996-2001) valued at US$ 8.3 million that concentrated its support at the district level, rehabilitating and equipping 20 priority district courts and promoting training for their judges. To complement the rehabilitation of the district courts, support was also given for law reform, in particular the revision of the procedural codes, considered one of the reasons for the poor administration of justice. Toward the end of the project DANIDA provided support for the strategic planning process. A US$ 8.5 million project was approved for the period 2002-2005, to be used to provide continuing support for integrated strategic planning, support for law reform through UTREL, training and research through the Centre for Legal and Judicial Training, access to justice and human rights through organisations in civil society and support for informal justice.

13 United Nations Development Program. The project 'Support to the Justice Sector in Mozambique' was initiated in 1999. Overall, this project received contributions from the UNDP itself, Norway, Ireland, Portugal and UNICEF of about US$ 4.9 million in its final year of implementation. The project had two components: (a) support for the establishment of the Centre for Legal and Judicial Training, equipment, training courses for judges and technical assistance; (b) support for the reform of the prison system. In 2002 another initiative aimed at fighting corruption was added to the project. The available funds (US$ 300,000) were used to organise a forum on corruption, train judicial inspectors and journalists and the first survey of the needs of the Criminal Investigation Police (PIC).

14 A financier through loans, the World Bank is one of the largest participants in the justice sector in Mozambique. Under its 1994-1999 US$ 6.6 million 'Capacity Building Program – Legal Component', funds were provided for training initiatives, Masters degree courses and equipment for the Ministry of Justice, the Administrative Court, the General Attorney's Office, the Supreme Court, the Law

Faculty of Eduardo Mondlane University, the Bar Association and some NGOs active in the sector.

15 The first USAID project in the justice sector (1997-2000, valued at US$ 580,000) focused on the civil section in the Maputo City Court, where a computerized case management system was introduced and proposals were prepared for the reform of the Civil Procedure Code. More recently, USAID has been supporting the Anti-Corruption Unit in the General Attorney's Office.

16 The source of information in notes 12 to 15 is Dagnino, F. et al., (2003). *The Justice System: Past and Present*. Maputo.

17 Created by Decree no. 22/89, of 5 August.

18 In 1996, court costs were composed of: legal charges, part of which were sent to the state; additional costs, which, in turn, included a surcharge of 30% on the legal charges; stamps; postage costs (when necessary); the cost of paper and journeys, or, in other words, the monetary value of the distances which a bailiff had to cover in order to carry out his/her work. In civil cases, there was also the 'payment of costs' corresponding to the amounts the courts levied in advance from the individual involved in a claim, which were subsequently deducted from the sum of the legal costs when the case ended. Legal costs relating to civil cases depended on the amount of money involved, whilst in criminal cases they depended on the seriousness of the crime, the type of case and the financial means of the accused. In terms of amounts, in summary proceedings the charges varied between a minimum of 5,000 *meticais* and a maximum of 40,000 *meticais*, whereas in uncontested divorce cases they were around 50,000 *meticais*.

19 However, in 2002 and 2003 there was a significant decrease in pending cases (a total of 90,153 for 2002 and 98,842 for 2003).

20 Proceedings which allow court to apply a mandatory prison term of over two years.

21 Proceedings which allow for the court to apply a short prison sentence (between one and two years).

22 There were no data available for Sofala Provincial Judicial Court for the 2002-2003 period.

23 For a comparison of different systems of civil justice and their problems, see Zuckerman, 1999.

24 On this subject, see chapter 9.

25 For the main characteristics of civil justice in Portugal, see Marques et al., 1999:413.

26 ADRM – alternative dispute resolution mechanisms.

27 According to Bourmaud (1997: 84), "the transposition of administrative structures into very different cultural universes, in which a relationship with modernity is largely unknown" and "in which there exists a manifest dysfunction between the means which the administrative apparatus possesses and its official objectives" leads to serious dysfunctioning and an inability to adapt, on the part of the administration, to the human context in African countries.

28 See chapters 2, 4 and 6, for a better perspective on the current changes and challenges which the Mozambican society is facing.

29 Resulting from the abolition of the APIE, the state real estate management in charge of the real estate that was nationalized immediately after independence (see chapter 2).

30 The topic of family conflicts is also covered in chapters 10 to 13.

31 On this subject, see chapter 9.

32 On this subject, see chapters 2, 9 and 10.

33 Many criminal cases are solved through 'informal', unofficial channels of conflict resolution, as analysed in different chapters of this book.

34 A proceeding which allows for the court to apply a quite short prison sentence (from three days up to one year).

35 Institute for Legal Assistance and Representation.

36 On this subject, see chapter 2.

37 In 2003, 28 districts remained without formally established district courts and in the districts where they did formally exist, 17 were not operational at the time (Supreme Court Statistical Department, 2003).

38 The district courts studied were: Namaacha and Moamaba (Maputo province); Homoíne, Maxixe and Vilankulo (Inhambane province); Dondo (Sofala province); Pebane and Alto Molócuè (Zambézia province); Angónia, Cahora Bassa and Moatize (Tete province); Chiúre, Mueda, Mocímboa da Praia and Pemba-Metuge (Cabo Delgado province). During the first research project, the provinces of Niassa, Nampula and Manica were not included. The latter two provinces were studied in the second project.

39 As a result of this observation, and following the creation of the Center for Legal and Judicial Training (CFJJ), several justice officials from district judicial courts have undergone training in recent years (see chapter 6).

40 It was difficult to evaluate the court flow due to the fact that there was no statistical data for the district courts at the Supreme Court. The data analysed in the project and discussed here result from counting archived cases, the court claims register, etc.

41 This general rrecovery took place after a greater fall which occurred between 1987 and 1992 (corresponding to the period of civil war that ravaged the country). In 1992 the Rome Peace Agreement was signed. See chapters 1, 2 and 4 for a broader understanding of the socio-political scenario in Mozambique over the last three decades.

42 Overall, for the characterization of the ten-year period (1987-1997) 1,282 cases were analyzed. Of these, in 1987, 72 were proceedings for serious crimes and for felonies, and the vast majority – 1,002 – proceedings for misdemeanor. In 1997, we identified 72 proceedings for serious crimes and 68 proceedings for felony. The remaining proceedings did not refer the type of case.

43 In the early years of our sample, attempts on life were more significant (16.5% of cases in 1987, against 2.6% in 1997).

44 See also chapter 9, where the issue of domestic violence (including gendered violence) is analysed in more detail.

45 In 1997 we observed an increase in felonies committed by younger men between the ages of 18 and 25 (30.8% in 1987 against 36.1% in 1997).

46 Towards the late 1990s we identified a significant trend in the increase of unemployed people among the defendants. This figure confirms the opinions of several interviewees who associated the social and economic problems of Mozambican society with a strong increase in unemployment and criminal activity.

47 We also identified cases in which at least a sentence of flogging was given when Law no. 5/83 of 16 March was in force.

48 On the multiple forms this relationship may take, see also chapters 10 and 11.

8

The Judicial Courts' Performance: Main Blockages in the Court System

João Carlos Trindade, João Pedroso, André Cristiano José
and Boaventura de Sousa Santos

Introduction

The patterns of litigation present in the judicial system – civil, juvenile or criminal – as well as the patterns of litigation absent from the judicial system analyzed in previous chapters, are in themselves indicative of the first major blockages in the system: the distance between citizens and the judicial courts, and the economic, cultural and social barriers affecting access to the law and the official courts. According to the interviews and observations carried out during our research, this gap between the judicial courts and the majority of Mozambicans is due to the following: the fact that written law is ill-suited to the Mozambican situation; a distrust for the workings of the judicial courts; the official, legal, written culture of winner/loser and sanctions, instead of a local culture of reconciliation; misunderstandings concerning the purpose of the funds raised from fines and bail.

This distance from the courts and the social discrimination affecting access to official justice are much more complex phenomena than they may at first appear to be. In addition to economic factors (which are always the most obvious), they also involve cultural factors resulting from socialization processes and the internalization of prevailing values which are very difficult to transform. It is up to the state and the judicial system to work to reduce the selectivity of the legal system and the economic, social and cultural barriers and to transform the potential citizen demand for legal protection into an effective demand.

Access to official justice is extremely selective. The state machinery is incapable of responding satisfactorily to the increasing needs of citizens because it lacks the financial, human, technical and organizational resources, as the previous articles in this section have outlined.

1. The Media View of the Judicial System

The assessment of public opinion concerning the problems of justice is a rather recent phenomenon, promoted mainly by organizations from civil society, donors and, in some instances, the institutions themselves. Listening to citizens' opinions reveals a somewhat new concept of justice in Mozambique, more akin to the provision of services than the exercise of power, which can help strengthen a democratic and participatory culture.

On the assumption that the official legal system is much more accessible to those who can read and write Portuguese (thus reflecting some school education), we analyzed articles on the institutions and activities of the official legal system published by the Maputo press in 1999.[1] Later on, we analyzed the results of several surveys on the attitudes and performance of the legal institutions.

In recent years, several Mozambican radio and television programs have been organizing discussions between representatives from the justice institutions and the public, raising questions about issues such as crime, the performance of the courts, family law, state corruption, etc. Although the public involved is only a small fraction of the urban population, this kind of discussion is indicative of a maturity of opinion and a clear perception of the inadequacies and abuses of the institutions that oversee law and public order.

Up to 1999, the media described the Mozambican judicial system as suffering from various problems that were destroying its foundations. Amongst other aspects reported by the media, there was repeated discussion of its lack of financial and human resources, mainly affecting the upper echelons of the judicial system. There were also accusations of a lack of political will to resolve these problems.

Judges and attorneys were also criticized, with accusations focusing mainly on the passivity of the judicial institutions. According to the press there were also suspicions that ethnic and religious biases had influenced the behavior of the judicial institutions, resulting in huge delays in the justice system that prevented the Mozambican courts from functioning properly.

More specific criticisms were made of the Supreme Court. One of the problems noted in relation to this Court was its excessive slowness and another was its lack of impartiality in rejecting a request by one of the Mozambican political parties to contest election results.[2]

The General Attorney's Office was also criticized in the press for its lack of action and the same questions were asked about the reasons for such inertia. In addition, the papers reported suspicions that state attorneys may have been involved in a large-scale case of corruption. As a result, in 2000 a new Attorney-General was appointed by the President.[3]

Several surveys have also directly or indirectly revealed the interviewees' views on their level of confidence in justice in a broader sense. For example, in March 2000, the Ministry of Justice promoted an opinion poll on human rights, covering such subjects as respect for fundamental freedoms, citizens' knowledge of their rights, police actions, the right to defense and representation in court and the main human rights violations in the country. The results showed that, on the whole, Mozambican citizens have little knowledge of their rights and relative confidence in the state as the guarantor of these rights. However, half of the interviewees felt that the police did not respect human rights and a significant majority (63%) was aware of the growing 'privatization' of justice in Mozambique, affirming that "in Mozambique justice is only for those who have money." With regard to the violation of rights, those mentioned most frequently were second generation social and economic rights such as the right to health, a reasonably-paid job and education. The main problems in relation to human rights violations were illegal detentions, mistreatment in prisons, the slowness of trials and corruption in the civil service and the courts. Another situation indicated as an example of the violation of human rights was violence against children and women.

When the first research was carried out, the murder of Carlos Cardoso, a renowned Mozambican journalist, had not yet taken place.[4] The media sought to transform the trial of Carlos Cardoso's murderers into the struggle of civil society against corruption. The trial became an example of the role of the judiciary for most Mozambicans, since it was widely publicized and broadcast. Newspapers, weekly publications, and radio and television news programs featured interviews with citizens about the trial. The attention paid by the media to the Carlos Cardoso case was justified by the fact that it was linked to a major bank fraud that he had been investigating which still has not been fully explained and which gave rise to suspicions about the possible involvement of public figures and their connections with organized crime.

In addition to the interest raised by the subject itself, the Cardoso trial offered a rare opportunity for citizens to observe closely how justice works, including its various different procedures. The way the trial was conducted – almost always in a simple, direct and sometimes 'didactic' manner – transformed this trial into a collective learning process on penal law, helping to demystify the unfriendly and distant character of official law in the eyes of the ordinary Mozambican.

One of the reforms to the Mozambican justice system which has received the most media coverage is the Labor Law, for reasons which are sometimes rather strange. Criticisms center on the ineffectiveness of labor jurisdiction. Although established by legal diploma, the labor sections operating in the common courts have not yet been transformed into real and effective labor courts. By 2005 this situation still had not changed.

The press also gave coverage to constitutional reforms.[5] Most of the criticism was leveled against the introduction of new institutions (such as the proposal for the creation of the Constitutional Court and the introduction of the position of

Ombudsman)⁶ without the adequate establishment and consolidation of those which already existed

2. Ritual and the Length of Justice

Ritual and the Chief Judge

The distance between citizens and the courts is also reflected in the formal nature of courtroom practice. Observation of both the provincial and district judicial courts led to the conclusion that the entire ritual of the hearing is conducted in an atmosphere of formality which distances the court from the parties and is filled with symbolism. The ritual and formalities are centered on the chief judge, to the detriment of cross examination and the active participation of the prosecution and the defense. The chief judge conducts the hearings in an inquisitorial and relatively discretionary manner. In effect, the prosecution and the defense barely participate, as previous chapters have shown.

It should, however, be emphasized that elected judges participate in trials as a form of popular participation in the administration of justice, in spite of the difficulties the courts have in mobilizing them, due mainly to the fact that they receive little or no payment.

In the judicial courts the ritual of the trial, which has essentially symbolic functions, still does not fully guarantee legality and debate, as it is a ritual that focuses on the chief judge.

The Length of Justice in Mozambique

The theoretical construction of the duration of a case must distinguish between its necessary duration – the reasonable period of time needed to defend individual or collective citizens' rights – and delay, *i.e.* the unreasonable or excessive duration of a case that is not required – and is sometimes even damaging – in order to protect the parties concerned. The necessary duration of the case should correspond to the legal duration of the case. However, according to previous research, in many cases it is the law itself which causes delay. Delays may also be organizational or endogenous to the system and may result from the volume of the work or routines acquired, as well as the (dis)organization of the courts.

Finally, the excessive duration of court cases can also be caused by the judicial actors (judges, attorneys, lawyers, parties, police, experts, legal officials, etc.). Such delays may, or may not, be unintentional. The former situation arises out of organizational delays resulting from involuntary negligent behavior on the part of the judicial actors. The latter is caused by one of the parties involved in the litigation, or someone acting on his/her behalf, defending his/her own interests.

In the lengthier proceedings we studied, for example, the progress of one of the civil cases analyzed — from the allocation of the judge to the hearing of the trial — occurred at the pace of procedural law, except for the documentary evidence, which got 'stuck' in the courts. The biggest delay occurred when the case was transferred from the provincial court to the Supreme Court. From the time the appeal was lodged with the Supreme Court to the time when it was allocated to a Justice, about 15 months had elapsed.

In addition to this, one criminal case analyzed had been running for over 10 years. Slightly less than five months had elapsed between the filing of the case by the police (November 7, 1986) and the date of the trial (April 10, 1987), with the judge having previously ordered a reformulation of the accusation and the release of the defendant. In addition to problems with the instruction of the case, the legal claim for the case and the inability to notify one of the interested parties has meant that it has been awaiting a verdict for over ten years. This was initially because of delays with the 'transfer from one instance to another' and later because the case was 'held up' for many years following an appeal to the Supreme Court. In Mozambique, as used to be the case in Portugal, criminal cases proceed whilst the defendants are in custody and come to a halt when there are appeals. This indicates that reforms to the penal procedure are imperative.

3. Delays in the Provincial Courts

An analysis of these cases and legal claims identified the following as determining factors in the crisis in the judicial system in Mozambique:

1) a legal culture based on normative abstraction and logical-formal deduction, which produces a form of self-sustaining, complete and coherent knowledge within the system itself, but is alien to the society;

2) a highly complex, bureaucratic procedural structure that relies almost exclusively on adjudication (involving a win/lose decision) to settle litigation, with no systematic recourse to mediation, negotiation or arbitration processes. In addition, the way in which cases are processed results in their dragging on for a long time (more on this below).

There is a general consensus that the accumulation and excessive duration of cases, particularly in the Supreme Court, combined with corrupt practices, are the main reason for the judicial courts' loss of credibility and legitimacy.

In spite of a relatively controlled civil and labor court demand, civil and labor actions on average take between three months and two years (196 cases in 1987 and 473 in 1997), although a significant number last between two and five years. In 1997, when the situation became more serious, the slowest cases were labor cases, litigation on housing and debt collection. By province, the greatest delays occur in courts with the most litigation, or, in other words, in the city and province of Maputo.[7]

In general, the situation regarding the time required for a decision on criminal cases brought before the provincial courts[8] has deteriorated. In 1997, a quarter of the cases lasted over a year. This apparent speed was due to the fact that, in almost all cases, the defendant was held in custody, so that the case became urgent and the trial had to be completed before the period of custody expired.

Table 8.1: Length of Civil and Labor Actions in Provincial Courts (sample of proceedings)

Duration	1987	%	1997	%
< 3 months	71	20.4	171	22.6
3 months–1 year	104	29.8	291	38.5
1 year–2 years	92	26.4	182	24.1
2 years–5 years	65	18.6	102	13.5
> 5 years	17	4.9	10	1.3
Total	**349**	**100**	**756**	**100**

Source: CEA/CES, 1999.

Table 8.2: Length of Criminal Proceedings in Provincial Courts (sample of the proceedings)

Duration	1987	%	1997	%
Up to 6 months	269	67.3	349	49.7
6 months–12 months	97	24.3	175	24.9
12 months–24 months	21	5.3	99	14.1
18 months–24 months	7	1.8	50	7.1
24 months–36 months	6	1.5	29	4.1
Total	**400**	**100.0**	**702**	**100.0**

Source: CEA/CES, 1999.

The increasing delays in cases and deteriorating criminal justice has been accompanied by a rise in the number of cases pending. This situation can only be explained in part by a severe deterioration in the performance of the judicial system from the late 1980s onwards, when many judges left the courts. In addition, the Supreme Court Justices became less able to supervise and monitor the provincial courts. Finally, the increasing inefficiency of the judicial system is also due to the poor performance of the court offices.

Although there has been some growth in the number of juvenile cases brought before the Nampula Judicial Court, child justice is specific to the city of Maputo. It should also be emphasized that, between 1987 and 1997, juvenile litigation was resolved more quickly. In spite of the increasing number of cases, it can be seen that most of these were resolved in less than 3 months.

Due to its specialized nature and, as a rule, the absence of contestation, juvenile justice is a type of jurisdiction which may be considered exceptionally rapid in comparison with the length of civil and criminal justice.

4. Reasons for Court Delays

The identification of the causes of delays must be the object of a study that is independent of the corporate civil interests of the various operators within the system. In terms of the legal duration and the delays resulting from excessive legal time limits, as previously stated, the law, namely procedural law, is a far more significant factor in delay than is necessary. The accumulation of different types of delays – legal, organizational (or endogenous) and provoked (unintentionally or intentionally) – means that a certain number of cases are held up in the system for years.

We have identified the following causes of endogenous (or organizational) delays and deliberate delays:

-   the organization of the judicial system and the concentration of competences in the judicial courts;
-   the rise, albeit slight, in demand;
-   the working conditions (premises and equipment);
-   the recruitment, selection, training and management of human resources;
-   inadequate legal and managerial knowledge;
-   negligent behavior – or behavior which causes delays – on the part of magistrates, court officials and lawyers or legal technicians and assistants;
-   inefficient organization and management of the court's work;
-   the weaknesses of the General Attorney's Office;
-   the inefficiency of criminal investigation;
-   the absence of any means of controlling the system;
-   the financial resources and lack of political will.

The judicial system is poorly and inappropriately organized and remote from most of its potential users. It only covers the provincial capitals and about two-thirds of the district capitals.

The size of the population and the socio-economic context of some of these districts means that, in practice, the geographical distribution of the courts sometimes does not coincide with the administrative divisions in Mozambique (and that therefore they should have more than one district court). In some districts, however, a district court is not warranted for the time being, as the demand for justice can be addressed by the community courts. There is also a need to consider the advantages and disadvantages of the effective application of the Organic Law, which classifies the district courts into first and second-class courts.

Table 8.3: Length of Juvenile Proceedings (sample of proceedings)

Duration	1987	%	1997	%
< 3 months	80	51.3	156	60.0
3 months–1 year	39	2.5	93	35.8
1 year–2 years	17	10.9	11	4.2
2 years–5 years	16	10.3	0	0.0
> 5 years	4	2.3	0	0.0
Total	**156**	**100.0**	**260**	**100.0**

Source: CEA/CES, 1999.

One of the specific and innovative features of the judicial system in Mozambique is that the management of the judicial system has been handed over to the courts themselves. This has had a paradoxical effect. On the one hand, it guarantees and symbolizes their independence yet, on the other hand, it has the adverse effect of judges accumulating obligations and thus having less time for their main job, which is to judge cases. Thus, the concentration of organizational and administrative management tasks in the Supreme Court, usually carried out by Supreme Court Justices, leads to a considerable dispersal of tasks and what should be the Justices' main activity – judging the appeals submitted to them – is relegated to second place. This situation is reflected in the declining number of cases closed annually in the highest judicial court.

The recognition that at this stage in the development of the judicial system, such a concentration of duties and obligations creates a bottleneck that affects the performance of the courts does not mean that it should be abolished. Retaining this function implies that the courts should be supported by auxiliary judges or advisors, so that pending cases and delays do not increase uncontrollably. As previously stated, delay is one of the main reasons for the judiciary's loss of credibility. As the highest instance in the court structure, the political and symbolic functions of the Supreme Court are of particular importance in legitimizing the system and preventing it from becoming trivialized or discredited.

At the moment, the growth in court litigation is more apparent than real, although it was the dominant topic in our interviews, as citizens are becoming more aware of their rights and there is a growth in new litigation arising out of the development of the market economy. The number of cases brought before the judicial system does not justify the increase in the number of cases pending in the judicial courts, which is disproportionate to the cases received. It is a sign that the courts are more inefficient. For some years now the courts have been unable to close even the same number of cases as have been filed and, as a result, there has been no reduction in cases pending. In some provinces, apart from civil and labor cases, demand has risen very little. The same cannot be said of the cases brought before the Supreme Court. The explanation for delays in the Supreme Court is the rise both in demand and in the volume of work. The number of cases has risen and the capacity to handle them has fallen.

An analysis of reports from the Judicial Council and Superior Council of the General Attorney's Office as well as interviews with the judicial stakeholders has led us to identify insufficient human resources, recruitment and training difficulties and low and irregular salaries as the main blockages in the system. Issues related to insufficient human resources include the accumulation of judicial duties, vacancies or the absence of positions and even a lack of movement.

Training magistrates and judicial officials is now a major priority, which has recently become the responsibility of the Centre for Legal and Judicial Training (CFJJ).[9]

One of the interesting characteristics of the Mozambican judicial system is the existence of non-professional judges. However, they are poorly motivated, as they usually receive no regular compensation, fee or remuneration in return for providing their time. Moreover, some judges, namely in the Maputo City Court, have started to hold trials without the presence of the elected judges. In addition to the fact that these trials are invalid – the grounds for some appeals to the Supreme Court – it seems that the abolition of elected judges would be a loss to the courts, since it would distance citizens even further from the administration of justice.

The low salaries paid to district and provincial magistrates (judges and attorneys), whether graduates or not, is a problem that must be analyzed in depth and reviewed in detail. The magistrates of the General Attorney's Office, who have no statutory law (since the Statute of the Magistrates of the General Attorney's Office is awaiting approval), also feel that their profession is underrated.

The very important role played by the justice officials, as auxiliaries in the administration of justice and in processing cases, has also been undervalued.

The most highly qualified lawyers in Maputo city attribute the excessive slowness of cases to the fact that judges have technical difficulties in deciding on some types of cases. Insufficient knowledge of the law and inexperience are therefore important reasons why cases drag on. The labor sections, the judges in charge of pre-sentence investigation and the district courts are mainly singled out for criticism. Inadequate legal knowledge is blamed primarily on a lack of adequate legal training.

In a metaphor used by one of the judges interviewed, the judge is the head, the court clerk the heart and the bailiff, the legs. Thus, the performance of the court office is fundamental to the overall performance of the system. The court notary is responsible for preparing cases for trial and for handling those already decided. The organization, management and modernization of notary offices is a priority factor in reducing pending cases and unblocking the workings of the judicial system.

Lawyers are blamed for applying various delaying tactics or for causing cases to accumulate (*e.g.* by appealing to pendency, provisional orders and the failure of parties to appear in court).

Criminal investigation, though not the object of this research project, is one of the factors influencing the performance of criminal justice. The main problems lie in the quality of the investigative work. In addition to criticisms of the Criminal Investigation Police (PIC),[10] there is also a consensus on the relative inactivity of the General Attorney's Office and the state attorneys. Their function is to direct the fight against crime and control and supervise legality in general, but they are usually passive and bureaucratic and thus jeopardize the individual and collective interests of citizens and other legal staff.

Throughout the first research project,[11] we also identified a feeling that the court sentences were not being properly administered, which was blamed on the court officials.

A complex organization such as the judicial system requires properly functioning internal control systems. The absence of active and operational court audits as instruments for controlling, inspecting and correcting the work of the judges and justice officials, thereby helping to improve the quality of the public service offered by the justice administration institutions, is one of the great problems which affect the system.

The low or (in the case of the district courts) almost non-existent budget allocation for courts does not allow them to develop. According to one of the people interviewed, "we are still at the first stage, the time of peace and macro-economic policies [...]. First, peace and economic stability. Then there will be a time for justice."

5. The 'Privatization' of Justice and Corrupt Practices

The 'privatization' of public practices and the occurrence of corrupt practices which are non-legal, illegal or criminal is 'the talk of the town' in Mozambican society, as stated earlier in this chapter. Embezzlement of funds, without doubt, lies behind the majority of corruption cases. Perpetrators range from government officials, or, in a wider sense, state employees, to customs officials, sports managers, etc. and cases can involve large or small amounts of money.

This image of corruption in its broadest sense has become firmly established, despite the reactions of the Superior Council of the Judicial System, the Judicial Council and the Supreme Court, as the rulings of the Supreme Court reveal. In his speech to the Judicial Council in 1997, the Chief Justice said:

> When illicit mechanisms are used in government offices or court registry offices – sometimes making use of bureaucracy – thereby forcing the citizen, whose resistance is exhausted, to give in to the intentions of a corrupt official, this is considered an act of violence against the citizen in a disguised form. Although judges and justice officials recognize the need for certain material conditions which the state is no longer able to provide adequately, this in no way justifies perverse acts directed against the rights of the citizen [...]. The material condition of the judges will not be remedied by corruption. The iniquitous judge, like the soldier using his sword as a source of revenue, will not be

moved to honesty by a larger salary or handouts. The need to improve our material conditions should not, under any circumstances, be a justification for iniquity, like a shield against spears [...].

The concept of corruption that features in this chapter is not used in the specific sense laid down by penal law as a 'legal type of crime'. It is a very relative concept. The social phenomenon which nowadays is seen to be widespread in public administration and in society not only violates criminal law but also other forms legislation, such as administrative legislation. Therefore we prefer the concept of *corrupt practices* and argue for a proactive response to these phenomena, with their immediate incorporation into current legislation. According to Graça (1992),

> It may be said that these practices occur, above all, in connection with the appropriation, possession and use of food and equipment, as well as funds. Areas such as the armed forces, the police force and the paramilitaries, as well as the important distribution and marketing chain, seem to be the ones most affected by corrupt practices. There is also a tendency on the part of professionals working in the public services sector, in which salaries are extremely low in relation to the current cost of living, to trade services in order to facilitate quicker decisions, documents, interviews and other services. This affects state housing, teaching appointments in secondary schools, health care, bureaucratic services and support from bureaucratic staff and public institutions. Corrupt practices also exist at management level, although their extent is not known. There has been publicity about irregularities involving directors of companies or autonomous institutions. This phenomenon of corruption is becoming more widely established, so that it is imperative to find measures to contain it.

It has, in fact, not been contained and since 1992 corrupt practices have also extended to the administration of justice, in spite of the reactions of the Supreme Court and the Superior Council of the Judicial System whenever facts are denounced to them which enable them to intervene. As acknowledged by the Judicial Council in its Fifth Session (from 9 to 12 September 1997),

> The wave of corruption, of reprehensible unethical behavior, of gross violations of professionally correct behavior, are not virtual realities but objective facts, which are part of the daily routine in our courts [...]. It is not only magistrates who are involved [in this] but also justice officials at various levels.

With the exception of the Supreme Court, all those interviewed always accused the other judicial courts of corrupt practices and referred to the total inability of the police to proceed with any credible form of investigation, thereby preventing penal justice from being just. Frequently the judge takes the initiative and asks the parties for money, even those whom he knows are in the right. Again according to Graça (1992), the following measures need to be taken:

> The legal system currently in force covers corrupt practices adequately, allowing for a 'passive' as well as an 'active' fight against corruption. However, there is a need to improve it and make it clearer, more comprehensive and more up-to-date. It is also important to think in terms of providing mechanisms for direct prosecution by citizens or legally constituted organizations and for legal action against those involved in criminal offences such as corruption and the embezzlement of property, funds and other items, which is very common. We should also consider creating a system of independent audits of the effectiveness of the administration and strengthen internal inspections in institutional terms. For a start, the areas of legal control and internal inspection are clearly lacking in human, financial and material resources and the government should attend to these minimum basic needs.

In addition to these measures, there is also a need for a permanent system for auditing and inspecting the judicial system that is both educational and disciplinary. The problem of corruption also affects the independence of the magistrates. This situation is obviously serious, given that magistrates are underpaid and sometimes very poorly trained. Avoiding corruption and guaranteeing the independence of the judges requires not only greater transparency and control over cases by the parties involved, but also improvements in the salaries and working conditions of magistrates and justice officials as well as efforts to build up the credibility of the judicial system.

Conclusion

According to our research, the distance between the judicial courts and the majority of Mozambicans is due to the fact that written law is ill-suited to the Mozambican situation, there is a distrust of the workings of the judicial courts and an official, legal, written culture of winner/loser and sanctions, instead of a local culture of reconciliation.

The excessive formalism of judicial justice, the delays in judicial procedures and corrupt practices are also key factors that create blockages in the overall performance of the judicial court system.

We have identified the following causes of endogenous (or organizational) delays and deliberate delays: the organization of the judicial system and the concentration of competences in judicial courts; the rise, albeit slight, in demand; the working conditions (premises and equipment); the recruitment, selection, training and management of human resources; inadequate legal and managerial knowledge; negligent behavior – or behavior which causes delays – on the part of the magistrates, court officials and lawyers or legal technicians and assistants; the inefficient organization and management of the court's work; the weaknesses of the General Attorney's Office;

the inefficiency of criminal investigation; the absence of any means of controlling the system; the financial resources; a lack of political will.

The judicial system is poorly and inappropriately organized, remote from most of its potential users – since it only covers the provincial capitals and about two-thirds of the district capitals – and reflects an image of corruption despite the reactions of the Superior Council of the Judicial System, the Judicial Council and the Supreme Court.

Notes

1 Nine newspapers were analyzed overall and 49 articles on judicial issues were considered.
2 *i.e.* the general (presidential and legislative) elections of 1999.
3 On this subject, see also chapter 6.
4 Carlos Cardoso was murdered on November 22, 2000.
5 This culminated in 2004 with the approval of the new Constitution.
6 The idea of a Constitutional Court was not reflected in the recent changes to the Constitution (2004). However, the office of Ombudsman has been established (Article 256 of the 2004 Constitution).
7 Although other provinces which have witnessed a strong economic recovery, such as the Nampula and Sofala provinces, are also indicating a substantial increase in case flow, with an escalating number of pending cases (data from 2002 and 2003).
8 For a description of the type of proceedings predominant in Mozambique, see chapter 7.
9 On the role of CFJJ in training the main actors of the judiciary, see chapter 6.
10 *Polícia de Investigação Criminal* - PIC, in Portuguese.
11 From 1996 to 2000.

9

Access to Law and Justice: Advocacy and Legal Assistance Between the State, the Market and the Community

Maria Manuel Leitão Marques, João Pedroso, André Cristiano José,
Boaventura de Sousa Santos and Terezinha da Silva

Introduction

In Mozambique, although the right to defense, assistance and legal representation is a fundamental right for all citizens (Article 62 of the present Constitution), this constitutional requirement has not yet become a reality.

Throughout the early revolutionary period in the country,[1] legal assistance was the monopoly of the state. In an attempt to redress the lack of defense lawyers, especially for the accused in criminal cases, the first 20 people's defenders were trained on an intensive course in the late 1970s. As state employees in the Ministry of Justice, they were sent to the country's various provinces and started practicing in the newly created People's Provincial Courts. Gradually, they were incorporated into the *Serviço Nacional de Consulta e Assistência Jurídica*[2] that became the only entity qualified to supply free legal assistance.

In 1986 the *Instituto Nacional de Assistência Jurídica* (INAJ) was founded, with its own statutes but still under the Ministry of Justice.[3] The INAJ was created to try to reconcile the growing demand for legal services (defense and representation in the courts and extra-judicial consultation) with the limited availability of qualified lawyers. By 1990, the INAJ was already establishing branches in the main provincial capitals.

With the reintroduction of private advocacy in the 1990s, the INAJ was replaced by the *Instituto de Patrocínio e Assistência Judiciária* (IPAJ[4]) in 1994, although its functions and performance remained similar.

According to the INAJ and IPAJ statutes, there were three categories of legal defenders: lawyers with a full law degree; legal technicians with a bachelor's degree in law; and legal assistants trained on *ad hoc* courses. These professionals could provide paid legal and extra-legal representation and consultation services, according to rates established by INAJ. However, free legal representation was provided for people who were unable to pay, in which case INAJ itself covered the fees.

Nowadays access to the law depends, to a great extent, on the work of the non-governmental organizations (NGOs). With the opening up of the political sphere since the late 1980s, the NGOs began to play an important role in defending human rights and denouncing their abuse by the authorities. In fact, it may be said that the right to legal defense and legal assistance has been guaranteed more by NGO initiatives than by the state institutions.

1. Advocacy and Legal Assistance

In 1994, private law practice was permitted once again and the law creating the Mozambique Bar Association[5] was approved (Law no. 7/94 of 14 September). In one sentence, Law no. 7/94 enshrined advocacy as one of the three pillars of the administration of justice. The Mozambique Bar Association is a collective body governed by public law, independent of any organs of the state and possessing administrative, financial and patrimonial autonomy. It reproduces the public organizational model of the Associations which exist in most continental European legal systems.

Simultaneously, the legislation deemed that the INAJ had already fulfilled the objectives which had led to its creation and also affirmed the need to "adopt legal mechanisms more suited to the new demands of society, in terms of practicing advocacy," in order to effectively guarantee that the right to legal defense was recognized for all citizens. Therefore, as the INAJ was brought to an end, it was replaced by the IPAJ in response to the need to create an organization that could guarantee access to justice for citizens who were economically disadvantaged (a Constitutional right).[6]

Rules of Access and the Practice of Private Advocacy

The Association is entrusted with certain obligations, namely those of defending the rule of law and individual rights, liberties and guarantees, collaborating in the administration of justice, contributing towards the development of the legal culture and perfecting the law, the obligation to pronounce on drafts of legislation of interest to the practice of advocacy; participation in the study and dissemination of the law, and the promotion of respect for the legal order (Article 4). The statutes of the Bar Association also establish norms which provide for the independence of lawyers in relation to other professions by identifying practices incompatible with the exercise of advocacy. In addition they emphasize the ethical-social role of advocacy by establishing the moral obligations by which lawyers should regulate their professional and civic conduct.

The Bar Association exercises its prerogatives through its organs, which are the presidency, the general assembly, the jurisdictional council and the governing council. Each one of these exercises disciplinary action over its members, in accordance with its statutes and regulations. Official ceremonial honors, similar to those of the Attorney General's Office, are conferred upon the president.

Only lawyers and trainee lawyers[7] enrolled in the Bar Association can practice professionally, or, in other words, exercise their judicial mandate or offer legal consultations as a paid member of the liberal professions. The beginning of legal practice has to be preceded by a training period. Law graduates from Mozambican universities, as well as graduates from foreign universities whose diplomas have been officially recognized, can request to enroll as trainee lawyers. Enrollment as a lawyer is also offered to foreign citizens awarded a diploma by a Law Faculty in Mozambique. Foreign lawyers who have qualified in faculties abroad can also enroll in the Association if there are government agreements which establish a reciprocal regime and satisfy the necessary requirements.

In certain cases, legal technicians[8] and legal assistants are also allowed to practice as lawyers if there are not enough lawyers in their area.

Legal technicians are allowed to intervene in cases in which the amount involved does not exceed the range of the provincial judicial court or in criminal cases which do not involve prison sentences of more than two years, with or without a fine. Legal assistants may defend cases which do not exceed the range of the second-class district court or crimes which do not involve a prison sentence of more than one year, with or without a fine.

Power of attorney, in principle, corresponds to a paid activity and the criteria for determining fees, to be paid in cash, are the time involved, the difficulty of the case, the client's means and the result obtained. A prior adjustment of fees is allowed, with the lawyer able to demand a sum of no more than half of the total. The *'quota litis'* (or 'contingent fee', in the North American system) — in other words, the setting of fees in relation to the final settlement, especially when this involves a purely monetary content – is forbidden. The sharing out of fees is also forbidden, except with colleagues who have collaborated on the case.

The Market for Legal Services in Mozambique

At present in Mozambique, an imbalance has been observed in the legal services market, with the number of lawyers low in relation to the potential demand for this type of service. At present, about 300 lawyers (and respective trainees) are enrolled in the Bar Association, almost all of whom are concentrated in the city of Maputo. Some also go out to the provinces; however, in 2000 only about half a dozen lawyers were established outside the capital and today the numbers remain strikingly similar. This imbalance shows that the Bar Association only guarantees the right to judicial or extra-judicial legal representation and assistance for a clientele belonging to the urban elite living in the capital. If we consider only the most well-known or those who work professionally on a full-time basis, this imbalance becomes even more evident. This situation allows many to specialize, almost exclusively, in sophisticated business law, preferably working for large companies (especially those with foreign capital) and public institutions, and to do consultancy work. Apart from this, some civil economic litigation and large-scale economic crimes are the only other cases handled by these law firms.

The cost of a lawyer's services is therefore extremely high, both in absolute and relative terms. Moreover, the fee system of payment by the hour practiced by some lawyers makes legal services even more expensive.

Up until 2000, the majority of lawyers interviewed had either had a European training acquired abroad (particularly in Portugal) or at the Eduardo Mondlane University, whose faculty and curriculum are still Portuguese-influenced.[9] Consequently, for the time being law firms have foreign partners, predominantly Portuguese law firms. Portuguese lawyers also have a direct presence in the Mozambican legal services market, through their own law firms and in partnership with Mozambican lawyers. There is little regional integration within the SADC area,[10] evident in the type of training lawyers receive and in the absence of regional networks of law firms. Even interpenetration in professional practices is weak, except for the embryonic influence of Anglo-Saxon legal practice in the drafting of contracts for South African investors.

The Bar Association still has little legitimacy among the most well-known lawyers in the city of Maputo, where it has its headquarters. Its model is that of a classical corporate civil organization, with rules controlling access to the profession. Consequently, apart from the habitual disadvantage of this kind of organization in terms of limiting competition, there is the additional fact that the market itself is already not very competitive.

The Bar Association and the Legal Technicians and Assistants

Legal technicians and assistants with inadequate training and without any institutional framework continue to share part of the legal services market with lawyers, whilst struggling against the Bar Association in Maputo city in order to maintain their professional status. Since lawyers prefer consultancy work and business advocacy (which does not require their presence in court), and taking into account their reduced number, there is reasonable potential demand for legal technicians and legal assistants, whether for minor civil litigation – which they prefer – or in the penal field. This is due, above all, to the fact that their fees are much lower than those of the lawyers and also because lawyers are inaccessible to the majority of citizens and small businesses. It is these professionals who defend almost all interests outside Maputo city. Although the position of the Bar Association is more restrictive, some judges and even several lawyers recognize the need for these kinds of professionals to continue working in the judicial arena of Maputo city and in the provinces.

The Institute for Legal assistance and Representation (IPAJ)

Access to justice is extremely selective, as stated above. The state legal assistance system is incapable of responding satisfactorily to the increasing needs of citizens because it lacks the financial, human, technical and organizational resources.[11]

Over the years following its creation, several branches of the IPAJ have opened in all the provincial capitals and their members (legal technicians and assistants) have been assigned to the provincial courts to ensure public defense. However, these legal aid services are marginal, functioning under poor conditions and are hardly known or recognized by most citizens.

As an institution dedicated to providing legal assistance and representation for the needy, the IPAJ has been unable to ensure that legal defense is actually free of charge for the citizens that resort to its services. Most of its members have no institutional, contractual link with the IPAJ. They are left to their own devices, charging low fees for their work.

In 1999 the IPAJ had approximately 360 registered members: 232 legal technicians and 128 legal assistants. However, the Ministry of Justice acknowledged that these figures had to be read cautiously. Their current number throughout the country is impossible to obtain; however, we estimate that in 2004 there were around 400 IPAJ members. Of these, only ten legal technicians actually held a formal contract with the IPAJ head office in Maputo.[12] The Institute does not cover the salaries of the remaining assistants.

Our research has shown that five main problems affect access to the public system of defense and legal assistance in Mozambique: a lack of political commitment; inefficient leadership and management in the IPAJ; a lack of resources; a lack of dialogue and links with the NGOs; the *de facto* privatization of the system.

The lack of political commitment on the part of the Ministry of Justice has meant that the (human, material, financial and organizational) institutional resources available to the state are insufficient to meet the growing needs of citizens. The IPAJ's inadequate funding, together with a high turnover of senior staff has led to its present day inefficient management (characterized by a lack of rules and procedures) and poor quality service.

The lack of any links between the IPAJ and other associations which promote and defend human rights is one of the weaknesses of the system given that, as previously stated, these are the organizations which citizens resort to most frequently to defend their rights.

Most of the IPAJ's affiliates work privately, as 'lawyers' for example, being less well-paid than the licensed lawyers and offering a barely adequate service.[13] They have to live off the income from their profession, which means that legal technicians and assistants end up giving priority to civil cases for financial reasons and neglect criminal cases, even though these account for most of the courts' activities and the accused are almost always needy or even poor. Therefore, neither the legal technicians nor the legal assistants, much less the lawyers and trainees, actively intervene in official defenses, which are left up to *ad hoc* appointments, sometimes even clerks of the court. This situation is particularly serious given the almost total absence of lawyers in the courts, particularly in criminal cases. People with limited resources therefore have no chance of obtaining legal representation, and if the quality of defense in the courts is weak in general, public defense is much worse. These factors have led us to question whether the actual IPAJ is, in fact, capable of offering a service to the public for whom it was created, namely the most disadvantaged citizens. In effect, given that the geographical area covered by any of the alternatives (lawyers, legal assistants and legal technicians) is very restricted, and the costs prohibitive, most individuals using the courts are prevented from resorting to any specialist professional service to defend their rights, either at the pre-trial stage or during the trial itself.

In Mozambique, access to justice and the law is therefore very selective – given the inability of the public defense system (the IPAJ) to provide an adequate service and to function efficiently and the difficulty of hiring lawyers due to cost and scarcity – so that the constitutional objective guaranteeing this right has yet to materialize.

It is not surprising therefore that the human rights NGOs are the most prestigious organizations in the eyes of citizens, due to the defense and legal information services they offer.

Sometimes these NGOs are actually the only support organizations people are aware of (see below). More recently, the Law Faculties (*e.g.* Eduardo Mondlane University and the *Instituto Superior Politécnico e Universitário*, ISPU) appear to have altered their views on the effectiveness of the right to justice by creating legal clinics for needy citizens, an institutional innovation also geared toward giving practical training to final year students. Despite this, there is little close or regular collaboration between this type of organization and the IPAJ or the Bar Association.

2. The NGOs, Access to the Law and the Defense of Human Rights

The Mozambican League of Human Rights (LDH)

Given that, at the moment, access to the law and justice is largely dependent on NGO activities, the research project included a case study on the Mozambican League of Human Rights (LDH).[14]

The LDH was the first institution in civil society created with the fundamental aim of offering legal assistance to the most disadvantaged citizens and leading and promoting the campaign for the defense of human rights. Its central role in this struggle – with all the socio-political implications this involves – and the evident popularity it enjoys in the country, justify its inclusion in this work.[15] The aim of the study was to analyze the League's performance and its importance to citizens and to the consolidation of human rights policies in the country. In fact, in contemporary Mozambique the LDH stands as an example of a NGO which takes the defense of human rights as its central objective.

The Organization of the League

The League is a relatively new institution with a highly centralized structure. The majority of its human and financial resources are concentrated in its head office, located in Maputo city. Moreover, it is an organization personified by its president, Alice Mabota, whose courage has enabled her to resist pressures and external obstacles. The structure and the profile of the League are, to a great extent, defined by its President's powerful personality.

Moreover, this stance also characterizes relations within the institution – which are vertical – with paralegal staff and support services personnel subordinate to lawyers and these, in turn, to the president.[18] The very image of the institution is safeguarded by the rigor imposed by the president. Misbehavior by members that might damage the organization's prestige is promptly sanctioned by the president.

However, from the outset the LDH has always struggled with a lack of full-time lawyers. It only has professionals who are hired and paid for the work they do. There are strong indications that this situation can result in some of them practicing privately as lawyers within League premises and transferring the cases that involve less money to the institution itself.

Finally, the paralegal centers (PCs) located outside Maputo struggle with difficult conditions, both in terms of premises and equipment. Sometimes paralegal staff even lack basic working conditions, such as chairs and office desks.

Figure 9.1: Organization of the League's head offices (in 2000)

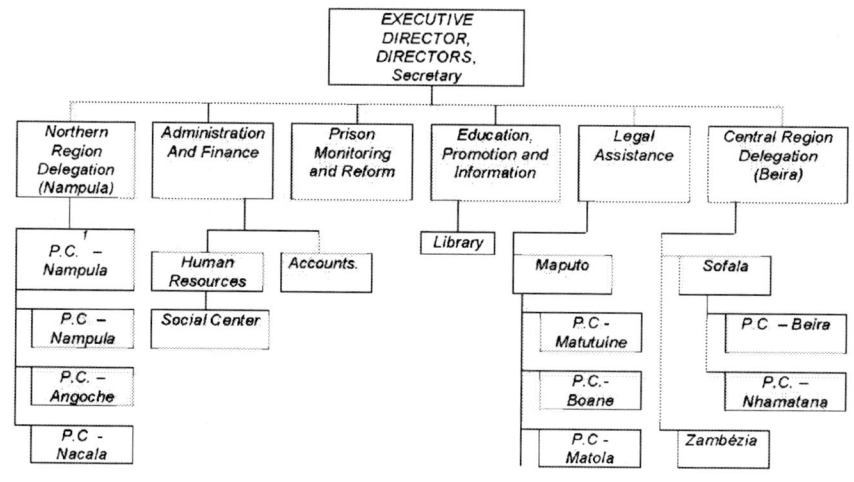

The Development of the League

The League has extended and developed its structure and, at the time when the research was carried out, covered large areas of the country.[10] This situation requires very tight and very much more visible coordination. However, financial and staffing constraints mean that there is inadequate supervision of the paralegal centers.

In addition, centralization in the head office, accompanied by bureaucratic procedural rules, can constrict the activities of the paralegal staff. For example, the credentials of paralegal staff in the Matola Center (Maputo province) must be obtained from the head office in Maputo. In cases where these credentials are required by other entities, this bureaucratic condition makes proceedings even slower. Even in the head office, as solicitations are increasing, the supervision and sanctioning of paralegal staff is inadequate. Furthermore, there are no guaranteed mechanisms for any ongoing interaction that could anticipate errors arising out of the inadequate training of the paralegal staff.

The Scope of the League's Activities

Given the general lack of action on the part of the higher state institutions to put an end to human rights violations by public and private entities, the League appears as the main denouncer, and therefore mobilizes national and international public opinion on the human rights situation in Mozambique. Following the creation of the LDH, the issue of human rights has begun to be debated in the country in a much more open and incisive way. The pressure that the League exerts on the state has, to a certain extent, found a response, if we consider the substantial reduction in cases of police abuse in recent years. The coverage of the so-called *Tchembene case* by the LDH was instrumental in forcing police authorities to initiate criminal proceedings; it precipitated the downfall of the Minister of the Interior at the time, who was strongly suspected of illegal conduct.

According to the League's 2001 Annual report, the Maputo office handled 731 cases, two thirds of which were classified by the LDH as labor and civil matters. The great majority of civil matters are filed by women and involve questions of child custody, child support, alimony or separation payments and inheritance matters. It should be pointed out that, out of 252 labor cases, about half of them (128 cases) were settled by out-of-court mediation conducted by the League's paralegal staff. Finally, 109 cases were classified as criminal (Liga de Direitos Humanos, 2001).

Nowadays the LDH is an essential point of reference as an institution that defends human rights. Its legitimacy in the community is unquestioned. Moreover, the maturity and credibility of its programs of action has helped mobilize financial resources from international agencies.

As reported, the League receives a very heterogeneous selection of cases and handles situations that extend beyond the legal sphere. The subjects under discussion do not follow rigid criteria, in contrast to the proceedings in judicial courts where discussion meets the criteria of *legally relevant material*. Ordinary citizens have problems and face social conflicts which need to be resolved. They usually find a response in the League, regardless of the legal nature of their problems. User participation is much more widespread. The absence of solemn formalities when dealing with people permits broad-based participation in the relevant hearings. In addition, there are no so-called limits to the cases on trial. Cases can be discussed and (re)discussed several times. Everyday language and the national languages predominate, so that there is no need for an interpreter, facilitating free dialogue between members and users.

The Mozambican League for Human Rights plays a substantial role, not only in improving the conditions for citizens' access to justice, but also in denouncing actions and omissions which contend with the rights, freedoms and guarantees of citizens. The League often replaces the government and the courts, performing functions that, according to formal law, are reserved for them.

In Mozambique, as in other peripheral countries, the contingencies of democracy – intersected by long periods of war – and even the processes which gave rise to the third sector, have made relations between it and the state much more unstable and problematic. There is great resistance and many constraints on its activities, as is the case today with the LDH. Given that, on its own the extremely weak state is performing its role inadequately, new forms of collaboration with the community need to be found in order to guarantee that its power is extended more effectively. As Santos affirms, "complementarity between the third sector and the state is, in democratic countries, the other main way of creating a public, non-state arena. For this to happen, however, it is necessary to distinguish between complementarity and substitution" (1999: 46). In addition, the LDH can grant Mozambique very important subsidies in its field of activity.

3. Domestic Violence: Gendered and Child Violence – the Role of the NGOs and the Maputo Juvenile Court

The emergence of the League has provided an impetus for the creation of other NGOs with identical aims, although with very different profiles in relation to their specific objectives. There are various organizations which defend the rights of the most vulnerable groups in society in general and the rights of women and children in particular.[20]

Gendered and child violence has become a worldwide problem covering all aspects of the lives of women – the family, the workplace and the public arena. Although efforts have been made to understand the nature and global dimensions of violence in order to define more efficient strategies to combat it, it is only very recently that gender theories have been incorporated into an analysis of violence.

The International Context

The United Nations Decade for Women (1975-1985) triggered a focus on the problem of gendered violence. During this decade, world summits and conferences took place, organized by the United Nations, during which themes relating to equality, development and the need to increase the role of women in production and development were presented, both by governments and NGOs. However, even in the mid 1980s it was recognized that in spite of the integration of women into development, they continued to play a subordinate and dependent role, which led the feminist movement to raise the issue of violence against women and the violation of human rights.

Even at world events dedicated to women, where the theme of gendered violence was on the agenda, there were few speeches delivered on the subject (*e.g.* the Copenhagen Conference); five years later at the Nairobi Conference (1985) the theme of violence received more attention, although it was not considered relevant to development.[21] By 1986, during a meeting in Vienna, the theme of violence against women within the family was given priority, resulting in the United Nations Convention on the Elimination of All Forms of Discrimination Against Women. The Declaration of the Elimination of Violence Against Women (December 1993) defined violence as one of the gender-based forms of discrimination and inequality. The culmination of this process occurred at the Beijing Conference in 1995.[22] Discussions on violence against women within the family, within marriage, in the workplace, in the public arena, and against children took place, examining different perspectives. The very active participation of Mozambican NGOs and government organizations at the Conference, which contributed towards the theme receiving the attention it did, should be emphasized. In addition, the networks that were established after Beijing became an inspiration for the start of an open process of challenging and combating violence.

The Debate on Domestic Violence in Mozambique

The debate on domestic violence in Mozambique has been particularly intense since the start of 1996. At that time various public figures and particular members of various women's organizations were deeply involved in debating the issue, both on television and in the newspapers.[23] The debate was highly indicative of the ideas which common sense conveys of domestic violence and the place of women within the family. That is to say, the 'preconceived ideas' about violence were full of meanings based on presuppositions about the construction of masculinity and femininity and about the relative positions of women and men. It should be noted that when we speak about common sense, we are referring to the dominant discourse which is imposed and conveyed by social institutions and which, by gaining the appearance of a consensus, becomes even more effective.

However, in general, one of the areas of litigation absent in the courts is that of domestic violence, due to the barriers which its victims experience in terms of access to the law. Domestic violence constitutes a particularly visible manifestation of the imbalance of power between women and men and occurs at all levels, regardless of any specific cultural, religious or class characteristics, even when it assumes different forms. Domestic violence is revealing of the system of male dominance, particularly at the level of the institutions of marriage and the family. As the research carried out — as part of a project on domestic violence[24] — has shown, this phenomenon can only be understood through the social roles that men and women are destined to play, which attribute decision-making responsibilities and control of resources to the former. We aim to treat domestic violence not only descriptively but also by considering the representations of the agents involved, which can contain different perceptions according to whether they are male or female. Nevertheless, they are based on an acceptance of common presuppositions, such as the subordination of women to male authority.

It is only through this perspective, which contextualizes domestic violence as part of gender relationships and as yet another mechanism of social control and preservation of the patriarchal order, that social acceptance of this phenomenon can be explained. Throughout our study we saw that fathers, family members, neighbors and even professionals from legal and social services institutions became accomplices to domestic violence by preaching acceptance or minimizing the complaints made by victims of violence. This is one of the reasons why many women feel intimidated and incapable of asking for help in exercising their rights to life and physical integrity.

Although gendered violence may be increasingly incorporated into the human rights agenda and is becoming increasingly recognized in universal models for equality and social justice, these models are ignored when applied to women.

The Increasing Visibility of the Problem and Political Will

The increasing participation of women and men in the struggle for respect for human rights has, to a certain extent, influenced the visibility of the problem of domestic violence. Campaigning strategies will only be effective if there is the political will to put domestic violence into its true perspective, given that it affects over half the population of the country. It is necessary to recognize publicly, and without any ambiguity based on cultural or traditional justifications, the unacceptability of gendered violence. Often public discourse condemning violence does not, in itself, generate change, but it may be decisive in facing up to the resistance of patriarchal institutions, since women have no real power to alter the situation.

It therefore becomes crucial that legal mechanisms are created for combating domestic violence, which, as has already been mentioned, must envisage a change in the political will of the government.

Our research has shown that there is an important relationship between domestic violence and the legal system. Currently there is no law that makes domestic violence a crime in Mozambique. Many women believe their spouses have the right to beat them and cultural pressures discourage women from taking action. As a result, domestic violence is only judged as a minor physical offence. In fact, the Penal Code[25] today has still not been updated with regard to punishment for bodily harm committed by one spouse against another or by parents against their children, the crimes of abuse, rape and procurement for prostitution, adequate protection for women who are victims of violence and the ill treatment of women within the family.

However, once again, the NGOs are playing an extremely important role by publicly defending women's rights and denouncing their abuse, both in public and private arenas. For example, the recently approved Family Law may serve as a precedent on which future gains in gender-related legal reform can be consolidated.[26] In fact, the work carried out by a network of women's organizations has already succeeded in establishing domestic violence as grounds for divorce. Today, it is advocating new legislation to criminalize spousal abuse. The network is also seeking to enforce inheritance laws for polygamous unions. The Constitution states that all wives in a polygamous union should be treated equally when their husband dies and should inherit property. Yet only too often these women are left with nothing.

The Role of the Maputo Juvenile Court:[27] An Emerging and Localized Justice

In addition to women, domestic violence also victimizes children through lack of parental support or negligence and the psychological, physical and sexual abuse they may suffer.

The Maputo Juvenile Court is a good example of how the rights of children may be promoted through the combined actions of the NGOs and the General Attorney's Office, who have already brought many cases involving family conflicts before the courts in order to defend the rights of minors and their mothers.

Until 1998 less than one thousand juvenile cases were filed annually, but this figure rose in 1998 to 1,210, a figure that represented over half the civil cases filed in the city (2,182 civil cases).[28]

It is essentially women (domestic employees, workers, etc.) who resort to the Maputo Juvenile Court in order to obtain alimony for children under 12 or to sue for divorce, as a result of a family separation.

The Maputo Juvenile Court responds to a specific demand in the city of Maputo, as a result of an increased awareness of women's and children's rights through access to the General Attorney's Office and some of the NGOs, such as the Mozambican League of Human Rights or MULEIDE. In a sentence, the promotion of child justice in Maputo is the result of a combination of four factors: the role of the NGOs in raising awareness of children's rights; the existence of a specialist court; the legal role of the Attorney's Office in this jurisdiction; and the speed of the proceedings.

Conclusion

In Mozambique legal representation and defense were nationalized after independence (1978), when private advocacy and legal representation were banned. Following the Peace Agreements and a change in the political regime, in 1994, private advocacy was once again sanctioned and the Mozambique Bar Association was founded. At the same time the National Institute for Legal Assistance (INAJ), which later became the Institute for Legal Assistance and Representation (IPAJ), was created with the aim of providing a state system for access to justice and the law for those who were unable to contract the services of a lawyer.

The legal services market may be defined as a market which contains few lawyers, almost all of whom are based in Maputo, offering services which are prohibitively expensive for the vast majority of the population.

The state system of access to justice and the law (IPAJ) does not cover the whole country either, since it centers on Maputo, functions poorly and is inefficient. We identified five major problems: inefficient leadership and management in the IPAJ; a lack of political commitment; a lack of financial and human resources; a lack of dialogue and links with the NGOs; and the *de facto* privatization of the system, as a result of which the IPAJ technicians operated according to market principles.

In Mozambique, access to justice and the law is therefore very selective – given the inability of the public legal defense system (the IPAJ) to provide an adequate service and to function efficiently and the difficulty of hiring lawyers due to cost and scarcity – so that the constitutional objective guaranteeing this right has yet to materialize.

The human rights NGOs are the most prestigious organizations in the eyes of citizens, due to the legal information and defense services they offer. Their geographical base is also distinctively different, since some, such as the Mozambican League of Human Rights (LDH), are represented in all the provincial and some of the district capitals. In 2003, for example, the LDH in Maputo accepted over 1,000 cases of varying types (labor, civil and criminal). These NGOs receive international aid and operate with a combination of lawyers and paralegal staff. The former carry out all the activities that are defined by law for their profession. The paralegal staff are responsible for providing supplementary legal information and support services and for extra-judicial conflict resolution.

The activities of the League have provided an impetus for the creation of other NGOs with identical aims. There are various organizations which defend the rights of the most vulnerable groups of society in general and the rights of women and children in particular.

The Maputo Juvenile Court responds to a specific demand in the city of Maputo and is essentially used by women to defend the rights of children under 12, and to sue for divorce, as a result of a family separation. The emergence of child justice in Maputo is the result of a combination of factors: the role of the NGOs in raising awareness of children's rights; the presence of a specialist court; the legal role of the Attorney's Office in this jurisdiction; and the speed of the proceedings.

In sum, the endemic lack of legal defenders is a feature of many African countries. On the one hand, for legal assistance to be provided effectively to the needy there must be enough trained defenders and they must be paid for the services they provide. On the other hand, it would be illusory to expect the Government to be able to pay civil servants in sufficient numbers, given the fact that the entire justice sector receives only a very small share of the overall state budget. Therefore, privileged legal actors must be involved in reforms, but must not be allowed to take them over, much less obstruct them.

The picture present in Mozambique is merely a much sharper and more severe image of what happens in other countries and continents. It is therefore important to avoid certain errors made elsewhere – with excessive corporate professionalism blocking reforms leading to increased dejudicialization or anything else that may affect the potential income of lawyers. Consequently, initiatives that combine the efforts of public institutions, NGOs, universities and private lawyers are extremely important, so that the most pressing demands can be addressed, especially in the criminal field where personal freedom is at stake.

Notes

1   On this subject, see also chapter 2.
2   National Service for Legal Consultation and Assistance.
3   National Institute for Legal Assistance.
4   Institute for Legal Assistance and Representation, approved by Law no. 6/94 of 13 September. The organic statute of the IPAJ was only approved a year later, in 1995 (Decree no. 54/95 of 13 December).
5   In Portuguese, *Ordem dos Advogados de Moçambique* – OAM.
6   i.e. with the aim of guaranteeing economically unprotected citizens the right to defence.
7   All Law Faculty graduates have to dedicate some time to clerkship before becoming full lawyers.
8   Currently, a legal technician is someone who has attended classes in a law faculty. He/she does not need to hold a Bachelor's degree to be admitted to the IPAJ (see below).
9   Since the late 1990s various new Faculties of Law have opened in the country. On this subject, see chapter 6.
10 The Southern African Development Community SADC – is a regional organization uniting fourteen countries from southern-central Africa, aimed at coordinating development projects. On this subject, see chapter 4.
11 The Ministry of Justice – which as an institution supervises the activities of the IPAJ – cannot even pay the minimum IPAJ operating costs at central and provincial level.
12 Also, over the last few years, the IPAJ Nampula office has been supporting another 20 legal technicians through regional governmental funding.
13 However, the statute of IPAJ clearly states that their members must give adequate legal assistance and aid free of charge for those who, for economic reasons, are unable to engage their own attorney (Article 8 of Decree no. 54/95).
14 *Liga Moçambicana de Direitos Humanos*, in Portuguese.
15 Due to lack of time and financial resources and because it had not been created when the research work was planned, it was not possible to develop the same type of work on the *Associação Direitos Humanos e Desenvolvimento* (Association for Human

Rights and Development – DHD), an organization whose formal objectives are identical to those of the MLHR. Moreover, since 2000 the activities of the DHD have declined dramatically for several reasons and the association has almost disappeared from the political landscape.

16 Paralegal Centers. The category of paralegal assistant was inspired by the experiences in several Third World countries where citizens without full technical training give legal support to fellow citizens – above all, the most needy – in situations where state and even private legal assistance is scarce. Paralegals dedicate themselves mainly to providing defence and legal assistance; in many cases they also develop conciliation and mediation activities, make new laws known (mainly in the field of human rights), denounce situations of arbitrary arrest, etc.

17 Maputo city has the status of a province; therefore it is divided into five municipal districts, previously known as 'urban districts'.

18 The League's activities have spread through Mozambique, through the complex networking of paralegal centers, both in the central and northern part of the country. Each of these regions constitutes a regional head office. Each regional head office controls various subordinate centers.

19 In 2002 the League had 20 offices spread across the country, employing a total of 40 paralegals and a significant number of activists.

20 Among the very active NGOs one could refer MULEIDE (Women's Association, Law and Development), aimed at promoting and defending the legal rights of women, particularly as they pertain to improving social conditions and ensuring participation in the development process; ORAM (Rural Association for Mutual Support), and UNAC (National Peasants' Union, coordinating various grassroots associations); these two main peasant organizations have been pivotal in the defense of land rights of peasants (women are the primary cultivators of family land in rural areas).

21 Reference to the World Conferences on Women, held in Copenhagen and Nairobi, which have contributed to the progressive strengthening of the legal, economic, social and political dimensions of the role of women (editor's note).

22 Corresponding to the fourth United Nations World Conference on Women.

23 In relation to this, see the article by Meneses and Adam (1996).

24 This study was carried out under the scope of the program 'All against violence', initiated in 1996 by *Forum Mulher* (a Mozambican network of women's organizations).

25 The current Penal Code, with several changes, dates back to 1886.

26 The new Family Law approved in 2004 raises the minimum age for marriage from 14 to 18, allowing women to inherit property in divorce cases. This legislation represents a step forward for the women of Mozambique, who have long suffered from profound discrimination. It also legally recognizes traditional marriages, which constitute the great majority of marriages in Mozambique.

27 In Mozambique, juvenile justice is administered by outdated legislation dating from colonial times. Whether dealing with minors 'in moral danger', minors who are 'undisciplined or abandoned' or minors 'in conflict with the law', measures are always applied to protect and defend minors, seeking to prevent them from turning to a life of crime. Promoting the well-being of deprived, abandoned, ill-treated, neglected or traumatized children, as well as the education and correction of juveniles who commit crimes, therefore forms part of the instrumental, social control and resolution of litigation functions.

28 For 2002 and 2003 the figures are: 2,132 cases filed in 2002 and 1,764 the following year.

10

Community Courts

**Conceição Gomes, Joaquim Fumo,
Guilherme Mbilana, João Carlos Trindade
and Boaventura de Sousa Santos**

1. The Creation of Community Courts

In the process of breaking with and dismantling the colonial state after independence, the new Mozambican state created a new judicial system (Gundersen and Berg, 1991; Gundersen, 1992; Lundin, 1994).[1] In this judicial system – the main objective of which was to serve all Mozambicans – the popular courts, at different levels and with different forms of organization, were the guarantors of the implementation and reproduction of popular justice.[2]

The Mozambican Constitution of 1990 abandoned the judicial system of 'Popular Justice' and created a new paradigm. The new political-constitutional framework adopted a judicial organization "consistent with the new philosophy of the organization of the State and the many democratic institutions in the country" (Preamble to Law no. 10/92 of 6 May – the Organic Law of the Judicial Courts).

The community courts created by Law no. 4/92 of 6 May remained outside this judicial organization. The main objective of these courts was to fill, at the base level, the void created by the formal abolition of the popular courts. Defending the supremacy of social justice, equal rights for all citizens, social stability, the value of tradition and many other social and cultural values, the Law recognized that the country's experiences of a community style of justice "indicated the need to value and deepen it, taking into account the ethnic and cultural diversity of Mozambican society." It therefore justified the creation of "bodies which enable citizens to resolve small differences within the community and contribute towards harmonizing the various practices of justice and enriching rules, habits and customs, thus leading to a creative synthesis of Mozambican law" (Preamble to Law no. 4/92).

Despite defining the parameters within which the future community courts should develop their work, Law no. 4/92 was never regulated, which means that the Mozambican state never formally fulfilled its desire to create these courts.[3] For almost all the judges in the community courts, this legislative omission represents a strong sign of delegitimization on the part of the state.[4] Compared to the former popular courts, which formed the base of the official judicial system, the community judges interviewed considered that the state, by not establishing a legal framework of operations for the community courts and by not making support available, particularly material support and training, delegitimized them both in the superstructure and in the communities.

Although the available data regarding the distribution of community courts in Mozambique is quite feeble, figure 10.1 is indicative of their strong presence in the country (a total of 1,740 community courts).[5]

Figure 10.1: Distribution of Community Courts by Province (2004)

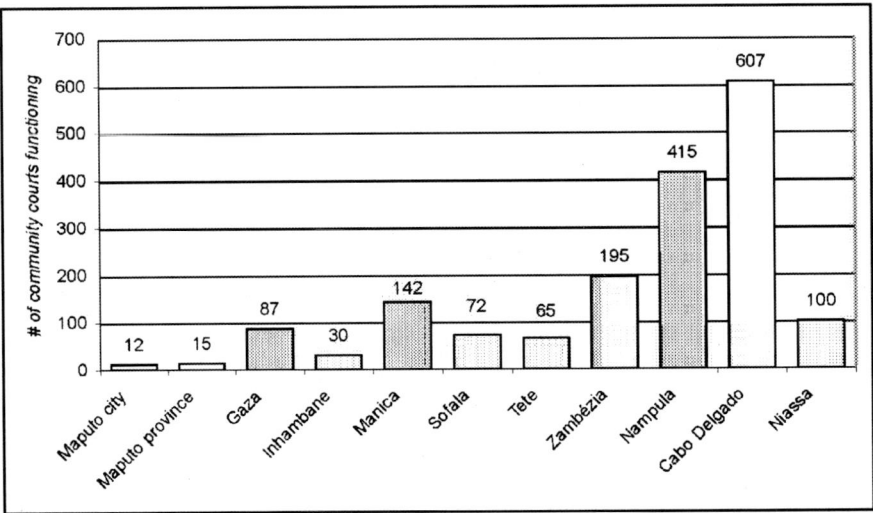

Source: Ministério da Justiça (2004). *Relatório ao X Conselho Coordenador*. Tete, 13-15 July 2004.

The Relationship Between Community Courts and Official Courts

In general, the provincial courts do not have any links with other non-judicial bodies involved in the resolution of conflict. As for the district courts, their relations vary according to geographical proximity, the personal bent of the judge in the judicial court, the legitimacy and efficiency of the other bodies, their willingness to cooperate (particularly in the case of the traditional authorities) and the implementation of research and support projects specifically for the community courts, which can also benefit the judicial courts and the judges themselves (as was observed in the province of Cabo Delgado).

There are cases of close collaboration between the district courts and community courts which may assume various forms. In the district of Mueda (Cabo Delgado province), for example, the district court and the community courts in the district headquarters have maintained a stable relationship which has progressed from discussion and clarification of the responsibilities of community courts to the joint definition of the sanctions to be applied in various cases and the rapid handling of cases emanating from the community courts. Although on a different level of intensity, a similar situation was observed in the district of Alto Molócuè (Zambézia province). Here the relationship had developed mainly into the presentation of monthly reports to the district court and the depositing of the revenue collected in the Bank.

The official judicial system does not wish to function as an appeals body or an alternative to community justice when the latter is not efficient or when its decisions are not accepted by one of the parties involved. For instance, in trial sessions observed in a provincial court, the judge refused to hear family conflicts (in one case, this involved the crime of bodily harm in which the victim was the sister of the aggressor and in another, material damage carried out by a husband) and sent the parties involved back to their neighborhood. According to the judge, these types of conflicts "are not for a judge to hear, but should be resolved within the family or in the neighborhood". He was referring to the structures of the local *grupos dinamizadores*,[6] the community courts and the families themselves. In both cases the accused[7] benefited from legal defense by being appointed a legal assistant. However, in these situations, denial of access to the law affected the victim and had nothing to do with any problem on the part of defense, since both cases had been brought before the court by the attorney's office.

The Law that created the community courts was never regulated. This law limited itself to defining the courts' institutional framework. It determined that the judges of the former popular courts at the level of the localities and neighborhoods would continue to exercise their functions until the first elections for judges for the community courts were held.[8] However, as there have been no elections, the judges at the time kept their positions. Due to reasons arising out of normal occurrences and circumstances of life, such as death, illness, migrations caused by the long civil war and professional moves, the body of judges naturally suffered some reductions. These reductions were also affected by some people leaving their posts due to the loss of social prestige attached to the position and to the feeling of having been 'abandoned' by the government, which was (and is) the case of many of the judges, as well as the unpaid nature of the work. In some courts these absences were filled by new members. In the absence of any regulatory law to define the rules of recruitment, these replacements were made from within the same socio-political environment as that of the previous judges. The new judges were elected through the local *grupos dinamizadores*, proposed by neighborhood structures or by the direct intervention of individuals connected with the Frelimo party.[9] It may therefore be said that the creation of community courts by the state, to function as a bridge between the judicial system and the community, failed due to a lack of political will or attention. A vacuum was created at this level, which, as soon as political conditions allowed, has been filled by other social regulation mechanisms, the most important of which are the traditional authorities.[10]

2. Brief Characterization of the Community Courts

The community courts are, therefore, a hybrid legal entity which combines the characteristics of official justice with those of unofficial justice. As the law that instituted them was never regulated, in sociological terms the characteristics of unofficial justice predominate.

In the areas in which they remain active and operational, community courts are entirely maintained by the strength of their previously conquered legitimacy. Throughout our period of research we had the opportunity to observe some courts which were very active and involved with the community. Among these, we wish to highlight the community court of Vilankulo-Sede (Inhambane province) and those in the neighborhoods of Mafalala, in the city of Maputo and Munhava-Central, in the city of Beira. However, exceptions do not make the rule. The human and infrastructural needs which, in general, affect the community courts, and the competition they face from the other entities involved in the resolution of litigation (the police, local *grupos dinamizadores*, the religious authorities, the traditional authorities, etc.) are contributing to their gradual disappearance as the favored centers for the *creation of a new law* and as the disseminators of rights. The crisis in their legitimacy is evident in the number of cases they handle: in many of the courts observed there is less than one case a month. According to many of the judges interviewed, the main causes of this crisis are that the state does not provide material resources (paper, pencils, pens) and financial compensation for their work, that there is a lack of training or guidelines on working rules, and that the judicial courts do not give them any support in social cases. In other words, there is no adequate institutional integration.

The Judges

As established in Article 7 of Law no. 4/92, the community courts are composed of eight judges, five of whom are full members and three are substitutes. However, in seven community courts in various regions of the country, namely Ingonane, Mafambisse, Chipangara, Morrumbala-Sede, Sansão Muthemba, Chingodzi and Dómuè, there were not even enough judges to allow the court to function with its minimum legal *quorum* (two members, in addition to the presiding judge). Other courts, although composed of three judges, are very often forced to function without a *quorum* whenever one of the judges, for some reason, is unable to attend. For example, in the Maimio Court (Cabo Delgado province), when two judges were ill, the *quorum* was made up by the secretary of the neighborhood *grupo dinamizador*, a situation which, as we observed, was considered normal.[11] The reasons for the lack of judges in the community courts have already been discussed. About half the courts have a clerk or a messenger or both in their service.

It should also be pointed out that there is an overwhelmingly male presence. Of the 174 individuals who make up the 34 courts initially observed, only 19% (33) were women.[12] This percentage is even lower in relation to judges. Only 26 of them were women, which amounts to only 18%.

The judges, whether men or women, tend to be over 40 years of age. Even when they are replaced, recruitment does not, as a rule, alter the age group. However, in some cases, particularly when the replacements are women, they do tend to be younger. In societies with a strong rural element, as is the case in Mozambique, age is very significant in relation to the exercise of authority and this is the main reason why people in such positions tend to be older than the legally stipulated minimum age.[13]

In terms of occupation, the majority are peasants (they work in the fields at their *machamba*, including most of the women), whilst others are retired people, artisans and workers. In four courts the stated profession was head of the district market, post-office worker, school functionary, health authority worker and police officer. In Murrébwè (Cabo Delgado province) one judge also stated that he was a *régulo* (traditional leader) and in Muélé (Inhambane) one was a member of Ametramo.[14]

The Politicization of the Community Courts

Given the socio-political context in which the community courts have been functioning, there is no discontinuity with the popular courts (for instance, the judges are, in most cases, still the same). Almost all of the judges in the courts observed said they belonged to the Frelimo party and many of them also participated in party organizations such as the OMM[15] and the local *grupos dinamizadores*. This duality is one of the reasons why the courts have a party identity and also a degree of ambiguity. It is also the source of the problems they confront in the exercise of their duties. The persistence of this connection – both in terms of the political loyalties of the judges and the human component and also the community court premises in which the courts operate – encourages the courts' widespread identification with the Frelimo party.

This fact, combined with a certain marginalization of the traditional power structures, has led to the increase of political bipolarization, with the community courts regarded as the instruments of Frelimo and the traditional authorities as instruments of Renamo.[16]

This identification has led a group of judges in one community court in Mocímboa da Praia (Cabo Delgado province), presumably supporters of Renamo, to create a parallel community court.

In 2004, observations of several community courts in Angoche – a municipality won by Renamo in the 2003 elections – revealed an intensification of the political differences between the parties (Renamo and Frelimo), a situation that was dramatically affecting the existence of the local community courts. Accused of being controlled by Frelimo, the judges seemed incapable of attracting litigants. In fact, the extreme politicization of these courts had resulted in a profound distrust, by the parties, of the community courts' ability to judge their cases with the impartiality they required.

Working Conditions in the Community Courts

The vast majority of community courts observed operate in the same premises as the former grassroots popular courts. One characteristic common to all the courts is the precarious condition of the buildings where they function. Out of the total number of courts studied during the first research project, eight were held in the open air, eighteen worked in buildings offered by the *grupo dinamizador*, the Frelimo party, the Administrative Post, the school director or the Municipal Councils, and two functioned in the house of the presiding judge – one on the veranda and the other in the yard. Only six courts have their own premises.

The fact that a court operates in the open air obviously influences its activities, making them seasonal – sessions must be interrupted every time it rains.

When courts operate in buildings that are loaned, usually by the local *grupo dinamizador*, they have to be shared. This situation displeases the majority of judges interviewed. From the outset, it affects the working hours of the court. In several sessions and in various courts observed, the judges warned the parties or the witnesses during the trial session of the need to adhere to the session schedule because the room was due to be occupied 'by others' later. In addition, as observed during the trial sessions, sharing facilities means that trials are frequently disturbed by members of the *grupo dinamizador* consulting documents filed there, fetching papers, etc.

The lack of premises of their own prevents community courts in general from having any space for their own exclusive use, to keep and file their documentation. For this reason, in many of the courts the case files and other documents were stored in the house of the presiding judge or the court clerk. This situation also occurred in cases where the community courts had their own premises. Their advanced state of disrepair meant that no materials could be stored in them. Quite apart from practical concerns, sharing premises with structures linked to political parties naturally makes it difficult for the community courts to function autonomously, as well as to affirm their status as independent structures.

Even when courts operate in buildings, the furniture is very simple and sparse, generally consisting of a table or desk, chairs for the judges, one or two long benches for the parties and, in some cases, a cabinet. In some courts the parties had to bring their own benches or sit on the floor. In others, the furniture for the trial session was loaned from other nearby entities, either the local *grupo dinamizador*, the Frelimo party or others or, in cases where the courts functioned in the open air, the residents of the nearby houses. It is, however, interesting to note that, within the general precariousness in which the community courts operated, there were substantial differences in the material assistance they requested. For example, whilst the community court of Bairro Sansão Muthemba[17], in Tete city, requested a typewriter – because "the modern world has an advanced technology" – and the "Penal Code", the community court of Vilankulo and the community court of Bairro de Machavenga (both in the Inhambane province) asked for notebooks and pencils.

Working Hours

The court schedules vary considerably. Few courts are open every day. Most are only open twice a week and on those days, few function throughout the day, usually only in the morning or in the afternoon. This situation is a result of the fact that the great majority of courts observed did not have their own premises, but had to share a building with other structures.

The fact that they cannot operate on a daily basis prevents community courts, from the outset, from intervening in urgent situations such as minor disputes between spouses or neighbors which in turn can result in many people 'running straight to the police', a frequent complaint of many community court judges. The population does not, therefore, have easy access to community court justice.

3. The Nature of the Cases

For reasons previously explained, it was only possible to gather, by random sampling, documents and data on 436 cases in 15 courts (see table 17.1). Using a form to describe the cases, we obtained data relating to the characteristics of the parties involved, access to the courts and the nature of the problems dealt with.

The socio-legal demand is dominated by marital issues (35%), followed by theft, slander, and bodily harm. There are also cases relating to debt, land and housing issues. In a more fragmentary manner, cases of suspicion of witchcraft, abuse of trust, and labor issues (related to contracts and indemnities) also occur. Additionally, the survey encountered cases involving lack of hygiene, a complaint about a large fine, a disturbance at work, the attribution of a name and the formation of a partnership, a case of sexual harassment, a rape, arson, the sale of another person's property, and an accusation of cutting firewood without authorization.

Conflicts involving relations within the family have significant weight in our sample, particularly marital conflicts, although there are also issues relating to minors, the division of property and the breach of promises of marriage (the latter amounting, on the whole, to 169 cases – 48% – out of a total of 350).

Marital issues were the most frequent type of litigation in all the community courts observed. The great majority of cases involved adultery, domestic violence, abandoning the home, lack of support from husbands and divorce claims. In the community court of Mafalala (Maputo city), for example, the plaintiff wanted a divorce "because the first wife is possessed by a bad spirit".

Table 10.1: Types of Issues in the Community Courts Studied (1996–2000)

Type of issues	Number of cases
Marital conflicts	121
Marriage	9
Minors	23
Family conflicts	10
Division of property	6
Housing	13
Burglary (petty theft)	34
Bodily harm	24
Abuse of trust	8
Witchcraft	10
Land tenure	18
Debts	21
Contracts	4
Compensation	6
Labor issues	5
Other	9
Total	**350**

Source: CEA/CES, 1999.

There are major differences in the working conditions of the community courts and in the way in which they operate. However, these differences, as we shall see, exist mainly in terms of emphasis and degree. In fact, as we are dealing with a community justice which is not professionalized, aside from being informal and not subject to predefined standard rules and procedures – as is the case in the judiciary and the procedural codes that govern formal justice –, this operational diversity is only natural. Moreover, their non-professional nature and the structural differences confer different competences on the community court judges and result in specific kinds of behavior. For example, a presiding judge who is more familiar with the judicial courts, as is the case with the presiding judges at the Bairro da Liberdade community court (Inhambane city) and the Mafalala community court in Maputo city (who are both also elected judges in the judicial court), will be more likely to reproduce the procedures of formal justice. Naturally, the level of education is also reflected in the litigation procedures, particularly in relation to written records.

The Parties

Plaintiffs comprise a more or less equal number of men and women, with men slightly outnumbering women.[18] At first glance this information does not seem to correspond to the nature of the conflicts, which predominantly constitute marital litigation, with most of the complaints being brought by women. In fact many of the cases, particularly those in which a wife has been abandoned, are presented not by the woman concerned but by her father, who appears at the trial as the plaintiff.

In terms of the accused, men predominate substantially, representing 68% (285 men and 132 women). Accused males are the majority in samples from all the courts, with the exception of the community court of Bairro da Liberdade (Inhambane city), in which both men and women brought forward complaints in identical numbers.

There were no differences in relation to the age of the plaintiffs and of the accused. In both cases, the most common age group is between 20–40 years, followed by the 40–50 group. However, the main incidence for both plaintiffs and accused was in the 20–30 age group.

Housewives predominated amongst the plaintiffs – which is explained by the high number of cases relating to family conflicts – followed by workers, service sector employees, and small farmers. On the side of the accused, there were no significant differences in terms of occupation, although they included fewer housewives and more unemployed people. There also appeared to be more security agents (police and military), as well as more senior officials and retired people. This distribution seems to indicate that the socio-economic status of the clients of the community courts, whether plaintiffs or accused, is similar.

The Complaints

Complaints submitted directly to the court predominated – 57% of the complaints were presented directly to the community court; in other words, the plaintiff had not previously resorted to any other community body to resolve the dispute. There were, however, a significant number of cases in which the offended party had previously presented a complaint to the local *grupo dinamizador* or to the police (24% and 14%, respectively). In addition, some other cases had been brought before the community court via the judicial court or Ametramo.

This absence of reference to an intermediary structure does not mean that it did not exist. In the sessions observed we found various cases in which, although it was not reported that the case had been taken up by another community body, this was in fact what had happened. In general, when a case is transferred from another community body a document is created (a "guide" to the transfer of the case) which is directed to the community court. As the transfer documents show, the deescription of the case can be very brief or more detailed. The document is signed by a representative from the body that is forwarding the case and bears its stamp.

Court Proceedings

In the judicial courts, the procedural formalities required by procedural law constitute one of the pillars on which official, formal justice rests and represent one of the fundamental guarantees for those who have recourse to them. The procedural rules are uniform and the assumption is that they are known and used by all agents of justice. In contrast, community justice is a non-professional form of justice based on oral, informal and, naturally, non-uniform procedures. For this reason, it is a very heterogeneous form of justice in terms of proceedings. In the case of the community courts, this heterogeneity also arises out of the fact that they operate outside any formal, organizational context, and are left to their own devices and to the local ability to improvise, innovate and reproduce.

There are, in fact, significant differences between the courts, whether in terms of the organization of proceedings or the language used. In some courts, as is the case in the community court of Mafalala (Maputo city), Munhava-Central (Beira city), Bairro da Liberdade (Inhambane city) or Chipangara (Sofala province), the very close relationship with formal justice has led to a selective adoption of the formulae, styles and language inherent in that type of justice. The proceedings are more formal, with all complaints recorded in writing as a document of notification or formal complaint.

The court record sometimes contains other notes, such as an indication that a given party or witness has been notified, the terms for payment of compensation, or the setting of a trial date. Proceedings are, in general, handwritten. However, in most courts we observed, the complaints are registered in a much more summary form: on a school notebook, merely recording the identification of the parties and the object of the litigation.

It is interesting to see that, even in the most formal of proceedings, the use of legal terminology was combined with the use of simple language, directly linked to the oral nature of the surrounding culture. In any case, this formality did not influence the outcome of the litigation. It seemed, above all, that the prime objective was to establish a distance vis-à-vis the parties and to legitimize the power of the court. When the statements were written down, they were signed by the party who had made them and by the presiding judge or his/her substitute. Having received the complaint, the accused was notified to appear on a particular day and time at the court.

In this respect, too, there are many differences between courts; whilst in some courts notification may be written on any sheet of paper (including, in one case, the blank space on an election leaflet), in other courts embossed sheets of paper existed. In addition, in these notifications, the procedural law of the judicial courts was used as a means of imposing the power of the community court. In the cases to which we had access, these notifications always ended with the threat of punishment in accordance with the law.

There were no significant differences in terms of proceedings during the hearings. Once again, the differences were, above all, those of emphasis and depended very much on the presiding judge. The judges use their resources in the way they feel is most effective in order to impose the power and the decision of the court. Consequently, the hearings can be ritualized to a greater or lesser extent, with greater or lesser recourse to the 'threat' of the law. The hearings always created an effect of distance between the parties and the court, achieved mainly by the distinction between the area reserved for the court and that of the parties.

All the hearings observed took place in a context dominated by rhetoric, translated into verbal expressions, silences and gestures. National languages predominated in the hearings; Portuguese was very seldom used. The court used the same language as the parties; there was no need for interpreters or rephrasing. On rare occasions there was recourse to the concepts and formulae of judicial law, and when this happened, it was always done very selectively and instrumentally, with the aim of legitimizing the court. The parties never intervened spontaneously. In many courts, excessive gesturing by the parties was punished.

The Decision

The most common verdict was condemnation (58%), irrespective of the nature of the conflict concerned. The sentence could consist of the payment of a fine, the payment of compensation, the restoration of a situation to its normal order, the termination of marital or family problems, or the authorization of the payment of alimony. There were, however, cases in which the guilty verdict was reversed, that is to say that the plaintiff rather than the guilty party was condemned if it was proved that the plaintiff had been lying, had behaved in an offensive manner during the trial, or had presented a complaint without proof against the accused. In many cases, the payment of a fine or an indemnity was associated with other sanctions, such as, for example, community service and *levar chamboco* (a beating with a wooden stick).

Many complaints arising out of family conflicts ended in agreement between the parties, especially when they involved child support payments and the payment of compensation by either the plaintiff or the defendant. Reconciliation of parties is most frequent in marital conflicts. The judges always sought to obtain reconciliation between the couple or between the accused and his relatives. When this was unsuccessful, the conflict ended with the separation of the couple and the subsequent division of property. Our sample contained very few examples of cases being withdrawn – only 6 out of 291 cases.

In various situations the court decided that cases had to be dealt with by another entity which had more specific powers to resolve the conflict. The dispute could therefore be sent back to the family, to Ametramo or to the judicial courts.

In situations specifically involving pending cases, the reasons given for this were as follows: in five cases this was due to the non-appearance of parties or witnesses; in six cases the court decided to delay the trial; in one case it was decided, on the request of the plaintiff, "that she should be submitted to certain traditional investigations to determine the truth about whether she had sent evil spirits to her nephew's house, as the spirit has said"; finally, in another case, this was because the wife of the accused "had acquired a pregnancy".

Analysis of the documentation enables us to verify that pecuniary sanctions have become, in recent years, the standard measure for all types of litigation. The courts have virtually ceased to apply the other measures envisaged in the law – such as community service, or the loss of any right whose immoderate use had led to the transgression of Article 3, no. 2, of Law no. 4/92 (paragraphs b and d) – as was often the case at the time of the popular courts. Although it is not acknowledged by the judges in these courts, it may be stated that very frequently the amounts of the fines and legal charges levied considerably exceeded those stipulated by law, which certainly affects the access to the justice offered by the community courts.

Conclusion

Community courts in Mozambique today are entities for resolving very complex litigation. They have taken over the human and institutional legacy of the popular courts, but not their formal organizational legacy. Unlike the formal courts, they are not part of the judicial structure nor do they receive any technical and material support from the judicial courts. Under these circumstances, wide variations in the way community courts work are only to be expected. With all kinds of human and infrastructure shortages, and faced with competition from other litigation settlement mechanisms – from the police to the *grupos dinamizadores* to the churches to traditional authorities –, the community courts have been left to their own devices and to the local capacity for improvisation, innovation and reproduction. This explains the almost chaotic variation in the way in which they operate. The absence of any recognition of this *de facto* situation has led to the absence of any mutually beneficial interaction between official justice – which is almost exclusively at the service of the urban population – and a form of justice that is not official but reaches the areas where most of the population live.[19] This poses the risk of formal justice becoming more and more formalized and of informal justice not having a regulatory framework in which constitutional principles and respect for human rights represent the limits of its autonomy.

As legal hybrids community courts are producing a 'creative synthesis of Mozambican law'. However, the uncertain environment in which they operate, if not corrected soon, could in the short term jeopardize their very existence. In light of this, Mozambique has been developing a broader project for legal reform since 2003, which is aimed at democratizing and decentralizing the court system whilst improving access to law and justice and this project includes, as one of its pillars, the reform of the community courts.

Notes

1   On this subject, see chapters 1 and 2.
2   The popular courts were considered the instrument which enabled the people "to resolve the problems and difficulties arising out of daily life in the community, the

local area and the village and neighborhood communities." The popular courts were also considered to be a guarantee of the consolidation and unity of the Mozambican people, "the great forge in which the people create the new law which continues to drive out the old law of colonial-capitalist feudal society" (Preamble to Law no. 12/78).

3 The Law of the Community Courts is currently (2005) being reformulated, as part of a broader reform of the justice system in Mozambique (see below). It should be pointed out that the new constitutional reforms of 2004 defined the existence of several categories of courts, including community courts (Article 223).

4 This chapter refers mainly to the study carried out during the first research project, from 1996 to 2000.

5 Law no. 4/92 defines the institutional framework of the community courts. For example, it clearly states that the provincial governments are responsible for establishing these courts (Article 12). However, throughout the first research project little was known at provincial court level about the activities carried out by these courts.

6 See note 34 in chapter 1.

7 When communicating in Portuguese, community courts tend to use the word 'accused' instead of 'defendant', the word in use in the judicial courts.

8 Law 4/92 states that the provincial governments should establish the mechanisms and time frames for the election of community court members (Article 13) and that the district judicial courts are responsible for controlling the process.

9 The party in power since Mozambique became independent. After the introduction of a multi-party system in the early 1990s, Frelimo has won both the presidential and the legislative elections.

10 The subject of traditional authorities is analyzed in more detail in chapter 11.

11 Of the 34 community courts studied during the first project, less than half of them had five or more judges. The data available since 2003 indicates a clear deterioration in this situation.

12 In some community courts, in addition to judges, there were also other counsellors, treasurers, etc.

13 By law, the minimum age for a judge in a community court is 25.

14 AMETRAMO – Mozambican Association of Traditional Healers. On the role of traditional healers in conflicts involving accusations of witchcraft, see chapter 3.

15 *Organização da Mulher Moçambicana* (Organization of Mozambican Women), an organization which is part of Frelimo.

16 Renamo is the main opposition party in Mozambique.

17 *Bairro* corresponds to a large neighborhood. See note 18 in chapter 1.

18 In the cases analysed up to 2000, 195 of the plaintiffs were male and 202 female.

19 According to the last census, the rural population accounts for the vast majority of the population in Mozambique (77%).

11

Traditional Authorities

**Maria Paula Meneses, Joaquim Fumo,
Guilherme Mbilana and Conceição Gomes**

Introduction

As argued earlier in this book, the landscape of justices in Mozambique is heavily defined by legal plurality. In addition to the community courts, our study also analyzed, although in less detail, traditional authorities as entities involved in the resolution of conflicts.[1] The subject of tradition and traditional authorities, widely discussed today within the context of the social sciences and politics in Africa, is extremely complex and diverse (Ranger, 1988). Although the practices and content of these concepts vary from one setting to another, in Mozambique they are both, in general, meant to connote autochthony and authenticity. By invoking local/regional cultural practices vis-à-vis the modern state, groups create and reinforce legitimacy and authority through their own cultural constructs. However, the transformations that these entities have experienced and been subject to have imbued the content and nature of both with ambivalence.

The Mozambican state is not strongly established and has a weak ability to intervene in large parts of the country, especially rural areas. This power vacuum was filled in the colonial era by co-opting the local authorities through a system of 'indirect rule' (Mamdani, 1996a). This explains the presence of traditional authorities (tribal leaders, chieftains, *régulos*, etc.) and their subordinates,[2] whose authority, in the countryside and often in periurban areas, is legitimately recognized. Since the colonial period, therefore, traditional authorities have been a subaltern power, a form of subordinate power by which a subordinated people were ruled. Being a subordinate power, their ability to resist the interference of the dominant powers was limited.

1. The Traditional Authorities in a Postcolonial Context

In the post-independence era, the attempt by the Frelimo government to institute a modern state free from any ties to the colonial state led to the distancing of the traditional authorities as local administrative bodies. Their formal ban resulted in the need to create new local organizations, such as the *grupos dinamizadores*.[3] However, as some of the case studies show, the hostile politics of Frelimo were felt more strongly in the urban areas or areas close to the centers of power, where the state was more firmly established. This explains the fact that traditional authorities (and the other bodies of local power)[4] managed to keep functioning on the margins of official discourses and practices, by developing their own mechanisms for social reproduction. If the opposition of the Frelimo government toward traditional authorities had already weakened the penetration of the state into the rural communities, the civil war made its presence militarily unviable. Another structuring factor of the armed conflict was the party affiliations of the traditional authorities (Geffray and Pederson, 1986: 316-318; Clarence-Smith, 1989).[5]

The non-acceptance, from below, of a state structure mirroring the colonial one, together with the ongoing persistence of traditional authorities in the political landscape, led to increased resistance and opposition – on the part of community members – to the excesses of power demonstrated by the new 'modern' leadership in the country (Geffray, 1990; Lundin, 1998; Dinerman, 1999). This fact, combined with the state's docile compliance with neo-liberal impositions from the mid-1980s onwards, fuelled the process by which the traditional became a way of claiming an alternative modernity.

During our fieldwork[6] we identified the presence of a complex blend of local ancestral authorities and those imposed by the colonial state (tribal headmen, 'elders', *régulos*), which has produced an intricate fabric with distinct cross-threads in terms of actors, functions, etc. In terms of cooperation with the political-administrative local state, the present situation is extraordinarily heterogeneous. Some authorities collaborate constructively with local state administrative structures, as is the case with the Luís and Mafambisse *régulados* (both in the Sofala province) and the Cumbana *régulado*, in the Inhambane province.[7]

At the same time, there are *régulos* who have stopped working and await institutional 'integration', *i.e.* from above. This was the case of the *régulo* Salgado (Tete city) and *cabo de terra* Jorge in the Zavala district of Inhambane. Others functioned almost 'independently' of the official administrative structures, either because they did not exist or because they felt themselves in competition with them (as was the case with some of the *régulados* in the district of Matutuíne, in the extreme south of Mozambique, or the *régulo* Zintambila in the province of Tete).

Since the early 1990s, the Frelimo government has been trying to neutralize the hostility of traditional authorities,[8] co-opting them by granting them some kind of subordinate recognition and participation in local administration, both in rural and periurban areas.[9] This process was most evident in Decree no. 15/2000, which recognized local community authorities.

The same political party that once banned all traditional authorities, rituals and beliefs under the auspices of 'anti obscurantist' socialist modernization reintroduced the possibility of incorporating – as legitimate, decentralized local government – those same 'traditional' chiefs once held to be the instruments of the colonial State. In fact, according to Article 1 of this Decree, "community authorities are understood to be the traditional chiefs, the neighborhood or village secretaries and the other legitimate leaders recognized as such by their respective communities or social groups". At the same time, this prepared the way for a broader understanding of the figure of the local, community leader.[10] Prompted by the Mozambican Ministry of State Administration, a two-stage process has taken place: initial recognition – by local communities – of their local leaders, followed by official recognition – by the state – of these leaders. By mid-2003 this process had resulted in more than 13,500 legitimately identified leaders from rural and urban communities. Of these, about one and a half thousand (roughly 10.7%) had by then been recognized by the state as official community leaders.[11]

2. The Traditional Authorities in Action

In the cases analyzed it can be seen that, in terms of customary law, traditional authorities act mainly to prevent conflicts from emerging, whilst the object of modern state law is to resolve situations of open dispute.

As dispute resolution mechanisms, traditional authorities are particularly important in issues involving access to land, the family (including adultery and, in some cases, divorce), debt, bodily harm, damage to property, health/sickness, witchcraft and petty theft – in fact, a very broad range of issues (Alexander, 1994; Carrilho, 1995; Cuahela, 1996; Dinerman, 1999). In all these matters the traditional authorities are the key node in a network of institutions that may include the district or even the provincial courts, the police and the local political and administrative agencies. Sometimes they are the first ones sought out by the parties, at other times they function as appeal institutions, and in yet other cases they provide advice or evidence in cases being dealt with by other institutions.

As mentioned above, the sample we used shows the extreme heterogeneity of current proceedings, although it is possible to detect some common aspects (Meneses *et al.*, 2003).

In terms of 'traditional justice', it can be seen that the *régulo* does not function as the lower instance in the resolution of conflicts.[12] Cases are normally brought before subordinates (*cabos de terra, tinduna*, etc.) and are only sent to the *régulo* if the latter are incapable of dealing with them.

From the cases studied, we observed that one of the great strengths of the justice provided by traditional authorities is its immediate, public, collective, face-to-face, and relatively transparent character.

The hearings normally take place in the house of the traditional authority[13] or near it, on the porch or in the garden. The frequency of these hearings varies. Certain days might be selected for the hearing, or hearings might occur when people solicit the help of the *régulo* to solve a difficult and unexpected situation. In the cases we observed, most of the *régulos* tended to hold the hearings on the weekends, particularly on Sundays. Conflict resolution is dominated by rhetoric and orality, as in the community courts. Additionally, like the community courts, the language used is, by and large, the local language of the parties involved and there is no need for interpreters. The participation of the *régulo* and his associates is essential. The *régulo* (and occasionally the *madoda* – his counselors) sit at a raised table. The parties are seated below, either in front or to the side of them. The audience sits on benches or mats. The *régulo* leads the hearing. After the session has been opened, the person leveling the complaint and the person accused normally make their case. Because the sessions are open to the public, members of the audience are usually invited to participate by presenting their explanations of the problem. This is a very important part of the process of conflict resolution and adults are, in fact, allowed to question witnesses and give their opinion on the case.

The *régulo's* counselors also offer their appraisal of the conflict. In the regions surveyed, no example was found of a woman being a *régulo*. However, among the counselors of the *régulo* there are normally one or two women and a significant number of women are also traditional healers.

When the case involves accusations of witchcraft, the opinions of the *madodas* pertaining to the decision to appeal to healers or to Ametramo,[14] the Mozambican Association of Traditional Healers, are important.[15] At times the healers intervene and give a deposition.

After hearing and considering the problem, the *régulo* deliberates. In most cases, he attempts to obtain acceptance of the sentence from both sides in order to maintain the social equilibrium.

The main forms of sentencing, when that is the case, translate into fines, community service or physical punishment (for example, head shaving and *chambocadas* – a beating with a wooden stick). Despite being forbidden by law, corporal punishment still seems to be practiced. Several *régulos* expressed a nostalgia for these sanctions: "in the old days the authority could take action. The person was tied up and beaten. Now the authority can't beat people any more".[16] In the case of the régulado Luís (Sofala province), there was a cell in his headquarters. In Inhambane we also saw that sentencing involving physical punishment still exists, although usually the sentence also mentions the fact that the punishment can be replaced by a fine.

Case records are also variable. As this is an environment in which rhetoric predominates, we only observed one case where the sentences and the agreements reached were recorded in writing (*régulo* Luís, in Beira city). Although some *régulos* claimed that they lacked utensils (as in the community courts), it was clear that many did not know how to read or write. In some cases the notifications were written.

When the chieftains handed them out, they also explained the contents orally to the parties concerned; in other cases notification was only given orally.

All the traditional authorities levied taxes for their services. However, the amounts were extremely variable, a fact which was confirmed by some *régulos*.

The language of the hearings is vernacular and the national languages are mainly used. Portuguese seems to be used only rarely, although it is the official language of the country.

Throughout our research we found evidence that relations between the community courts and the traditional authorities in the same geographical location were sometimes conflictual and sometimes collaborative. The *social division of labor* usually ends up determining a certain 'specialization' for each of the entities, with traditional chiefs solely responsible for accusations of witchcraft and complex extended family issues and community courts solely left in charge of petty crime, whilst both share litigation linked to the demarcation of land and family conflicts.

The typology of these cases and the process of reaching a decision, based mainly on mediation and the reconciliation of the parties, are very similar. From what we could observe there seems to be a tendency toward compensation. Although in neighboring countries 'traditional justice' is normally described as being very 'cheap', this is not the case in Mozambique. Fines and the justice tax applied by traditional authorities tended to be higher than those in the community courts.

Relationships with other Institutions

In the field of conflict resolution, the relationships between traditional authorities and other local authorities are quite complex and not always free from conflicts or tensions. Forms of cooperation also exist: many *régulos* send divorce cases to the community courts and serious crimes − such as homicide − are sent to the police. In other situations, cases are presented to the *grupos dinamizadores* and the other community structures which compete and collaborate both with the community courts and the traditional bodies whenever conflicts break out.[17]

Although they have not been studied in detail in this research, mention should be made of the role of traditional medical practitioners as entities for resolving conflicts. In fact, countless cases are sent, both by the traditional authorities and the community courts, to Ametramo, especially those involving the identification of the guilty parties in cases of witchcraft. The *tinyàngà* (traditional healers) play a key role in producing proof in these cases, as they are central to the identification of the guilty party. They therefore constitute another entity within the set of traditional authorities which should be studied more closely in future.[18]

The power discourse relating to traditional authorities is currently extremely controversial in the country. Many of the *régulos* complain that there is no consultation on who should become the *régulo* of a particular area, or if there is, this often involves people who do not represent the community (although this is covered by the above-mentioned Decree no. 15/2000). It is essential that conditions be granted to the traditional authorities to enable them to decide on these issues as they see fit and be able to do this independently of any political, or any other, tutelage.

Political Parties and Traditional Authorities

Within the main political parties, positions on the traditional authorities are also unclear. Opinions waver between a minimalist concept (which sees traditional authorities as a reactionary institution, enclosed within anti-democratic practices and barely represented in the local community) and a maximalist concept (which recognizes the specific nature of the traditional authorities as an expression of a social and religious power that transmits ancestral protection and rightly favors them over other local organizations).

This brings us back to the discussion on the party affiliations of the traditional authorities. Although they are normally identified with Renamo, this is not always the case, as with the *régulo* Phata, in Inhambane province, for example.

During the presidential and parliamentary election campaigns of 1999, both Renamo and Frelimo attempted to invoke the 'traditional authorities' and traditional values in their campaigns. A case in point was the political struggle between Frelimo and Renamo for control of the influential *régulo* Luís in Beira city. Both parties attempted to convince him to support their campaigns, but *régulo* Luís himself wavered to and fro. Nevertheless, the struggle triggered a dispute for the succession in which his nephew proclaimed himself the new *régulo*, and a clear supporter of Renamo, after his uncle finally refused to take sides. The struggle for the succession was only settled after the elections were over and *régulo* Luis is still in power in Bairro Manga-Loforte, in the city of Beira (2004). The current trend in politics at the national level of involving local and regional traditional authorities such as *régulo* Luis imbues tradition locally with a renewed ambivalence derived from (or at least strengthened by) national political practices. The move by both Renamo and Frelimo into the domains of tradition creates a tension between, on the one hand, the political reframing of and call to tradition, and the local situation in relation to development practices on the other.

In terms of the resolution of conflicts, however, and faced with the complexity of the structures surrounding the struggle for power, it is worth emphasizing that fieldwork observations showed that positions can nevertheless be broken down, with traditional authorities being more inclined toward Renamo and the community courts while leading local groups are the favored arenas for Frelimo activity. In any case, the competition for power and the superimposition of the spheres of intervention of the different structures involved in the resolution of litigation are well known, since *"people don't know how to resolve conflicts. Nobody's role is clearly defined"*, as many of the interviewees affirmed.

The struggle for recognition of the multicultural political and legal landscape that exists in Mozambique has led to recognition, in the new Constitution (2004), of the various normative and conflict resolution systems that coexist in Mozambique (as long as they do not contradict its values and fundamental principles – Article 4).

Together with recognition of traditional authorities (Article 118), this represents a significant departure from earlier ideas on the nature of the Mozambican state.

Conclusion

The framework of justices in Mozambique consists of a series of institutions whose work depends on the fluidity of the interaction between them. The better defined their respective roles are, the better they can carry out the functions attributed to them by society in general and by local communities in particular, the more efficient their performance will be and the more fully citizens' rights will materialize and the state's interests be realized. In fact, although official discourse does not recognize them, the *régulos* and other instances of traditional leadership very often operate in close cooperation with the state. Many *régulos* are called upon to intervene in vaccination campaigns, civic education, etc.

The path of the various cases analyzed in our research demonstrates a simultaneous recourse to diverse mechanisms for the resolution of litigation, forming a complex network. This means that all are necessary, since their common denominator is offering perspectives for solving and/or preventing problems. They are proof that legal hybridization has been developing in Mozambique for a long time. It is a hybridization that accepts, inclusively, the official, modern, legal model and even makes room for its work. Seen from this perspective, the vitality of the types of justice into which traditional authorities are integrated is the mirror image of the difficulties of official justice, which seems unable to achieve its objectives.

Traditional authorities manipulate certain 'traditional' aspects as legitimizing marks of their authority while also using 'modern' elements – such as the political parties – to consolidate their power. It is this subtle dialectical relationship between tradition and modernity that animates traditional authorities and allows them to develop. Rather than personifying the fixedness of an imagined past rewritten in the present, this landscape of justices is the symbol of another modernity which is eminently complex and calls for further study.

Extending the community's participation in the resolution of its problems is one of the requirements of the process of democratization taking place in the country. It is vital to make the constitutional principles and administrative organization of the state compatible with the models of action, cultural presuppositions and normative structures of the traditional authorities.

Today, an ongoing legal reform is taking place in this complex, and even conflicting context. It recognizes a myriad of ways of settling informal disputes encompassing a large percentage of the country's population. Legal projects should seek to provide an integrating framework for these conflict resolution mechanisms, given that the absence of rules has negative implications, as this chapter has aimed to show.

Notes

1   The issue of traditional authorities is also analysed in chapters 1 and 3.

2   Although the most common term is *régulo* (chieftain), the local expressions are extremely varied: for example, *mwene* in the Amakhuwa regions, *nyakwawa* in the provinces of Manica and Sofala, *samasuwa* in Zambézia, *hosi* for the Machangana, etc.

3   See note 34 in chapter 1.

4   In this research, local notables, such as traditional healers, local religious authorities, heads of lineages or heads of production, are understood as part of the concept of 'local, traditional authorities', despite the fact that their political importance seems to be less visible.

5   In this regard, the plasticity of the traditional authorities is eloquently illustrated by the institutional innovation of the *régulo* of Mafambisse (Sofala province) during the civil war. During the course of the war, the *régulo*'s territory was torn apart by the conflict between Frelimo and Renamo. In order to preserve the traditional leadership in the zone, the territory was divided into two zones. The zone under the control of Renamo continued to ruled by the titular *régulo*, Manuel Dique Mafambisse, who came from a prestigious family. In the zone under government control, traditional authority was represented by the then local political leader, José Dique Mafambisse, the younger brother of the titular *régulo*.

6   Field work for the first research project took place from 1997 to 2000. Complementary information from the second research project (since 2003) is also provided.

7   This climate of cooperation amoug the members of this web of legal and administrative entities does not prevent those intervening from remembering past grievances and from voicing them when deemed appropriate. *Régulos* and other notables were intimidated and humiliated by former subjects who came to occupy party secretary positions within Frelimo, or by other higher level state and party authorities (Geffray, 1990). During interviews several traditional authorities (*régulos*, healers, etc.) referred to the persecution they had suffered for political reasons and the climate of animosity towards them. As a result, many were arrested or even deported to the northern provinces during the infamous *Operação Produção* in the early 1980s, to be 're-educated through labor action' in order to become 'new human beings' (Meneses *et al.*, 2003).

8   See chapter 1. One must also be aware of the fact that the position of the main political parties toward the customary remains undefined. While traditional institutions were normally identified with the Renamo, nowadays this is not the case. For example, Frelimo and Renamo seem to share a common perspective of fear in relation to witchcraft, which results in non-recognition as part of the state system. Both parties resent the role of this leadership, since traditional authorities may stand in the way of their plan to enhance centralized political action.

9   What is particular to Mozambique is that these authorities are present both in rural and periurban contexts. In some areas covered by our field work, even in areas close to the urban centres – such as Jangamo and Inhambane (*régulos* Patha and

Nhampossa), Beira city (*régulo* Luís) and Dondo in Sofala province (*régulo* Mafambisse) – the traditional chiefs contacted were extremely active, either in collaboration with the political-administrative authorities or with their knowledge and agreement. See also note 18 in chapter 1.

10 Because they are not recognized as part of the state, however, these community authorities are not entitled to salaries paid by the state. Instead, the state allows them to retain up to 5% of the taxes collected by them from members of the community, as a means of supporting their activities.

11 The local authorities elected/chosen by communities include not only *régulos* and other *traditional* structures, but also neighborhood or village secretaries (*i.e.*, the former *grupo dinamizador* secretaries, the remains of a power structure introduced by Frelimo after independence to replace the customary institutions – Chichava, 1999). Today, due to their reputation for wise counsel, they are elected through a process whereby they compete with other local institutions. A very small proportion of these recognized leaders are women. After returning to the field in mid 2004, we observed that in several districts the process of recognition of these authorities had been fully implemented. Before then, however, no leaders from urban or periurban settings had been officially recognized. The leaders – upon formal recognition – have received national flags and personal badges.

12 Although the *régulo* and his counselors stand at the apex, various other assistants help him on a daily basis. In southern Mozambique, for example, in each area of the chiefdom there is usually a *cabo de terra* (*nduna*). He hears cases, solves problems, etc. and reports directly to the *régulo*. Several *tinduna* are also part of the *régulo*'s council. Some people bring their problems directly to traditional counselors, who may intervene initially in a conflict in order to solve community problems.

13 I.e. the *régulo, cabo de terra*, etc.

14 *Associação Moçambicana de Médicos Tradicionais*, in Portuguese.

15 The power of the *nyángà* (traditional healer) lies in his or her ability to identify existing social tensions, contradictions, and areas of distrust, as well as possible anti-social hostilities that may manifest themselves as sickness, bad luck, or even death in the community (Meneses, 2004). The process of identifying the witchdoctor, locating the agent of evil and making him or her confess to their actions, is also the process by which the witchdoctors are cleansed of the burden of evil, thereby paving the way for the restoration of stability and good health in the community. Even in the revolutionary period the popular courts would often turn to traditional healers to solve cases involving accusations of witchcraft.

16 Interview with the *régulo* Phata, Inhambane province.

17 Ministerial Decree no. 107-A/2000 defines the interaction between community courts and the community chiefs. Article 5(b) outlines one of the tasks of these authorities as "interaction with the community courts, wherever they exist, in the resolution of minor conflicts of a civil nature, based upon local habits and

costumes, within the limits established by law", clearly recognizing the existence of a complex network of interaction in local administrative areas.

18 Ametramo also has a fairly hierarchical structure, mirroring the pyramid of formal justice. Cases addressed to Ametramo can go to appeal from a 'local' to a 'higher' level (the district or provincial structure of the association), by requesting other more experienced and knowledgeable *tinyàngà* to 're-evaluate' the case.

12

Solidarity Networks as Entities for Resolving Conflicts

Teresa Cruz e Silva

Introduction: Neighborhood Networks at Mafala (Maputo City)

The successive crises and transitions which marked the 1980s and 1990s in Mozambique played a significant role in the process that brought about the weakening of the state. The state's inability to supply basic services to the population (Santos, 1998b: 11) meant that part of this social management was transferred to "civil society," which has begun to exercise many functions linked to the production of economic and social well-being – through non-governmental organizations (NGOs), associations and a variety of solidarity networks originating out of the networks of primary relationships (family and neighbors, professional, ethnic and friendship groups, etc.) existing in society (Nunes, 1995: 10-11). It was the weakness of the state, rather than its authoritarian power, that undermined its authority, and it was its absence and inability to produce basic services that led to an increase in alternative forms of social management.

The 'network approach' was used successfully for several decades to analyze urban social phenomena. Nowadays it is applied to the study of wider phenomena, such as situations of conflict, political power or even the analysis of problems such as hunger, vulnerability and poverty, as it improves understanding of the different types of existing strategies, particularly the aid networks developed to deal with these problems (Loforte, 1996; Andrade *et al.*, 1998; Ministry of Planning and Finance, 1998).

In Mozambique, where a process of urbanization marked by a large country-to-city migratory flow can be witnessed, the social relations created within society are vital, since they generate mechanisms that can deal with daily life and develop strategies over a longer period of time. The impact of social urban space on the structuring of social bonds between people in relation to the economic, social and political situation that has characterized Mozambique during recent decades is not easy to measure. If, on the one hand, it is not possible to ignore the fact that many of the norms relating to a rural environment have been transferred and adapted to an urban context (and are relevant for an understanding of the systems of rights and obligations which are part of many of these urban groups, in which 'customary norms' continue to offer a certain security in the process of social relations), on the other hand we can also encounter cases in which these various survival strategies have been redefined. This not only reinforces 'customary norms', but also recreates new relationships based on solidarity, in which, for example, neighborhood relationships begin to play an essential role in developing bonds of solidarity and mutual help.

The networks constitute a social capital which may be defined in terms of the reciprocal relationships existing in society, based on social bonds in which factors such as the sex, age, religion and social position of their members define hierarchies and power relationships, and in which existing norms and relationships of trust, aid, cooperation and coordination work to the benefit of all (Loforte, 1996; Andrade *et al.*, 1998).

The study of alternative forms of social management involving the use of the network approach, in the context in which we propose to analyze such forms, necessarily entails using and working with concepts such as family and parenthood,[1] due to the essential role which cooperative relations established through the family represent in the construction and reconstruction of solidarity networks. Thus, while it is not our intention to analyze the various forms of theoretical approach which can be applied to the concept of family, we cannot ignore the fact that it represents a privileged space for the social construction of reality, in which, through the relationship between its members, socialization is produced (Saraceno, 1997), and in which relational dimensions (relationships of a family nature, affectivity or affinity), spatial dimensions (expressed as cohabitation) and economic dimensions (the common budget) all play an essential role in defining the strategies of the *amakhuwa*[2] in the Bairro da Mafalala (Mafalala neighborhood),[3] even if we consider that the applicability of these relationships may vary, according to the complexities that characterize the country (Andrade *et al.*, 1998).

1. Social Management and Its Alternatives in an Urban Context

Using the case study of the Mafalala neighborhood in the city of Maputo, we proposed to identify the role played by solidarity networks in the resolution of litigation, within a situation of legal plurality such as the existence of community courts and traditional authorities. It is necessary to extend the vision of the administration of justice in Mozambique, in this case with specific reference to the urban forms of informal conflict management.

Actors and Networks

Starting with the option of working in an urban environment, the study of Mafalala, a community mainly composed of a Muslim population of *makhuwa* origin, enabled us to identify a privileged socio-cultural space in which the dynamics of solidarity networks could be understood. Since in the analysis of networks we are always confronted with contexts and social processes which can change at any moment, this case study makes visible the effects of the economic and social policies introduced in the country over the last two decades, as well as the alternatives used by this community to face situations of need produced by the fact that the state is not able to offer a number of basic services. In the process of establishing alternative strategies to deal with existing needs and access to basic services, the study identified: i) a set of primary solidarity networks (parenthood, co-residence, neighborhood and religion) that members appealed to in order to receive material or extra-economic support in situations of crisis; ii) societies and mutual aid groups of an informal nature (funeral societies, savings and mutual aid groups as well as women's committees); iii) formal associations with recreational and supportive aims, which functioned as resources in cases of need.

Social control and Mechanisms of Conflict Resolution

The informal systems of social control, which normally include mechanisms for the resolution of litigation, are therefore managed within the various networks which we have identified, functioning as first or second instances, according to each individual case. Working as mediators, members of these networks use rhetoric to persuade the different parties involved in disputes, since their authority is restricted to the power to arbitrate conferred upon them by the parties involved. The most frequent types of disputes include marital conflicts, conflicts between parents and children and conflicts between neighbors. Although these may be considered exceptions, the research team also observed that cases such as crime, robbery and commercial types of litigation were also submitted to arbitration through these networks, without the intervention of state justice, and also involved the use of persuasion. The Mafalala study showed that most litigation rarely leaves the community area, where it is settled, and is only rarely resolved by other bodies, such as the police or the courts. Cases involving some types of economic conflict and disputes over property or the custody of children are normally reserved for the latter institutions and only after the parents and the religious community have been consulted. We are looking at a situation in which legal demand is preferentially met through informal mechanisms, not just for economic and social reasons but also due to the cultural weight of Islam.

Notes

1 Seen as relationships based on solidarity and reciprocity.
2 A matriarchal society from northern Mozambique.

3   Because Maputo city holds the statute of a province, it is divided into several municipal districts, mirroring the overall administrative division of the country. Each of the municipal districts (five in all) is divided into neighborhoods. Mafalala is part of Municipal District 3. For further details see also note 18 in chapter 1.

13

Customary Land Systems and the New Land Law (1997): An Epistemological Note

José Guilherme Negrão

Introduction

In Mozambique and else where in Africa, for the poor peasants – who constitute the vast majority of the population – the land is the only certainty of continuity they have at their disposal.[1] It is on the land that they produce the food they eat and the few surpluses or industrial cultures they are able to get, on it they converse with the spirits of their ancestors, on it they find wood and stakes to build their houses, on it they allow the cattle to graze and they look for healing herbs, on it they identify themselves with the origin of life which is carried by the waters of the rivers. The land is the heritage of the family, the lineage and the community; their ability to resist outside intrusions resides in the sustainability of the use of the land in the fight against poverty and for the increase of wealth.

There fore, the land is inseparable from work, human capacity and capital. Empirical evidence showed that among rural families[2] the land used for various types of consumption could not be perfectly replaced by the land geared for the market; in addition, the market does not work exclusively through the convertibility of assets into capital, but also through the convertibility of the latter and the social obligations networks. In other words, there are social relationships that are based on the land. In this way, the function of distribution on the land is intrinsically connected to the functions of production and consumption, and of these with the rural family. The rural family's function of consumption corresponds to the access to land; the function of production is equivalent to the security of possession; and the distribution function is related to the division of the land in function of the multiplicity of networks which are established by means of blood ties, marriage and inheritance.[3] Thus, for them, above any other interest group, the maintenance of inter-generational returns in the use of resources is of paramount importance, because it is essential for their reproduction.

1. The Customary Law Systems in Mozambique

In any one of the existing customary law systems relating to land in Mozambique – the system of preferential marriage, entrusted territory, stability of nuclear descendents, security over three generations and group dependency (Negrão, 2003: 230-251) – enormous adaptability can be seen in relation to the social and legal changes that have taken place throughout history, in which communities have no direct decision-making powers but of which they are an integral part. The versatility of these customary law systems can also be seen in relation to the interactions, whether complementary or opposing, established at the heart of communities.

If it is true that diachronic adaptability and synchronic versatility are two characteristics of the customary law system existing in Mozambique, the same cannot be said of the legal practice of written law.[4] With about 80% of all land use managed by customary structures, however, during and since the post-war resettlement period, it made sense to give these systems legitimacy under Mozambican law.

2. The Land Law and the Legal Structures of Mozambique

Not infrequently, judges in the district and provincial courts have been seen refusing to apply the new Land Law in disputed cases (*e.g.* in relation to rights of occupation), while the judges of community courts and traditional and community authorities do so without having received any specific training for that purpose. In addition to personal reasons (ignorance of the law, parallel interests, etc.) in the appointed judicial judges' non-application of the new Land Law, what is at issue is the link between the oral and the written in legal concepts and practice. Written law, as it exists, is based on a philosophy of science wherein deductive logic is the only vehicle for thought worthy of consideration (Sayer, 1992). Just as deductive logic, so too oral law (like all rhetoric) has 'non-logical thinking' as an integral part of its practice. While formal logic deals with the inferences and implications between premises and conclusion as the reasoning behind truth, the 'non-logic' of customary law deals with the establishment of premises, the criteria adopted for their selection, the methods employed for gathering them and the relationship between facts and forms of abstraction on the route toward rationalizing opinion.

The new Land Law's incorporation of non-codified customary systems into formal law to be applied by any court is the first sign of an epistemological rupture in legal science in Mozambique.[5] The shift from a rupture to an epistemological cut in legal practice depends on each and every one of us in the coming years.[6]

This incorporation of customary law systems has had implications on the production of legal science. Gradually, everywhere, the method of production of knowledge relating to the land problem in Mozambique has been successively questioned. In their analytical as well as their normative and political discourse, conventional theories on the rural world and its development are less and less accurate in their predictions of what will happen when various kinds of options are adopted. Whenever the accuracy of the prediction of a scientific theory (or set of theories) begins to decline, there is nothing more to do but return to empirical evidence to redefine presuppositions and build a new theory. This is what currently can be seen in Mozambique, as this book illustrates.

Analytical and normative discourse were both questioned when the Land Law began to be implemented at a national level. For the first time, professionals and scholars from a wide variety of scientific and technological areas were called upon to take part in seminars, promote debates and write articles on questions such as what a rural community is, which models of community management of resources exist, how women's rights to land can be ensured in the context of customary law systems, which spatial options should be followed and how the emergence of group dynamics should be facilitated within the context of the dissemination of the new Land Law.[7]

Rural sociology questioned the approaches to social space and causality, as it was forced to ponder the notion of local community. The classic search for the internal dynamics of a cohesive social space gave way to the identification of interactions between social areas. The mono-causal explanation of an economic, technological or political nature so much in vogue in African academic circles evolved, out of the Aristotelian dualities taught in the universities, into the multi-causalities of a dialectical nature which orality imposes by not recognizing the primacy of the conceptual definition over the construction of the notion revealed in the self-defining act of the community.

Time and space emerge once again in an analysis of the modernist discourse which presupposes that the traditional is equal to the primitive and that modern equals civilized. Post-modernism re-questions cultural identities in the community management of natural resources, and wavers between renunciation of the traditionalism of local cultures (which, as such, are the object of political and economic bottom-up autonomy) and affirmation of the symbolic nature represented through discourse (which, as such, is the object of decentralization ruled by constitutional principles and party interests).

Conclusion

The options available in planning the use of land confront each other and range from a technical vision of registered law, in the form of a land deed, as the only means of guaranteeing property rights (and, as such, in attracting investment), to the interpretation of the acceptance of current models of use requiring only compliance with the oral clause of the Land Law in order to recognize already acquired property rights (lowering the costs of the transaction) as a means of preventing conflict and avoiding the rise of the 'landless'.

Finally, the facilitation of the emergence and strengthening of local dynamics at the community level soon comes up against the debate between representative democracy, which the local government project implies, and participative democracy in decision-making processes, in which power is exercised though interest groups and not through urban political parties.

We are far from being able to speak of an epistemological break in the production of science in Mozambique, but, without a doubt, the incorporation of customary law systems into formal law has brought implications which indicate a rupture in the monopoly of deductive logic in theoretical ideas.

Notes

1   The vast majority of the Mozambican population lives in rural areas (77%, according to the 1997 Population Census).

2   By rural family we mean the smallest unit of production, consumption and distribution of the African rural societies.

3   In Mozambique, about 90% of married people are married according to customary law.

4   For a discussion of the fabric of community justices in Mozambique, see chapters 10 and 11.

5   The law that established community courts (Law no. 4/92) was the law no. 19/97. of 1 October first step toward the recognition of local norms and customs in the legal, formal structure. However, it differs from the Land Law in that, it (i) only applies to community courts, and (ii) defends the principles that these norms and customs should be mutually enriched, recognizing state law and the superior form of law.

6   See Mondlane's reflection (1997) on alternative means for resolving conflict, by resorting to common law forms of mediation, conciliation and reconciliation of parties.

7   Among the countless initiatives under way, one movement, called the *Campanha Terra* (Land Campaign), has emerged as a catalyst. It was an initiative of civil society, involving around 200 NGOs, churches of all denominations, associations, cooperatives, public and private research institutions, and other civil society organizations. The Land Campaign reflected civil society's contributions to securing the land tenure of rural populations, acting not only at the level of conceptualization, but also in disseminating information among rural populations, the private sector and state institutions. In less than two years, more than 15,0000 people voluntarily spread the text of the new Land Law through theatre, short courses, cartoons, video cassettes, audio cassettes, music, newspapers, posters and pamphlets, using 20 national languages.

14

Conclusion

**Boaventura de Sousa Santos,
João Carlos Trindade and Maria Paula Meneses**

In recent decades the interest generated throughout the world in the supremacy of the law and the judicial system is a political phenomenon of the greatest importance. Whether it is the product of internal dynamics or of high-intensity global pressures or even – more than ever before – the product of a combination of internal dynamics and global pressures, the reform movement is closely related to the emergence of a new form of state, which can be characterized as a post-Welfare State (in the core, developed countries) or a post-developmentalist state (in the peripheral and semi-peripheral countries, as in the case of Mozambique). It is a state that intervenes very little in the processes of social change, aims to be efficient and is dedicated to ensuring regulation of an economic and social life essentially based on the market and the private sector. This new model of development, which apparently enjoys a global consensus – leaving open the question of how solid this consensus is – is based on the idea that social change is no longer a political issue and that social inequality has to be accepted as part of a process of development that is basically impelled by the market. The supremacy of law and the primacy of the judicial system appear to be the ideal instruments for a depoliticized concept of social change. At the same time, representative democracy, stripped of its mechanisms for social redistribution, has been promoted as the political regime which best guarantees the stability, manageability and social legitimacy of the weak and efficient state and makes depoliticized capitalist social change possible. The supremacy of law and the primacy of the courts are converted into the main pillars of this political project, which we term low intensity democracy.

This democratic project is doubly vulnerable. Firstly, the historical experience of the core countries shows that democratic stability depends on a reduction in, or at least, the non-aggravation of, social inequality. However, this has been increasing dramatically in recent decades. It is an open question when this increase will reach breaking point – the point beyond which turmoil will replace democratic stability. Secondly, the liberal democratic public sphere presupposes the existence of basic rules which guarantee equality for all citizens and a reciprocal responsibility on the part of the government in relation to them. However, in the neo-liberal model of development, social agents have emerged who are so powerful that they control political and economic activities and shape the laws or manage to alter them to suit their own interests. The principle of equality can thus be subverted beyond that which is politically tolerable. Moreover, at the same time that this model of development makes nation-states more responsible to international agencies and multinational corporations, it enables, or even forces, them to become increasingly less responsible to citizens. The combination of these two tendencies can contribute towards transforming democratic capitalist societies into shrinking islands of democratic public life afloat in a sea of despotisms.

The performance of the courts in peripheral and semi-peripheral countries depends, in part, on the level of economic and social development, which affects their working conditions in two main ways. On the one hand, the level of development affects the type and level of social and, therefore, judicial types of litigation. A rural society dominated by a subsistence economy does not generate the same type or volume of litigation as a heavily urbanized society with a developed economy. On the other hand, due to political changes in the peripheral countries, the consolidation of civil and political rights (or law) is embryonic but, nevertheless, superior to that of economic and social rights. This discrepancy is fundamental to an understanding of judicial performance in these countries and the difficulties of the struggle for independence from other powers.

The level of social and economic development alone does not explain the level and type of performance of the courts, since countries with similar levels of development reveal very distinctive judicial profiles. Attention must, therefore, be paid to other factors, one of these – perhaps the most important – being the dominant legal culture in the country, which is almost always articulated as a political culture. Legal pluralism and the concomitant subject of the plurality of instances of conflict resolution – the focus of this book – were the object of intense debate during the late 1980s, both in Africa and in other parts of the world.

The information available suggests that the propensity to initiate legal actions is greater in some societies than in others and these variations may, at least in part, be anchored culturally, since this propensity does not necessarily increase on a level with economic development. If, in certain societies, individuals and organizations demonstrate a clear preference for consensual solutions, or, at any rate, solutions obtained outside the judiciary, in others, the option of litigation is easily chosen. In addition to this, what also varies from country to country is the ability to adapt judicial supply to judicial demand. When this ability is totally absent, judicial supply does not cease to act on judicial demand. It continues to do so by discouraging it, thus increasing the discrepancy between potential demand and actual demand. In some countries, a fall in demand for judicial protection in certain areas has no other justification than the lack of an incentive for demand, due to the poor quality of supply.

Faced with the current crisis in modern legal systems, whose more obvious symptoms are the slowness, inefficiency and lack of quality in access to justice and administration of justice, one should ask whether the answers should not incorporate a plurality of solutions – a combination of diverse dispute resolution mechanisms – respecting the proportionality of means to achieve goals and the equity of citizens with regard to their cultural differences. This process should be carried out bearing in mind the promotion of citizens' access to law and justice. In Mozambique, it would be incongruous not to make use of the several means of non-formal conflict resolution currently in place in society.

Our study has pointed out that the formal, official legal system in Mozambique is only a part of the legal system in the country. Supranational laws also exert an influence on its implementation, especially with regard to issues involving public law, including legal institutions and the legal profession, just as much as 'local' laws continue to influence the conduct of the majority of the Mozambican population. Indeed, our study has shown that in the vast majority of situations, before resorting to the courts, the parties involved in legal disputes try, whenever possible, to resolve matters through the unofficial and more accessible, more informal and less culturally distant bodies which ensure a satisfactory level of efficiency.

Community courts, in Mozambique, are a significant part in the whole system of alternative mechanisms of conflict resolution. Our research has shown that these courts, although suffering from a lack of human resources and other infrastructures, represent a body that promotes access to the law and to justice that is widely legitimized by Mozambican society.

In addition to the community courts, other informal institutions – for example, a member of the family or a respected neighbor, the *régulo* (chieftain), a community organization, association or club, or even a professional, who might be a lawyer, a priest, a *xéhè* (Muslim priest), a social worker, a *nyàngà* (traditional healer), or a teacher, are all potential third parties and can function efficiently as such, depending on various factors. The choice has, above all, to do with the relationships between the parties in dispute, the social area of the dispute, the levels of socialization of both parties, the means of resolution and the means at their disposal to make the best possible choice. Economic, social and cultural factors of various types converge in the choice of a particular third party. Recourse to the judicial courts as the favored specialist entity for the resolution of litigation in contemporary societies therefore occurs within a range of various alternatives, to the extent that the lower court called upon to resolve the litigation is, sociologically, almost always an appeals court, that is, a means which is activated when all the other informal mechanisms used in the first attempt to resolve the case have failed. This factor is crucial in understanding judicial performance, since it shows that this does not occur in a social void, nor does it signify a starting point for the resolution of the disputes it is called upon to judge.

As this book illustrates, various legal orders and systems of justice are in existence in Mozambique. Their complexity is based on the intense interpenetration or reciprocal contamination existing between these different forms of law and justice. Therefore, since the plurality of legal systems is so wide, it is difficult to analyze them all, and some were not studied with the detail they require. In this book, we present what we consider to be the most important outlines of the plurality of law in Mozambique. We have grouped these into two categories: internal legal pluralism, and community justice and the traditional authorities. Internal legal pluralism defines a situation of extreme heterogeneity within state law and therefore within political-administrative state action and regulation. While internal legal pluralism occurs within official law and justice, community justice and the traditional authorities work outside the official domain. They are the conventional field of legal pluralism. Within this, we can distinguish two main subfields: the community courts and the multicultural and multi-ethnic systems of justice or, to be more precise, the so-called traditional authorities.

The community courts in Mozambique today are very complex entities for dealing with the resolution of litigation and, as such, merit special attention in this research project. They are a hybrid institution in terms of some of the previously mentioned variable dichotomies. The community courts have taken up the human and institutional legacy of the popular courts of the revolutionary period, but not the formal organizational legacy, since, in contrast, they are not part of the legal system, nor are they supported either technically or materially by the district courts, the official base of the judicial system in the country. Under these circumstances, it is only to be expected that there is a wide variety of models for the way in which community courts operate. Lacking in human resources and all kinds of infrastructures, and in competition with other mechanisms for resolving litigation – ranging from the police to the local *grupos dinamizadores* and from the churches to the traditional authorities – , the community courts are entrenched within themselves and dependent on local skills for improvising, innovating and reproducing themselves, to the extent that there is an almost chaotic dispersal of their operations. Thus, today, the community courts form 'a creative synthesis of Mozambican law', except that they create this under very precarious circumstances which, if not quickly corrected, will in the near future threaten their very existence.

Amongst all the entities involved in community justice, the traditional authorities and their law[1] have for a long time been the most significant. In our view, the greater visibility of the traditional authorities is related to the weakness of the state in two main ways: by its administrative inability and by the loss of the legitimacy of state power. The identification of various debates centered on traditional authorities today – Africanness and the politics of identity, the dual legitimacy of the power and appropriation of the state, its specificity and its recognition – serve to reveal the broad context in which the role of these authorities is discussed, as a mechanism for resolving litigation and as a pole for the creation and distribution of law and justice.

Therefore, our research comes out against the squandering of resources and experiences and in favor of capturing a wealth of legal resources that the developed world is trying to reinvent.

The question of spreading the legal offer to the whole country does not only depend on the human and financial resources (an obviously important issue) needed to guarantee to all citizens access to the official legal system. These circumstances have set the stage for the current debate on legal pluralism in Mozambique, a country that formally recognized its existence in the 2004 Constitution. It is our opinion that research, in association with the judicial system, must provide a forum in which the various legal discourses and theories can identify themselves and communicate with each other. The progressive and secure development of a genuine Mozambican legal system requires it to be formed at the point where the best legal practices in the country meet. This means giving due credit to African legal systems and African legal thought as a source for ideas, norms and local practices. Legal pluralism does not mean externally and clumsily trying to make state law more responsive by forcing it to open its eyes to other legal orders, but rather a radical rethinking of the way in which we perceive the law. This approach has laid the foundations for the current reform of the judiciary, initiated in Mozambique in 2003 under the supervision of the Centre for Legal and Judicial Training. The reform, seeking to address an understanding of the legal system in Mozambique as it exists today – a dynamically developing, complex system – combines research with the drafting of legislation.

The greatest challenge facing the legal system in Mozambique in the new millennium is therefore the issue of the legal incorporation – in terms of future development – of the components that will enable it to establish a truly unified legal system in the country.

We are certain that our readers will eventually draw other conclusions from our work that will form the basis of other proposals different from our own. Far from considering this a problem, we feel it is one of the more pleasing rewards of our work. If we have provoked a diversity of opinion and done so on the basis of reliable knowledge, we shall have contributed toward deepening the democratic debate in Mozambique. What better reward could there be?

Note

1 Traditional law, ancestral law, African customs and usage and common law are some of the terms currently used to define this.

References

Abrahamsen, R., 2003, "African studies and the postcolonial challenge", *African Affairs*, Vol. 102, No. 407, pp. 189-210.

Abrahamsson, H. and Nilsson, A., 1995, *Mozambique: The Troubled Transition*. London: Zed Books.

Abrahamsson, H. and Nilsson, A., 1996, *'The Washington Consensus' e Moçambique*. Gothenburg: Padrigu Papers.

Aguiar, C. de., 1891, *A administração colonial*. Lisboa, Typographia Lisbonense.

Alexander, J., 1994, "Terra e autoridade política no pós-guerra em Moçambique," *Arquivo*, 16, p. 5-68.

Anderson, P., 1996, "Balanço do Neoliberalismo", in E. Sader, P. Gentili, eds., *Pós-liberalismo: as políticas sociais e o estado democràtico*. São Paulo: Editora Paz e Terra, 3a edição, p. 9-23.

Andrade, X., Loforte, A. M., Osório, C., Ribeira, L. and Temba, E., 1998, *Famílias em contexto de mudanças em Moçambique*. Maputo, WLSAMOZ/CEA.

Ashforth, A.,1998a, "Witchcraft, Violence and Democracy in the New South Africa", *Cahier d'études Africaines*, 150-152(38), p. 505-532.

Ashforth, A., 1998b, "Reflections on Spiritual Insecurity in a Modern African City (Soweto)", *African Studies Review*, 41(3), p. 36-67.

Ashforth, A., 2001, "AIDS, Witchcraft, and the Problem of Power in Post-Apartheid South Africa", *The Occasional Papers of the School of Social Science*, 10.

Ayittey, G.B.N., 1991, *Indigenous African Institutions*. New York: Transnational Press.

Balandier, G., 1988, *Le désordre*. Paris: Fayard.

Baltazar, R., 1978, "Discurso proferido no encerramento do curso de preparação das brigadas de Justiça Popular". Maputo, *Revista Tempo*, 394 (23 de Abril).

Bayart, J.-F., 1993, *The State in Africa: The Politics of the Belly*. London: Longman.

Bekker, J.C., Labuschagne, J.M.T. and Vorster, L.P., eds., 2002, *Introduction to Legal Pluralism in South Africa. Part 1: Customary Law*. Durban: LexisNexis Butterworths.

Benda-Beckmann, F. von, 1988, "Comment on Merry," *Law and Society Review*, 22, p. 897-901.

Benda-Beckmann, F. von, 1991, "Unterwerfung oder Distanz: Rechtssoziologie, Rechtsanthropologie und Rechtspluralismus aus rechtsanthropologischer Sicht," *Zeitschrift für Rechtssoziologie*, 12, p. 97-119.

Bonate, L., 2003, "Women's Land Rights in Mozambique: Cultural, Legal and Social Contexts," in L.M. Wanyeki, ed., *Women and Land in Africa*. London: Zed Books, p. 96-132

Bourdieu, P., 1989, *O Poder simbólico*. Lisboa: Difel.

Bourmaud, D., 1997, *La politique en Afrique*. Paris, Éditions Montchrestien.

Bragança, A. de and Depelchin, J., 1986, "Da idealização da Frelimo à compreensão da história de Moçambique," *Estudos Moçambicanos*, 5/6, p. 29-52.

Cahen, M., 1996, "Unicidade, unidade ou pluralismo do Estado?", in J. Magode, ed., *Moçambique: Etnicidades, Nacionalismo e o Estado. Transição Inacabada*. Maputo: CEEI, ISRI, p. 18-39.

Carrilho, J., 1995, *Administração local e administração tradicional de terras. poder e autoridade tradicional* (volume 1). Maputo: Ministério da Administração Estatal – Núcleo de Desenvolvimento Administrativo, p. 109-121.

Castanheira, N., 1979, "Curandeiros espiritistas: desmascarar a mentira, educar o homem", *Tempo*, 474, p. 10-12.

Castrillo, M. C., 1997, *Crónica de un desorden. Notas para reinventar la justicia*. Madrid, Alianza Editorial.

Centro de Estudos Africanos, 1998, *O mineiro moçambicano. Estudo sobre a exportação de mão de obra em Inhambane*. Maputo: Imprensa Universitária.

Centro de Formação Jurídica e Judiciária, 2000, *Notas Sobre a Formação Jurídica e Judiciária*. Brochura de apresentação nas "Jornadas Sobre Formação Profissional na Área da Justiça. Maputo, 30 de Maio a 2 de Junho.

Chabal, P., 1997, *Apocalypse Now? A Post-Colonial Journey into Africa*. Inaugural lecture, delivered on 12 March 1997 in King's College, London. 10 October 2001. (http://www.kcl.ac.uk/depsta/humanities/pobrst/pcpapers.htm).

Chanock, M., 1998, *Law, Custom and Social Order: The Colonial Experience in Malawi and Zambia*. Portsmouth, N.H.: Heineman.

Chiba, M., 1989, *Legal Pluralism: Toward a general theory through Japanese legal culture*. Tokyo: Tokai University Press.

Chichava, J., 1999, *Participação comunitária e desenvolvimento: o caso dos Grupos Dinamizadores em Moçambique*, Maputo, INLD.

Chingono, M., 1996, *The State, Violence and Development: The Political Economy of War in Moçambique, 1975–1992*. Avebury: Aldershot.

Clarence-Smith, G., 1989, "The Roots of the Mozambican Counter-Revolution," *South African Review of Books*, April–May.

Coissoró, N., 1966, "A Abolição do indigenato e suas repercussões na evolução social dos africanos portugueses," *Separata da Revista Estudos Políticos e Sociais*, IV(3). Lisboa

Comaroff, J. and Comaroff, J.L., 1999, "Occult Economies and the Violence of Abstraction: Notes from the South African Postcolony", *American Ethnologist*, 26(2), p. 279-303.

Copans, J., 1990a, *La longue marche de la modernité africaine: savoirs, intellectuels, démocratie*. Paris, Karthala.

Copans, J., 1990b, "Preface", in C. Geffray, *La Cause des armes au Mozambique: anthropologie d'une guerre civile*. Paris: Karthala.

Correia, P.P., 1985, "*Uma Perspectiva sobre a descolonização.*" *Revista Crítica de Ciências Sociais*, 15/16/17, p. 549-58.

Covane, L.A., 2001, *O Trabalho migratório e a agricultura no sul de Moçambique*. Maputo: Promédia.

Cuahela, A., 1996, *Autoridade tradicional em Moçambique*. Maputo: Ministério da Administração Estatal.

Dagnino, F., 1980, "Sobre a constitucionalidade", *Justiça Popular - Boletim do Ministério da Justiça*, 1, 15.

Dagnino, F.; Cruz, L. and Muguambe, A., 1996, *Os Tribunais judiciais*. Maputo: Relatório da União Europeia.

Darian-Smith, E., and Fitzpatrick, P., eds., 1999, *Laws of the Postcolonial*. Ann Arbor: The University of Michigan Press.

Dezalay, Y. and Garth, B., eds., 2002, *Global Prescriptions: The Production, Exportation, and Importation of a New Legal Orthodoxy*. Ann Arbor: The University of Michigan Press.

Dinerman, A., 1999, "O Surgimento dos antigos régulos como 'chefes de produção' na província de Nampula - 1975-1987," *Estudos Moçambicanos*, 17, p. 95-246.

Douglas, M., 1977, "Introduction: Thirty Years after Witchcraft, Oracles and Magic", in M. Douglas, ed., *Witchcraft Confessions and Accusations*. London: Tavistock, ii-iv.

Ela, J.-M., 1994, *Restituer l'histoire aux sociétés africaines. Promouvoir les sciences sociales en Afrique noire*. Paris: L'Harmattan.

Ennes, A., 1946, *Moçambique: relatório apresentado ao governo*. Lisboa, Imprensa Nacional.

Esteva, G. and Prakash, M.S., 1998, *Grassroots Postmodernism: Remaking the Soil of Cultures* London: Zed Books.

Facio, A., 1994, "De necesidades básicas a derechos básicos," *Fempress*, 158, accessed on 15 May 1999.
http://www.fempress.cl/base/ne_feminismo.htm"
http://www.fempress.cl/base/ne_feminismo.htm.

Faria, F. and Chichava, A. (1999). *Descentralização e cooperação descentralizada em Moçambique, Documento de reflexão ECDPM 12*. Maastricht, ECDPM. (http://www.ecdpm.org/pubs/dp12_fr.htm). 12 September 2002.

Fisiy, C. and Goheen, M., 1998, "Power and the Quest for Recognition: Neo-traditional Titles among the New Elite in Nso', Cameroon," *Africa*, 68, p. 383-402.

Fitzpatrick, P.,1983, "Law, Plurality and Underdevelopment", in D. Sugarman, ed., *Legality, Ideology and the State*. London: Academic Press, p. 159-82.

FNUAP (Fundo das Nações Unidas para a População), 1999, *A Situação da população mundial 1999*. New York, FNUAP.

Fortuna, C., 1985, "Descolonização, o fim de um ciclo: Portugal, a África e a economia capitalista mundial," *Revista Crítica de Ciências Sociais*, 15/16/17, p. 469-99.

Francisco, A. A. S., 2003, "Reestruturação económica e desenvolvimento", In B.S. Santos, J.C. Trindade, eds., *Conflito e transformação social: uma paisagem das justiças em Moçambique.* Porto: Afrontamento, p. 141-78.

Fry, P., 1990, "Between Two Terrors," *Times Literary Supplement,* 9/15 Novembro.

Gable, E., 1995, "The Decolonization of Consciousness: Local Skeptics and the 'Will to Be Modern' in a West African Village," *American Ethnologist,* 22, p. 242-57.

Galanter, M., 1981, "Justice in Many Rooms: Courts, Private Ordering and Indigenous Law," *Journal of Legal Pluralism,* 19, p. 1-47.

Geffray, C., 1990, *La Cause des armes au Moçambique: Anthropologie d'une guerre civile.* Paris: Credu-Khartala.

Geffray, C. and Pederson, M., 1986, "Sobre a guerra na Província de Nampula. Elementos de anàlise e hipóteses sobre as determinações e consequências socio-económicas locais," *Revista Internacional de Estudos Africanos,* 4/5, p. 303-18.

Gentili, A. M., 1999, *O Leão e o caçador: uma história da África sub-saariana.* Maputo, Arquivo Histórico de Moçambique.

Geschiere, P., 1997, *The Modernity of Witchcraft. Politics and the Occult in Postcolonial Africa.* Charlottesville, University of Virginia Press.

Geschiere, P., 1999, "Globalization and the Power of Indeterminate Meaning: Witchcraft and Spirit Cults in Africa and East Asia", in B. Meyer, P. Geschiere, eds., *Globalization and Identity: Dialectics of Flow and Closure.* Oxford: Blackwell, p. 211-37.

Geschiere, P. and Nyamnjoh, F., 2000, "Capitalism and Autochthony: The Seesaw of Mobility and Belonging," *Public Culture,* 12, p. 423-453.

Ghai, Y., 1991, "The Role of Law in the Transition of Societies. The African experience," *Journal of African Law,* 35, p. 8-20.

Gomes, C.; Fumo, J.; Mbilana, G.; Santos, B. de S., 2003, "Os tribunais comunitàrios", in B. S. Santos, J. C. Trindade, eds., *Conflito e transformação social: uma paisagem das justiças em Moçambique.* Porto, Afrontamento, vol. 2, p. 189-340.

Gonçalves Cota, J., 1944, *Mitologia e direito consuetudinàrio dos indígenas de Moçambique.* Lourenço Marques: Imprensa Nacional.

Gonçalves Cota, J., 1946, *Projecto definitivo do Código Penal dos indígenas da Colónia de Moçambique.* Lourenço Marques: Imprensa Nacional.

Graça, J., 1992, *Pràticas corruptivas.* Maputo (mimeo).

Green, M., 1994, "Shaving Witchcraft in Ulanga: Kunyolewa and the Catholic Church". In Abrahams, R.G., ed., *Witchcraft in Contemporary Tanzania.* Cambridge: African Studies Centre, p. 23-45.

Griffiths, J., 1986, "What Is Legal Pluralism?" *Journal of Legal Pluralism,* 24, p. 1-56.

Gundersen, A., 1992, "Popular Justice in Mozambique. Between the State Law and Folk Law," *Social and Legal Studies,* 1, p. 257-282.

Gundersen, A. and Berg, N., 1991, "Legal Reform in Mozambique: Equality and Emancipation for Women through Popular Justice?", in M. Vaa, ed., *Gender and Change in Developing Countries.* Oslo: Norwegian University Press.

Hall, M. and Young, T., 1991, "Recent Constitutional Developments in Mozambique," *Journal of African Law*, 35, p. 102-115.

Hanlon, J., 1991, *Who Calls the Shots?* London: James Currey.

Honwana, A., 2002, *Espíritos vivos, tradições modernas: possessão de espíritos e reintegração social pós-guerra no sul de Moçambique*. Maputo: Promédia.

Hooker, M., 1975, *Legal Pluralism: An Introduction to Colonial and Neo-Colonial Laws*. Oxford: Clarendon Press.

Horton, R., 1993, *Patterns of Thought in Africa and the West: Essays on Magic, Religion and Science*. Cambridge: Cambridge University Press.

Instituto Nacional de Estatística, 1999, *II Recenseamento geral da população e habitação 1997. Resultados definitivos*. Maputo: INE.

Isaacman, A., 1990, *Régulos, diferenciação social e protesto rural*. Maputo: RIEA.

José, A. C.; Araújo, S.; Cuhaela, A.; Fumo, J., 2004, *A Administração da Justiça em Macossa: As redes de resolução de conflitos (relatório de trabalho)*. Maputo: CFJJ/CES.

Khare, R.S., ed., 1999, *Perspectives on Islamic Law, Justice, and Society*. Lanham: Rowman and Littlefield.

Khatibi, A., 1983, *Maghreb pluriel*. Paris: Denoël.

Ki-Zerbo, F., 1996, "Colonialism and Private Law in Africa," *African Environment* X, 55-85.

Klug, H., 1996, *Constitutionalism, Democratization and Constitution-Making for a new South Africa*. Madison, LL.M. Dissertation, University of Wisconsin at Madison, Law School.

Klug, H., 2000, *Constituting Democracy: Law, Globalism and South Africa's Political Reconstruction*. New York: Cambridge University Press.

Last, M. and Chavunduka, G.L., eds., 1986, *The Professionalisation of African Medicine*. Manchester: Manchester University Press and International African Institute.

Le Roy, E., 1992, "Les Fondements anthropologiques des droits de l'homme - Crise de l'universalisme et post modernité," *Revue de la recherche juridique Droit prospectif*, XVII-48.

Liesegang, G., ed., 1966, *Respostas das questões sobre os cafres (1796) elaboradas por Carlos José dos Reis e Gama*. Lisboa, Centro de Estudos de Antropologia Cultural.

Liga de Direitos Humanos, 2001, *Relatório Anual de Actividades*. Maputo.

Lippman, M., 1985, "Multinational Corporations And Human Rights", in Jr. Shepherd, V. Nanda, eds., *Human Rights and Third World Development*. Westport: Greenwood Press, p. 249-72.

Loforte, A., 1996, *Género e poder entre os Tsonga de Moçambique*. Lisboa, Dissertação de Doutoramento em Antropologia Social, ISCTE.

Lopes, M. M., 1909, *Subsídios para um código de usos e costumes indígenas nos territórios da Companhia de Moçambique*. Beira, Imprensa da Companhia de Moçambique.

Lundin, I. B., 1994, *Global Coalition for Africa/Africa Leadership Forum*. Maputo: Centro de Estudos Estratégicos e Internacionais.

Lundin, I.B., 1998, "Traditional Authority in Mozambique", *Decentralization and Municipal Administration. Description and Development of Ideas on Some African and European Models*. Maputo, Friedrich Ebert Stiftung.

Macaulay, S., 1983, "Private Government," *Disputes Processing Research Program Working Papers*, 6. University of Wisconsin-Madison.

Machel, S.M., 1981, "A Escola: ... uma base científica", *Tempo*, 549, p. 37-42.

Machel, S. M., 1983, *A Luta contra o subdesenvolvimento*. Maputo, Partido Frelimo.

Magode, J., 1998, *La Formation de l'État postcolonial au Mozambique: structures sociales, conflits et changements*. Lyon, Mémoires de DEA en Sciences Politiques, Lyon II, IEP.

Mamdani, M., 1996a, *The Citizen and Subject: Contemporary Africa and the Legacy of Late Colonialism*. Princeton, Princeton University Press.

Mamdani, M., 1996b, "Indirect Rule, Civil Society, and Ethnicity. The African Dilemma," *Social Justice*, 23, p. 145-150.

Mamdani, M., 2000, "When Does a Settler Become a Native? Reflections on the colonial roots of citizenship in Equatorial and South Africa", in D.W. Nabudere, ed., *Globalisation and the Post-Colonial African State*. Harare, African Association of Political Science Books, p. 222-232.

Manor, J., 1997, *The Promise and Limitations of Decentralization*. Paper submitted to Consultoria Técnica sobre Descentralização. FAO, World Bank, Swiss Agency for Development Consultation. Rome, 16-18 December.

Mappa, S., 1998, *Pouvoirs traditionnels et pouvoir de l'État en Afrique: l'illusion universaliste*. Paris: Karthala.

Marques, M. M. L.; Gomes, C. and Pedroso, J., 1999, "The Portuguese System of Civil Procedures", in A. Zuckerman, ed., *Civil Justice in crisis*. Oxford: Oxford University Press, p. 413-41.

Marwick, M.G., 1965, *Sorcery in its Social Setting. A Study of the Northern Rhodesian Cewa*. Manchester: Manchester University Press.

M'Baya, K., 1995, "Crise économique, ajustement et démocratie en Afrique", in C. Eshetu, I. Jibrin, eds., *Processus de démocratisation en Afrique – problèmes et perspectives*. Dakar: CODESRIA.

Mbembe, A., 2000, "A Propos des écritures africaines de soi," *Politique Africaine*, 77, p. 16-43.

Mbembe, A., 2001, *On the Postcolony*. Berkeley, University of California Press.

Melland, F., 1935, "Ethical and Political Aspects of African Witchcraft", *Africa*, 8, p. 495-503.

Melissaris, E., 2004, "The More the Merrier? A New Take on Legal Pluralism," *Social and Legal Studies*, 13, p. 57-79.

Meneses, M. P., 2000, "Medicina tradicional, biodiversidade e conhecimentos rivais em Moçambique," *Oficina do CES*, 150.

Meneses, M. P., 2003, "Agentes do conhecimento? A consultoria e a produção do conhecimento em Moçambique". In Santos, B.S., ed., *Conhecimento prudente para uma vida decente: 'Um discurso sobre as ciências' revisitado*. Porto: Afrontamento, p. 683-715.

Meneses, M. P., 2004., "'Quando não hà problemas, estamos de boa saúde, sem azar nem nada': para uma concepção emancipatória da saúde e das medicinas." In Santos, B.S., ed., *Semear outras soluções. Os Caminhos da biodiversidade e dos conhecimentos rivais*. Porto: Afrontamento, p. 357-386.

Meneses, M. P.; Fumo, J.; Mbilana, G. and Gomes, C., 2003, "As Autoridades tradicionais no contexto do pluralismo jurídico", in B.S. Santos, J.C. Trindade, eds., *Conflito e Transformação Social: uma Paisagem das Justiças em Moçambique*. Porto: Afrontamento, p. 341-420.

Meneses, M. P. and Adam, W., 1996, "Senhores do seu nariz: Amor, Poder e Violência". *NotMoc* 76, de 7 de Abril de 1996. (http://www.mol.co.mz/notmoc/1996/76c.html). 12 September 1999.

Merry, S., 1988, "Legal Pluralism," *Law and Society Review*, 22, p. 869-896.

Ministério do Ensino Superior, Ciência e Tecnologia, 2004, *Dados Estatísticos do Ensino Superior e das Instituições de Investigação, 2003*. Maputo, MESCT - Observatório do Ensino Superior, Ciência e Tecnologia.

Ministry of Planning and Finance, 1998, *Understanding poverty and well being in Mozambique, the first National Assessment (1996-97)*. Maputo.

Minter, W., 1998, *Os Contras do Apartheid. As raízes da guerra em Angola e Moçambique*. Maputo, Arquivo Histórico de Moçambique.

Moiane, E., 1994, "Consuetudinary and statutory land law and administration in Mozambique", in R. Weiss, G. Meyers, eds., *Second national land conference in Mozambique: briefing book*. Madison - University of Wisconsin, Land Tenure Center, p. 48-55

Moita, L., 1985, "Elementos para um balanço da descolonização portuguesa," *Revista Crítica de Ciências Sociais*, 15/16/17, p. 501-509.

Mondlane, E.C., 1969, *Struggle for Mozambique*. London: Harmondsworth.

Mondlane, L.A., 1997, "O acesso justiça e meios alternativos de resolução de conflitos," *Revista Jurídica*, 2, p. 134-146.

Monteiro, O., 1999, "Governance and Decentralization", in B. Ferraz, B. Munslow, eds., *Sustainable Development in Mozambique*. Oxford: James Currey.

Moore, S. F., 1978, *Law as process: an anthropological approach*. London: Routledge and Kegan Paul.

Moore, S.F., 1994, *Anthropology and Africa*. London: The University Press of Virginia.

Mudimbe, V. Y., 1988, *The Invention of Africa*. Bloomington, Indiana University Press.

Mudimbe, V. Y., 1994, *The Idea of Africa*. Bloomington, Indiana University Press.

Muthemba, A. S., 1970, "Usos e Costumes do Sul de Moçambique", *O Cooperador de Moçambique*, 10.

Nader, L., ed., 1969, *Law in culture and society*. Chicago: Aldine.

Nader, L., 2002, *The Life of Law: Anthropological Projects*. Berkeley: University of California Press.

Ndegwa, S. N., 1997, "Citizenship and ethnicity: an examination of two transition moments in Kenyan politics," *The American Political Science Review*, 91(3), p. 599-616.

Negrão, J., 2003, "Sistemas Costumeiros de Terra", in B.S. Santos, J.C. Trindade, eds., *Conflito e Transformação Social: uma Paisagem das Justiças em Moçambique*. Porto: Afrontamento, p. 229-256.

Newitt, M., 1995, *A History of Mozambique*. London: Hurst & Co.

Newitt, M., 2002, "Mozambique", in P. Chabal, ed., *A History of Postcolonial Lusophone Africa*. Bloomington, Indiana University Press, p. 185-235.

Ngugi, J, 2002, "The Decolonozation-Modernization Interface and the Plight of Indigenous Peoples in Post-colonial Development Discourse in Africa", *Wisconsin International Law Journal*, 20(2), p. 296-351.

Nilsson, A., 1995, *Legitimidade, economia, conflito e a guerra. Autoridade e poder tradicional*. Maputo: Ministério da Administração Estatal – Núcleo de Desenvolvimento Administrativo, Volume 1, p. 127-44.

Niehaus, I. A., 2002, "Witchcraft in the New South Africa: From Colonial Superstition to Postcolonial Reality?", in H.L. Moore, T. Sanders, eds., *Magical Interpretations, Material Realities: Modernity. Witchcraft and the Occult in Postcolonial Africa*. London: Routledge, p. 184-205.

Nunes, J.A., 1995, "Como mal ou com o bem, aos teus te atém: As solidariedades primarias e os limites da sociedade-providência," *Revista Crítica de Ciências Sociais*, 42, p. 5-25.

Nsereko, D. N., 1996, "Witchcraft as a criminal defence - from Uganda to Canada and back", *Manitoba Law Journal*, 24(1), p. 38-59.

Nzouankeu, J.M., 1997, *Stakes and Perspectives of Decentralization as a Means of Achieving Democracy in Senegal*. Paper presented to the International Conference on Traditional Contemporary Forms of Local Participation and Self-Government in Africa. Nairobi, October.

O'Laughlin, B., 1992, "A base social da guerra em Moçambique," *Estudos Moçambicanos*, 10, p. 107-142.

O'Laughlin, B., 2000, "Class and the customary: the ambiguous legacy of the *indigenato* in Mozambique," *African Affairs*, 99, p. 5-42.

Pannikkar, R., 1984, "La notion des droits de l'homme est-elle un concept occidental?" *Interculture*, XVII(1), Cahier 82, p. 3-27.

Pannikkar, R., 1996, "Qui a peur de perdre son identité l'a déjà perdue?" *Le Monde*, 2 Avril, 13.

Pedroso, J., Silva, T., 2003, "A justiça de menores" in B.S. Santos, J.C. Trindade, eds., *Conflito e transformação Social: uma paisagem das justiças em Moçambique*. Porto, Afrontamento, volume 1, p. 449-74.

Penvenne, J., 1995, *African Workers and Colonial Racism: Mozambican strategies and struggles in Lourenço Marques*. London: James Currey.

Peek, P.M. (ed.), 1991, *African Divination Systems: Ways of Knowing*. Bloomington: Indiana University Press.

Ramirez, A., Ranis, G. and Stewart, F., 1998, "Economic growth and human development," Queen Elizabeth House, *Working Paper Number 18*.

Randeria, S., 2003, "Pluralismo jurídico, soberania fracturada e direitos de cidadania diferenciais: instituições internacionais, movimentos sociais e o Estado pós-colonial na ôndia", in B. S. Santos, ed., *Reconhecer para libertar. Os caminhos do cosmopolitismo multicultural*. Rio de Janeiro, Record, p. 359-95.

Ranger, T., 1988, "The Invention of Tradition in Colonial Africa", in E. Hobsbawm, T. Ranger, eds., *The Invention of Tradition*. Cambridge: Cambridge University Press: p. 211-62.

Ranis, G. and Stewart, F., 1999, "Strategies for success in human development." *First Global Forum on Human Development*, 29-31 July 1999. New York: Human Development Report Office.

Rita-Ferreira, A., 1967-1968, "Os Africanos de Lourenço Marques," *Memórias do Instituto de Investigação Científica de Moçambique*, 9 (Série C, Ciências Humanas), p. 94-491.

Roberts, C.C., 1935, "Witchcraft and Colonial Legislation", *Africa*, 8, p. 488-94.

Roesch, O., 1992, "Renamo and the peasantry in Southern Mozambique: A view from Gaza province", *Canadian Journal of African Studies*, 26, 3, p. 462-84.

Sachs, A. and H.W.G., 1990, *Liberating the Law: creating popular justice in Mozambique*. London, Zed Books.

Sanchéz, B.E., 2001, "El reto del multiculturalismo jurídico. La justicia de la sociedad mayor y la justicia indígena", in B. S. Santos, M. García-Villegas, eds., *El Caleidoscopio de las Justicias en Colombia*. Volume II. Bogot: Colciencias-Uniandes-CES-Universidad Nacional-Siglo del Hombre, p. 5-142.

Santos, B.S., 1992, *O Estado e a sociedade em Portugal (1974-1988)*. Porto: Edições Afrontamento.

Santos, B.S., 1995, *Toward a New Common Sense - Law, Science and Politics in the Paradigmatic Transition*. New York: Routledge.

Santos, B.S., 1997, "Por uma concepção multicultural de Direitos Humanos," *Revista Crítica de Ciências Sociais*, 48, p. 11-32.

Santos, B.S., 1998, "A reinvenção solidaria e participativa do Estado". Texto apresentado no *Congresso sobre a Sociedade e a Reforma do Estado*, São Paulo: Março de 1998.

Santos, B.S., 1999, "A reinvenção solidria e participativa do Estado," *Oficinas do CES*, 139.

Santos, B.S., 2002a, "Para uma Sociologia das Ausíncias e uma Sociologia das Emergíncias". *Revista Crítica de Ciências Sociais*, 63, 237-280.

Santos, B. S., 2002b, "Toward a Multicultural Conception of Human Rights". B. Truyol, ed., *Moral Imperialism: A Critical Anthology*. New York: New York University Press, p. 39-60.

Santos, B.S., 2002c, *Toward a New Legal Common Sense*. London: Butterworths.

Santos, B.S., 2003, "O Estado Hegemónico e o Pluralismo Jurídico", in B.S. Santos, J.C. Trindade, eds., *Conflito e transformação Social: uma paisagem das justiças em Moçambique.* Porto: Afrontamento, volume 1, p. 47-95.

Santos, B. S.; Marques, M. M. L.; Pedroso, J. and Ferreira, P., 1996, *Os tribunais nas sociedades contempor,neas: o caso portuguís.* Porto: Afrontamento.

Santos B. S. and Trindade, J. C., 2003, *Conflito e Transformação Social: uma Paisagem das Justiças em Moçambique.* Porto: Afrontamento, 2 volumes.

Saraceno, C.,1997, *Sociologia da Família.* Lisboa, Editorial Estampa.

Saul, J., 1990, *Socialist ideology in the struggle for Southern Africa.* Trenton, NJ, Africa World Press.

Sayer, A., 1992, *Method in Social Science, a Realist Approach.* London: Routledge.

Schapera, I., 1975, "Sorcery and Witchcraft in Bechuanaland", in Marwick, M. (ed.). *Witchcraft and Sorcery.* London: Harmondsworth, p. 108-120.

Sen, A., 1999, "Keynote speech; a decade of human development". *First Global Forum on Human Development,* 29-31 July 1999. New York, Human Development Report Office.

Sheleff, L., 1999, *The Future of Tradition: Customary law, Common Law and Legal Pluralism.* London: Frank Cass.

Seidman, R.B., 1965, "Witch Murder and *mens rea*: A Problem of Society Under Radical Change", *Modern Law Review,* 28, p. 46-61.

Sheth, D.L., 1989, "Nation-Building in Multi-Ethnic Societies: The experience of south Asia," *Alternatives,* 14, p. 379-388.

Soiri, I., 1999, *Moçambique: aprender a caminhar com uma bengala emprestada? Ligações entre descentralização e alívio a pobreza, Documento de reflexão ECDPM 13.* Maastricht, ECDPM. (http://www.ecdpm.org/pubs/dp13_fr.htm). 12 September 2002.

Spear, T., 2003, "Neo-Traditionalism and the Limits of Invention in British Colonial Africa", *Journal of African History,* 44, p. 3-27.

Starr, J. and Collier, J., eds.,1989, *History and power in the study of law.* Ithaca: Cornell University Press.

Tamanaha, B., 1993, "The folly of the 'social scientific' concept of legal pluralism," *Journal of Law and Society,* 20, p. 192-217.

Tate, N. and Vallinder, T., eds., 1995, *The Global Expansion of Judicial Power.* New York: New York University Press.

Teubner, G.,1992, "The Two Faces of Janus: rethinking legal pluralism," *Cardozo Law Review,* 13, p. 1443-62.

Tie, W., 1999, *Legal Pluralism. Toward a Multicultural Conception of Law.* Dartmouth: Aldershot.

Tonkin, E., 2000, "Autonomous Judges: African Ordeals as Dramas of Power". *Ethnos,* 65(3), p. 366–86.

Trindade, J.C., 1997, "A crise do paradigma dominante". *Metical,* 1.

Twining, W., 1999, *Globalisation and Legal Theory.* London, Butterworths.

UNDP (United Nations Development Programme), 1990, *Human Development Report 1990*. New York: Oxford University Press.

UNDP (United Nations Development Programme), 1994, *Human Development Report 1994*. New York: Oxford University Press.

UNDP (United Nations Development Programme), 1995, *Human Development Report 1995*. New York: Oxford University Press.

UNDP (United Nations Development Programme), 1996, *Human Development Report 1996*. New York: Oxford University Press.

UNDP (United Nations Development Programme), 1997, *Human Development Report 1997*. New York: Oxford University Press.

UNDP (United Nations Development Programme), 1998, *Human Development Report 1998*. New York: Oxford University Press.

UNDP (United Nations Development Programme), 1999, *Human Development Report 1999*. New York: Oxford University Press.

UNDP (United Nations Development Programme), 2004, *Human Development Report 2004*. New York: Oxford University Press.

Vail, L. and White, L., 1980, *Capitalism and Colonialism in Mozambique: a Study of Quelimane District*. London: Heinemann.

Van Rouveroy van Nieuwaal, I.A.B. and van Dijk, R., eds., 1999, *African Chieftaincy in a New Socio-Political Landscape*. Leiden: African Studies Center.

Verschuur, C., 1986, *Mozambique, dix ans de solitude*. Paris: L'Harmattan.

Werbner, Richard (1996). "Introduction: Multiple identities, plural arenas", in R. Werbner, T. Ranger, eds., *Postcolonial Identities in Africa*. London: Zed Books, p. 1-25.

Williams, J. M., 2004, "Leading from Behind: Democratic Consolidation and Chieftancy in South Africa". *Journal of Modern African Studies* 42(1), p. 113-236.

World Bank, 1995a, *Aide Memoir. Mozambique: Socio-economic reintegration of ex-combatants*. Washington, The World Bank.

World Bank, 1995b, *Aide Memoir. Mozambique: Provincial reintegration support program*. Washington, The World Bank.

World Bank, 1996, *Aide Memoir. Mozambique: Provincial reintegration support program*. Washington: The World Bank.

World Bank, 1999, *World Development Indicators 1998*. Washington, DC.: World Bank.

Young, C., 1994, *The African Colonial State in Comparative Perspective*. New Haven: Yale University Press.

Zuckerman, A. A. S., ed., 1999, *Civil Justice in Crisis: Comparative Perspectives of Civil Procedure*. Oxford: Oxford University Press.

Lightning Source UK Ltd.
Milton Keynes UK
UKOW03f2003260114

225282UK00001B/218/A